Thomas Hinton Burley Oldfield

An Entire and Complete History, Political and Personal, of the Boroughs of Great Britain...

Volume II

Thomas Hinton Burley Oldfield

An Entire and Complete History, Political and Personal, of the Boroughs of Great Britain...
Volume II

ISBN/EAN: 9783337069407

Printed in Europe, USA, Canada, Australia, Japan

Cover: Foto ©ninafisch / pixelio.de

More available books at **www.hansebooks.com**

AN
ENTIRE AND COMPLETE
HISTORY,
POLITICAL AND PERSONAL,

OF THE

BOROUGHS

OF

GREAT BRITAIN;

TOGETHER WITH THE

CINQUE PORTS.

THE SECOND EDITION, CORRECTED AND IMPROVED.

IN TWO VOLUMES.

VOLUME II.

LONDON:

PRINTED FOR B. CROSBY, NO. 4, STATIONERS COURT, LUDGATE STREET.

M.DCC.XCIV.

CONTENTS.

VOL. II.

	Page		Page
NOTTINGHAMSHIRE.		**STAFFORDSHIRE.**	
Nottingham County	1	Stafford County	91
Nottingham	2	Stafford Town	92
East Retford	5	Litchfield	94
Town of Newark	9	Newcastle under Line	97
		Tamworth	101
OXFORDSHIRE.			
Oxford County	12	**SUFFOLK.**	
Oxford	16	Suffolk County	102
Oxford University	22	Ipswich	104
Woodstock	23	Dunwich	117
Banbury	24	Orford	119
		Aldborough	121
RUTLANDSHIRE	26	Sudbury	122
		Eye	125
SHROPSHIRE.		St. Edmundsbury	126
Salop County	27		
Shrewsbury	29	**SURREY.**	
Bridgenorth	37	Surrey County	127
Ludlow	39	Southwark	129
Wenlock	41	Bletchingly	134
Bishop's Castle	43	Ryegate	135
SOMERSETSHIRE.		Guildford	136
Somerset County	44	Gatton	138
Bristol	45	Haslemere	140
Bath	49		
Wells	50	**SUSSEX.**	
Taunton	53	Sussex County	142
Bridgwater	59	Chichester	145
Minehead	61	Horsham	147
Ilchester	63	Midhurst	148
Milborne Port	73	Lewes	150

CONTENTS.

	Page
Shoreham	152
Bramber	160
Steyning	162
East Grinstead	166
Arundel	167

WARWICKSHIRE.
Warwick County	170
Warwick	171
Coventry	173

WESTMORELAND.
Westmoreland County	185
Appleby	187

WILTSHIRE.
Wilts County	188
Salisbury	190
Wilton	191
Downton	192
Hindon	197
Heytesbury	215
Westbury	216
Calne	218
Devizes	219
Chippenham	220
Malmsbury	222
Cricklade	223
Great Bedwin	234
Luggershall	ib.
Old Sarum	236
Wotton Basset	238
Marlborough	239

WORCESTERSHIRE.
Worcester County	240
Worcester	247
Droitwich	261
Evesham	262
Bewdley	264

YORKSHIRE.
	Page
York County	265
York	267
Hull	268
Knaresborough	272
Scarborough	274
Rippon	275
Richmond	276
Heydon	277
Aldborough	278
Boroughbridge	279
Malton	280
Thirsk	281
Beverley	ib.
Northallerton	283
Pomfret	285

HISTORY OF THE CINQUE PORTS.
Introduction	289
Hastings	294
List of the Electors of Hastings	308
Dover	311
Sandwich	313
Hythe	320
New Romney	323
List of the Freemen of New Romney	325
Rye	327
Winchelsea	338
Seaford	348

WELCH BOROUGHS.
Introduction	395

ANGLESEA.
Anglesea County	397
Beaumaris	ib.

CONTENTS.

	Page		Page
BRECONSHIRE.		**RADNORSHIRE.**	
Brecon County	398	Radnor County	416
Brecon	399	Radnor	ib.

SCOTLAND.

	Page
CARDIGANSHIRE.	
Cardigan County	399
Cardigan	400
CAERMARTHENSHIRE.	
Caermarthen County	401
Caermarthen	ib.
CAERNARVONSHIRE.	
Caernarvon County	404
Caernarvon	405
DENBIGHSHIRE.	
Denbigh County	405
Denbigh	406
FLINTSHIRE.	
Flint County	407
Flint	ib.
GLAMORGANSHIRE.	
Glamorgan County	408
Cardiff	409
MERIONETHSHIRE.	
Merioneth County	410
MONTGOMERYSHIRE.	
Montgomery County	411
Montgomery	412
PEMBROKESHIRE.	
Pembroke County	413
Pembroke	414
Haverfordwest	415

	Page
Introduction	419
Report of the Committee of the Friends of the People, on the Representation of Scotland	421
Table, &c. of Number of Electors in the Counties, &c. No. I.	438
Table of the Number of Electors in the Royal Burghs, No. II.	439
COUNTIES OF SCOTLAND.	
Aberdeenshire	440
Argyleshire	ib.
Ayrshire	441
Bamffshire	ib.
Berwickshire	ib.
Caithnessshire	442
Cromartyshire	ib.
Dumbartonshire	444
Dumfriesshire	ib.
Edinburghshire	ib.
Fifeshire	445
Forfarshire	ib.
Haddingtonshire	446
Invernessshire	ib.
Kincardineshire	ib.
Kinrossshire	447
Kirkcudbright Stewartry	ib.
Lanerkshire	ib.
Linlithgowshire	448
Elginshire	ib.
Orkneyshire	449

CONTENTS.

	Page		Page
Peeblesshire	449	District VII.	460
Perthshire	450	——— VIII.	461
Renfrewshire	ib.	——— IX.	ib.
Rossshire	451	——— X.	ib.
Roxburghshire	ib.	——— XI.	462
Selkirkshire	452	——— XII.	ib.
Stirlingshire	ib.	——— XIII.	463
Sutherlandshire	ib.	——— XIV.	ib.
Wigtonshire	453		
Buteshire	ib.	Table of the Counties,	
Clackmannanshire	454	Cities, and Boroughs of	
Nairnshire	ib.	Great Britain	465
		Correct Table of Parlia-	
SCOTCH BOROUGHS.		mentary Patronage	477
Edinburgh	455	Patronage of Peers	ib.
District I.	457	——— of Commoners	480
——— II.	ib.	——— of the Treasury	483
——— III.	458	——— of Peers, in	
——— IV.	ib.	Scotland	ib.
——— V.	459	——— of Commoners	
——— VI.	ib.	in Scotland	484

ERRATA.

Page 16, line 24, *omit* earl of Abingdon.
——— 22, — 10, *omit* ditto.
——— 35, — 24, *omit*, but neither, &c. to the end of the paragraph.
——— 37, *add*, after line 15, William Pulteney, Esq. partially.
——— 39, ————— 12, Patron—T. Whitmore, Esq. partially.
——— 52, line 24, *read* Number of Voters—115.
——— 119, — 15, *for* earl *read* marquis.
——— 148, — 18, *omit* duke of Norfolk and
——— 276, — 9, *for* Mr. *read* Mrs.

HISTORY

OF THE

BOROUGHS OF GREAT BRITAIN.

NOTTINGHAM COUNTY.

POLITICAL CHARACTER.

THIS county is entirely under the influence of aristocracy. The duke of Portland, the duke of Newcastle, lord Middleton, and Mr. Pierrepont, have large estates in this part of the country. These four, or a majority of them, can always dictate to the county who shall be its members. If an attempt, therefore, of the few independent party, should be made to exert their own rights in the choice of their representatives, it would, we fear, be unsuccessful.

Major Cartwright, who is the father of the Constitutional Society, and author of a plan of Parliamentary Reform, made an effort to restore this county to its natural independence; for which purpose he offered himself a candidate; but neither the eminent talents of this gentleman, nor the service he rendered his country, by the great number of persons which he employed in its manufactures, could avail any thing when weighed in the balance against that undue influence which has been so long complained of in this country.

This county is divided into eight hundreds, or rather six wapentakes and two liberties. It lies in the province and diocese of York, and has one hundred and sixty-eight parishes, and nine market towns, which are Nottingham, Newark, Mansfield, Blith, Bingham, Workfop, Tuxford, Southwell, and East Retford. It sends eight members to parliament, that is, two knights of the shire for the county, and two representatives for each of the boroughs of Nottingham, Newark, and East Retford.

NOTTINGHAM.

POLITICAL CHARACTER. This town is not under immediate influence of any kind; arising principally from the great number of inhabitants who are voters, and the increase of its commerce

and

and manufactures. It is subject to the same in‑
conveniences that Westminster, Bristol and Lei‑
cester are, owing to a coalition of the leading
men of each party, who, to avoid the expences
which would necessarily attend an opposition,
agree that each should return one member. These
unconstitutional unions, which owe their origin
to avarice, and the ambition of a few, who call
themselves the great men of the place, virtually
deprive the people of any representation at all,
because, upon every subject of importance which
is debated in the senate, the numbers, thus con‑
stituted, always vote on opposite sides of the
question. The only effectual prevention of this
grievance that can be devised, is, that each dis‑
trict should choose either one or three represen‑
tatives, by which their influence must be neces‑
sarily felt in every decision that takes place in
the legislature of their country.

The right of election in this town was anci‑
ently, according to Dr. Browne Willis, in the
inhabitant housekeepers paying scot and lot;
but, by a resolution of the house of commons of
10 June, 1701, this right is made so complicat‑
ed, and open to fraud and litigation, that every
freeman of this town, by a surreptitious indenture

of apprenticeship, executed in any part of the kingdom, may qualify any number of electors that may suit his convenience or his interest.

This town was incorporated long before king Henry II. gave it a charter; for in Edward the Confessor's time it had a hundred and seventy-three burgesses. Many of our kings have in this town kept their court, and assembled here several parliaments. It was anciently governed by two bailiffs, coroners, and a common council. King Edward I. impowered them to choose a mayor annually. Henry VI. in the twenty-seventh year of his reign, made it a county of itself, changed the bailiffs into sheriffs, and appointed it to be governed by a mayor, and burgesses. The town is divided into seven wards, answering the number of aldermen, each of these having one of them committed to his care, though he is not confined to live in it; and, as a justice of peace, his power extends throughout all the liberties of the town.

CORPORATION. It is governed by a mayor, 6 aldermen, a recorder, 2 sheriffs, and 24 common councilmen.

RIGHT OF ELECTION—June 10, 1701. Agreed, that the right was in the mayor, freemen, and
freeholders

freeholders of forty shillings a year; and that the eldest sons of freemen by birth, and the youngest sons of freemen, who have served seven years apprenticeship, whether at Nottingham or elsewhere, and also such persons as served apprenticeships to any freeman of Nottingham, were well entitled to demand their freedom.

Number of Voters—About 1700.
Returning Officers—The sheriffs.

EAST RETFORD.

Political Character. The right of election in this borough is in the bailiffs, aldermen, and an indefinite number of freemen, in whom the qualification of *residence within the town* is not necessary. The freedom is obtained either by patrimony, as being the eldest son of a freeman born within the borough; by servitude, in consequence of having served seven years apprenticeship to a freeman within the same limits; or by redemption, which is by gift of the bailiffs and aldermen. Those who obtain their franchise by this special favour of the junto of aldermen, must be inhabitant householders *at the time they are made free,* but may leave their habitations the next day; and by this method of qualification,

B 3 a single

a single house may, by the court of aldermen, be made the instrument of doubling the whole number of electors between one election and another, or of multiplying their own party, so as to secure the return of any candidate whose interest they may think proper to espouse. In every charter granted by the crown we find the same power has been invested in the *few*, to control the independence of the *many*, where a monopoly of the election right in the corporation does not exclude the people altogether from a share in the choice of their representatives.

The aldermen of Retford have not, however, been under the necessity of having recourse to the exercise of this power, like their brethren at Carlisle, Durham, Seaford, and many other places, who have incurred the correction of parliament, and the censure of the public, a mutual agreement between the aldermen and freemen, each to nominate a member, and a concurrence in the election of them, rendering this measure unnecessary.

The aldermen, being in the interest of the duke of Newcastle, receive with implicit condescension his grace's instructions for regulating their political conduct; and the freemen, with
a scrupulous

a scrupulous attention to *established customs*, select some neighbouring gentleman for their reprefentative.

In juſtice to the freemen, and in conformity to that line of impartiality which it is our anxious endeavour to keep, we cannot conclude our account of this borough without relating that, under the impreſſion of gratitude to major Cartwright, who employs upwards of ſix hundred of the inhabitants of this place in the manufacture of woollens, and out of reſpect to that eſtimation in which his public character and private virtues are univerſally held, they made him an offer of their unbiaſſed ſuffrages at the laſt election; but whether that gentleman conceived it inexpedient to waſte his time in mock-harangues, and dividing againſt deciſive majorities, or whether he conſidered the poſt of honour in the preſent ſtate of things to be a private ſtation, we cannot take upon us to determine; he declined the honour they intended him, but has not abated that patriotic zeal which he has ſo eminently diſplayed in the cauſe of liberty.

CORPORATION. By a charter of 5 James I. it is governed by 2 bailiffs and 12 aldermen. The bailiffs are diſtinguſhed by the titles of senior and junior; the former of whom is chosen out of the aldermen, and the junior out of such freemen as have been chamberlains. The bailiffs and steward for the time being are justices of the peace, and of the quorum within the borough.

Right of Election—1700, 15th April. Is as well in the burgesses non-residents, as in the burgesses resident within the said borough. Agreed to by the house.

1701, 17th March. The younger sons of freemen of the borough of East-Retford, have not a right to demand their freedom of the said borough.

1702, 28th November. Persons not inhabiting the said borough, are incapable of being made free of the same by redemption. All the sons of freemen have a right to the freedom of the said borough.

1705, 17th January. Is in such freemen only as have a right to their freedom by birth, as eldest sons of freemen, or by serving seven years apprenticeship, or have it by redemption, whether inhabiting or not inhabiting in the said borough, at the time of their being made free.

1710,

1710, 11th January. Is in such freemen only as have a right to their freedom by birth, as eldest sons of freemen, or by serving seven years apprenticeship, or have it by redemption, inhabiting in the said borough at the time of their being made free.

NUMBER OF VOTERS—112.

RETURNING OFFICERS—The two bailiffs.

PATRON—Duke of Newcastle.

TOWN OF NEWARK.

POLITICAL CHARACTER. A contest has existed here above a century, between those who were taxed, and those who were not taxed, but were of sufficient ability, and of course had a right to be so, as in the cases of Leominster and Seaford.

The house of commons, in 1699, came to a resolution, that all who paid, or *ought* to pay scot and lot, had a right to vote at elections of members of parliament; but a contrary one has since been passed in 1791, which states the right to be in the mayor, aldermen, and inhabitants paying scot and lot. In this resolution, the words "ought to pay," are omitted. The inhabitants who were not rated, have appealed to this

this last decision, and their appeal is now before the house.

If this last resolution should not be amended, the choice of the members of parliament will, in a great measure, depend upon the overseers, who will always be the creatures of the corporation, and who will put no persons in the poor rates, but those who are friendly to their own party. By these means a majority of the town, if inimical to their parliamentry connections, may be deprived of their legal franchise.

The influence here is chiefly that of the duke of Newcastle and the duke of Rutland. The interest of the former arises from the great number of houses which he has in this town; and that of the latter from the estates and principal mansion which he has in its neighbourhood. The leader of the opposition to these interests is William Dickenson Rastal, Esq. who supported William Paxton, Esq. the petitioner to the house, the last year, against the return of John Sutton Manners, Esq. and William Crosbie, Esq. and was unsuccessful on account of the last resolution which we stated above. Several actions for bribery were brought, the last Lent assizes at Nottingham, against Mr. Rastal, but being

ing unsupported by facts, a verdict was given in his favour upon each of them.

This borough is the last in England that received the privilege of sending members to parliament, *by charter*, granted April the 24th, 29 Charles II.

The borough of Wenlock, in Shropshire, was the first that ever obtained the same privilege by similar authority, 29th November, 1478, in the reign of Edward IV.

CORPORATION. It is governed by a mayor, twelve aldermen, and as many assistants.

RIGHT OF ELECTION. 1676, 21st March. By virtue of a charter granted to the town of Newark upon Trent, in the county of Nottingham, the town of Newark hath a right to send burgesses to parliament.

1699-1700, 11th January. The mayor, aldermen, and all the inhabitants within the borough of Newark upon Trent, who pay, or ought to pay, scot and lot within the said borough, have a right to vote at the election of members to serve in parliament for the said borough.

1791, March 22d. The right of voting for members to serve in parliament for the borough of Newark, is in the mayor, aldermen, and all
the

the inhabitants, paying scot and lot within the said borough.

NUMBER OF VOTERS—700.

RETURNING OFFICER—The mayor.

PATRONS—The duke of Rutland and duke of Newcastle.

OXFORDSHIRE.

POLITICAL CHARACTER.

THIS county is entirely under the influence of aristocracy. The duke of Marlborough always returns one of the members, and the earl of Abingdon, the earl of Macclesfield, lord viscount Wenman, Sir Henry Watkin Dashwood, and Sir Gregory Page Turner, the other. The great contest, in the administration of the duke of Newcastle, in 1754, between lord viscount Parker, now earl of Macclesfield, and Sir Edward Turner, on the ministerial, and lord viscount Wenham, and Sir James Dashwood, on the side of opposition, first brought the famous Mr. Charles Jenkinson, now lord Hawkesbury, into

political

political notice. Since that period the above noblemen have settled the members among themselves, without appealing to the freeholders. The above four candidates being returned members by the sheriff, instead of two of them, there was no sitting member for the county. Any member might have moved the house upon this, the very first day of the session; and the sheriff might have been ordered to attend, and give an account of his proceeding; however, no notice was taken of it till Nov. 18, so that the house was not legally such, till the county of Oxford was represented, though it met on the 14th, and did business. All the four candidates petitioned, viz. lord Parker, Sir Edward Turner, lord Wenham, and Sir James Dashwood.

The friends of the two former moved, that the matter of the petitions should be heard immediately; but those on the other side insisted, that the merits of the return ought to be first heard and determined, which was certainly reasonable. They therefore moved for the previous question, whether the question upon this motion should now be put? Because, if the previous question had been carried in the negative,

gative, they would have had an opportunity to move for appointing a fhort day to confider of the return, and ordering the high fheriff to attend. But this the court party were againft, and carried their point, that the matter of the petition fhould be heard on the third of December following. It was afterwards moved, by the oppofition, that the high fheriff fhould attend on the day of hearing; but this was carried in the negative. It appeared that the fheriff had given a very unfair advantage to the court gentlemen, by allowing them to make their objections to all the voters through the whole poll, before the oppofition gentlemen fhould object to one individual; of which it was impoffible to go through half before the end of the month, when the writ was returnable. The latter therefore infifted, that they were fairly elected, becaufe they had an acknowledged majority, which could not be fet afide by fuch an unfinifhed fcrutiny, in which fcrutiny befides they had not an equal chance. It was therefore incumbent on the court gentlemen's counfel to endeavour to overthrow the majority claimed by their antagonifts. It was carried, that the oppofition counfel fhould proceed

ceed to shew the general merits of their cause. They did so, and proposed to disqualify no less than 540 voters for the court gentlemen. Then witnesses were examined for proving the partiality of the sheriff, and for " proving lord Parker, and Sir Edward Turner, and their agents, guilty of bribery; for which purpose they likewise produced letters, which they proved to be the hand-writing of the said two gentlemen. Nine days were spent in proving voters on the court side disqualified. Lord Parker and Sir Edward Turner answered objections against the sheriff, and endeavoured to clear themselves of the accusation of bribery, which they retorted upon their antagonists. They then spent ten days more in endeavouring to clear their voters. After this they proposed to set aside 522 of the opposite voters, in which they spent eleven days. Finally, the opposition counsel spent nine days in the reply. Many separate questions were debated, " most, if not all of which, were determined, by a great majority, in favour of lord Parker and Sir Edward Turner, the court gentlemen."

A motion was made by the opposition, that all copyholders, holding by court roll, and not at the will of the lord, have right of voting for county members. This motion was made on purpose to have a negative put upon it; but it was put aside by the previous question; when lord Parker and Sir Edward Turner were declared duly elected.

This county is divided into fourteen hundreds: it lies in the province of Canterbury and diocese of York, and contains two hundred and eighty parishes, one city, and twelve market towns; namely, the city of Oxford, Bampton, Burford, Banbury, Bicester, Deddington, Chipping Norton, Islep, Thame, Henley upon Thames, Woodstock, Whitney, and Watlington; and sends nine members to parliament, viz. two knights of the shire for the county, two citizens for Oxford, two representatives for that university, two burgesses for the borough of Woodstock, and one for Banbury.

OXFORD CITY.

Political Character. The corporation and freemen at large are almost all under the influence of the duke of Marlborough and the earl of Abingdon, each of whom has a sufficient interest to return one of the members. This city

city is remarkable for an act of bribery, committed by almost all the members of the corporation. In 1767 Philip Ward, Esq. then mayor, in conjunction with Thomas Robinson and John Brown, the bailiffs of the said city, and several of the aldermen, wrote a letter to Sir Thomas Stapleton, Bart. and the honourable Mr. Lee, their members, stating, that they would elect them again at the next general election for a certain sum of money, stipulated in that letter, and acquainting them, that unless they complied with that condition, they certainly should not meet with their support. This letter was produced in the house of commons by the honourable members who received it, when, upon being read, it was agreed, that the persons concerned in writing that letter should be taken forthwith into the custody of the serjeant at arms. They were accordingly taken and brought to the house of commons, and were by them committed to Newgate; but after a confinement of some considerable time, upon their petitioning, and setting forth to the house their hearty sorrow and sincere contrition for their offence, they were discharged, after being reprimanded on their knees, by the speaker, in the following words:

"Philip Ward, John Treacher, Sir Thomas Munday, Thomas Wife, John Nicholes, John Philips, Isaac Lawrence, Richard Tawney, Thomas Robinson, and John Brown;

"The offence, of which you have been guilty, has justly brought you under the severe displeasure of this house. A more enormous crime you could not well commit, since a deeper wound could not have been given to the constitution itself, than by the open and dangerous attempt which you have made to subvert the freedom and independence of this house. The freedom of this house is the freedom of this country, which can continue no longer than while the voices of the electors are uninfluenced by any base or venal motive. For if abilities and integrity are no recommendation to the electors, if those who bid highest for their voices are to obtain them from such detestable considerations, this house will not be the representatives of the people of Great Britain. Instead of being the guardians and protectors of their liberties, instead of redressing the grievances of the subject,

subject, this house itself will be the author of the worst of grievances; it will become the venal instrument of power to reduce this happy nation, the envy and admiration of the world, to the lowest state of misery and servitude. This is the abject condition to which you have attempted to bring your fellow-citizens.

"Many circumstances concur to aggravate your offence. The place of your residence was a singular advantage. You had at all times the example of one of the most learned and respectable bodies in Europe before your eyes. Their conduct in every instance, but especially in the choice of their representatives in parliament, was well worthy your imitation.

"You are magistrates of a great city. In such a station, it was a duty peculiarly incumbent on you to watch over the morals of your fellow-citizens; to keep yourselves pure from venality; and to prevent, by your influence, those under your government from being tainted by this growing and pestilential vice. How have you abused this trust? You yourselves have set the infamous example of prostitution in the most public and daring manner: surely you must have felt some remorse from the generous disdain

disdain with which your corrupt offer was rejected by your representatives. They thought, and justly thought, that a seat in this house, obtained by a free and independent choice of their constituents, was the highest honour to which a subject can aspire; and that discharging their duty, as such representatives, **was the nobleft of** services. **Sorry I am to** say, that **these** considerations do not appear to have had **the** least weight with you. However, you have at last acknowledged **your guilt, and,** by your petition yesterday, you seem conscious of the enormity of your offence. This house, in the **terror of** its judgments, always thinks **upon mercy; nor do** they ever inflict punishment but for the sake of example, and to prevent others from becoming the objects of their resentment.

" The censure passed upon you will, they hope, have that effect. **You** are now the object of their mercy, **and are** brought to the bar to be discharged.

" May you be penetrated with a due sense of their justice and lenity!—May you **atone** for your past offence, by a constant endeavour to make a right use of the invaluable privileges which you enjoy as electors!—Consider these

privileges

privileges as a sacred trust reposed in you. Discharge it with integrity. But before you rise from your present posture, I do, in obedience of the commands of this house, *Reprimand you.*

"I am now to acquaint you, that you are discharged, paying your fees."

CORPORATION—Consists of a mayor, recorder, four aldermen, eight assistants, two bailiffs, and twenty-four common council-men. The mayor for the time being officiates at the coronation of our kings in the buttery, and has a large gilt bowl and cover for his fee. The magistracy of the city is subject to the chancellor and vice-chancellor of the university, in all affairs of moment, even in those relating to the city; and every year the vice-chancellor administers an oath to the magistrates and sheriffs, that they will maintain the privileges of the university: besides, on the 10th of February, the mayor, and sixty-two of the chief citizens, in a solemn manner, pay each one penny at St. Mary's church, in lieu of a great fine laid upon the city, in the reign of king Edward III. when sixty-two of the students were murdered by the citizens.

RIGHT OF ELECTION—1621, 19. Feb. Stated, that the right was in the mayor, fifteen more, called the magistrates, and common-council, making in all forty-eight, together with the freemen of the said city.

NUMBER OF INHABITANTS—About 14,000.

NUMBER OF VOTERS—About 650.

RETURNING OFFICERS—The mayor and bailiffs.

PATRONS—Duke of Marlborough and earl of Abingdon.

OXFORD UNIVERSITY.

POLITICAL CHARACTER. The political principles of the members of this university are, with a few exceptions, those of toryism. They have always assisted and given shelter to royalty, whenever it was distressed by the parliament or people. So little are they, however, to be influenced in the choice of their representatives, that they do not suffer any canvas to be made, nor either of the candidates to be, at the time of election, within ten miles of the jurisdiction of the university. Their representatives are men possessing the same sentiments respecting civil and religious government that they themselves

selves do, so that in all probability, their present members will be continued in the same honourable situation, as long as they are able to perform the duties annexed to it.

This place was first imprivileged to send members to parliament by king James I. by diploma, dated March 12, anno 1603.

RIGHT OF ELECTION—In the doctors and actual masters of the university.

NUMBER OF VOTERS—About 600.

RETURNING OFFICERS—The vice-chancellor and heads of colleges.

WOODSTOCK.

POLITICAL CHARACTER. This borough, which is adjoining to the wall of Blenheim park, is wholly under the patronage of the duke of Marlborough. There having been no opposition to so potent an interest, the right of voting has never come under the adjudication of a committee of the house of commons, but it is admitted to be in a mayor, four aldermen, sixteen burgesses, and the freemen at large.

The honour and manor of the town and hundred of Woodstock, were, in the reign of the late queen Anne, settled by parliament upon John Churchill, duke of Marlborough, who commanded the army of the grand alliance, formed by Great Britain, Holland, Portugal, and other powers, against France and Spain, and upon his descendants male and female, as a monument of national gratitude for his bravery and conduct. A palace was also erected for him at the public expence, in a very delightful situation, about half a mile distant from Woodstock, which, to commemorate the important victory he obtained over the French and Bavarians at Blenheim, was called **Blenheim-house.** It was built by Sir John Vanbrugh, and though a heavy building, like the rest of that architect's performances, must be acknowledged to be a magnificent structure.

CORPORATION—Consists of a lord high steward, recorder, town clerk, five aldermen, one of whom is always mayor, and seventeen common council-men.

RIGHT OF ELECTION—In the corporation and freemen.

NUMBER OF VOTERS—160.

RETURNING OFFICER—The mayor.

PATRON—**Duke** of Marlborough.

BANBURY.

POLITICAL CHARACTER. This borough, in common with Abingdon and Higham Ferrers, which

which were also incorporated by queen Mary, Bewdley, which was incorporated by James I. and Monmouth which was imprivileged to send members in the reign of Henry VIII. have only the election of one member each. The right of voting in this populous town is confined, by a resolution of the house of commons, to a mayor, six aldermen, and twelve burgesses, who like all other corporations, are under the influence and direction of an individual.

The number of inhabitant housekeepers in this town, who, like Bath, Winchester, Salisbury, Andover, Poole, &c. have only a nominal representation, are at least six hundred.

CORPORATION. This borough was first incorporated in the first year of queen Mary, and then imprivileged to return one member to parliament; by which charter it was governed by a bailiff, twelve aldermen, and twelve burgesses. In the reign of king James I. it was made a mayor town, with twelve aldermen and six capital burgesses; and it had a new charter from king George I. in the year 1718, by which it is now governed by a mayor, high steward, recorder, six capital burgesses, twelve assistants, a town-clerk, and a serjeant at mace.

RIGHT

RIGHT OF ELECTION—In the mayor, aldermen, and capital burgesses only.

NUMBER OF VOTERS—19.

RETURNING OFFICER—The mayor.

PATRON—Earl of Guildford.

RUTLAND COUNTY.

POLITICAL CHARACTER.

THIS is the only county in England which has no representatives, except the two knights of the shire; and, consequently, the inhabitant housekeepers, like those of the city of Ely, and the opulent and populous towns of Manchester, Sheffield, Birmingham, Leeds, Woolverhampton, Halifax, &c. are without any representation. Ninety-nine parts out of a hundred of the empire of Great Britain are in a similar situation; but the observation applies with peculiar force, when these places present themselves to our view, and are compared with Castle Rising, or Gatton, which have only two houses each, or with Old Sarum, which has not a house remaining, or with

the

the nominal reprefentation of thofe cities and towns, where the right of election is confined to a corporation of nineteen, twenty-four, or thirty, as is the cafe at Banbury, Andover, and Bath.

To complete the deformity of this fhadow of reprefentation, the influence in this county is, like moft others, in a few individuals, the earl of Exeter, earl of Cardigan, earl of Winchelfea, and earl of Gainfborough.

This county is divided into five hundreds, but has no city, and contains only two market towns, namely, Okeham and Uppingham. It is in the province of Canterbury, and diocefe of Peterborough, and contains forty-eight parifhes, but fends only two members to parliament, who are the knights of the fhire.

SALOP COUNTY.

Political Character.

THIS county is not under ariftocratic influence, which may be imputed, in fome degree, to the fmall number of nobility who refide here. There are many gentlemen of comfortable fortunes, who like their anceftors of old, poffefs
independent

independent spirits, and have not as yet learnt to bow their neck to a yoke fabricated by despotic power.

They have, on this account, been branded by their enemies with the epithet of the proud Salopians; but if the definition of that pride be independence, in its fullest and completest sense, our wish is that all our fellow-citizens were in possession of it; aristocratic oppression would then cease, and cheerfulness and plenty would succeed in its room.

This county is seated in the province of Canterbury; and that part of it which lies south of the Severn, is under the jurisdiction of the bishop of Hereford; that which lies north, is under the bishop of Coventry and Litchfield, except Oswestry, and a few other places, which are under the bishoprick of St. Asaph: the archdeacon of Shrewsbury is archdeacon for the three dioceses.

It is divided into fifteen hundreds, containing one hundred and seventy parishes, and fifteen market towns: it sends twelve members to parliament, two knights of the shire for the county, and two burgesses for each of the following towns; viz. Shrewsbury, Bridgenorth, Bishop's Castle, Wenlock, and Ludlow.

SHREWS-

SHREWSBURY.

POLITICAL CHARACTER. The right of election in this town was anciently popular and free; so late as the year 1709, we find by the journals of the houfe of commons, the franchife extended not only to the burgeffes inhabiting within the town, paying fcot and lot, but alfo to thofe inhabiting fix other parifhes, and forty-fix vills in its fuburbs and neighbourhood. Thefe were however disfranchifed by a fubfequent refolution of the houfe, on the 9th of April 1723, and the right was limited to the burgeffes inhabiting the precinct of the borough only.

The corporation afterwards attempted to confine this right ftill further, as will appear by the following cafe, on the petition of certain electors in the intereft of William Pulteney, Efq. tried by a committee of the houfe of commons, on the 7th of March 1775.

The queftion was, whether a clafs of men, coming under the two following defcriptions, who had been refufed admiffion to their freedom by the mayor, were entitled to vote at that election?

1ft, All perfons of the age of one-and-twenty, and who have ferved a feven years apprenticefhip

ship to one of the trades, which form fourteen ancient companies by prescription or incorporation in this borough, have a right to demand, and be admitted to, their freedom, on paying five pounds and all the usual fees.

2d, All persons born within the borough, are, at the age of one-and-twenty, entitled in like manner to demand, and be admitted to, their freedom, on payment of five pounds and the usual fees.

The fact, that the rejected voters came under the description of one or other of those two customs, was not disputed.

It was proved, that more than a year before the election, they had tendered the fees to the persons whose province it is, by the law of the place, to admit freemen; that they had claimed to be admitted, and were refused. It was likewise proved, that they had tendered their votes at the election. But the two customs were called in question.

In 1771, one Baxter, claiming his freedom under those customs, had brought a mandamus in the court of King's Bench; on the trial of that cause, the corporation contended, that the two customs, which the plaintiff alledged to be immemorial, were only introduced by a bye-law

of

of 1642, which bye-law was repealed in 1733. The plaintiff maintained, that the bye-law was only declaratory of the ancient custom, which could not therefore be affected by the repeal of such a bye-law. The jury found for the plaintiff.

Baxter, in consequence of the judgment in his favour, sued out a peremptory mandamus, and was admitted to his freedom. But the corporation, after that decision, still refused to admit the other persons who claimed under the same customs.

In the case of Baxter they had moved for a new trial, which was refused; but a second mandamus being obtained against them, they moved that this new cause might be tried at bar; this was granted by the court; and, on that occasion, the judge who tried the first, said, he thought, that on the trial it had not been properly understood.

This second *mandamus* was depending, in the court of King's Bench, at the time of election. It was tried in Michaelmas term, 19 November, 1774, and determined in like manner as the former; and there was no application for a new trial.

On

On this state of facts, the counsel for the sitting member insisted, that the right of the controverted votes were still open to the discussion of the committee; that the two *mandamuses* were only conclusive amongst the parties, and that on the trial of new mandamuses, the two former verdicts, although they might have great weight as evidence, would not conclude the jury. They suggested, that since the last trial, and after the four days had elapsed, which the court allows for moving for a new trial, they had discovered fresh evidence, which if laid before the committee, would overturn the customs.

The counsel for the petitioners contended, on the contrary, that under circumstances like those of the present case, two verdicts, free from all suspicion of collusion (the two mayors against whom both the verdicts had been found, having continued to be warm partizans of the sitting members at the election, unimpeached and not disapproved of by the judge) would be conclusive evidence *as to the customs*, even in a court of law, because the parties to be bound by them on a new *mandamus* would be the same; viz. the corporation of Shrewsbury; that on two such verdicts, a court of equity would make a decree to establish a custom, and would not grant a third trial; but that if this were otherwise, a committee of the house of commons would never suffer two solemn verdicts, and consequent judgments, of the only court competent to such causes, to be called in question before them. They said, that even in the Middlesex case, nobody had ever attempted to impeach the verdict, finding Mr. Wilkes guilty of the libel.

The counsel for the sitting members cited several cases, where courts of law had granted new trials after two concordant verdicts, and others, where courts of equity had done the same. But they were all shewn to be cases where the judge, who tried the cause, signified his disapprobation of the verdict; and besides it was said, that a verdict *before judgment*, once set aside, is considered as if it never had existed.

On the other side, the cases of the duke of Beaufort, and of Manchester Mills, were cited among others. The latter came on in the duchy court before lord Kinnoul, assisted by lord Mansfield, who said on that occasion, that a verdict in the time of Charles I. (which was produced in the cause) was conclusive evidence of the custom. After this point had been argued, and the counsel directed to withdraw, the committee, after a short deliberation,

Resolved, Not to admit any evidence to impeach the two verdicts, but to consider them as conclusive evidence of the customs.

The sitting members' counsel then endeavoured to prove,

That the rejected voters had not applied in the proper manner, and according to the established usage, to be admitted to their freedom.

But it came out from the evidence, that the mode of their application was regular.

They then contended, That, as the title of those men to their freedom was in suspense, and under litigation in Westminster-Hall, when their votes were rejected, they could not be of any avail as to this election; for that in instances where the votes of men, who had applied for their freedom and were refused, and have been allowed on proving their titles, the case had been always such as to satisfy the committee, or the house, that there was no just ground for refusing them, and that it was done by concert with a candidate, and in order to affect the election.

The committee, however, on the same day, (Wednesday the 8th of March) informed the house,

house, by their chairman, that they had determined, that William Pulteney, Efq. was duly elected, and ought to have been returned.

The burgeffes and freemen, who elect the members for this town, are compofed of three claffes — gentlemen of fortune, independent tradefmen, and mechanics and labourers; the latter defcription are the moſt numerous, and being the moſt dependant, are provided with houfes by the two former, and depend upon the feptennial harveft of an election for the payment of rent and arrears.

The two great defects in the reprefentation of this place are, thofe of many of the moſt refpectable houfekeepers being excluded from the birth-right of Englifhmen, by the odious limitation of corporate rights; and feveral parifhes in the town being deprived even of the corporate privileges by the refolution of the houfe of 1723.

Mr. Pulteney poffeffes the caftle of Shrewfbury, which commands a profpect of twenty miles, and is defervedly an object of pride and admiration to its owner; but neither he, or any other individual, has yet obtained poffeffion of the political influence which can command its reprefentation.

CORPORATION—Confifts of a mayor, recorder, fteward, town clerk, 24 aldermen, and 48 common councilmen, who have a fword-bearer, 3 ferjeants at mace, and other inferior officers. They have the power of trying caufes within themfelves, even in capital cafes, high treafon excepted.

RIGHT OF ELECTION.—1709, 20 December. Is only in the burgeffes inhabiting within the faid borough, or in the fuburbs thereof, paying fcot and lot, and not receiving alms or charity.

1714, 27 May. Is in the mayor, aldermen, and burgeffes of the faid borough.

1723, 9 April. Is only in the burgeffes inhabiting in the faid borough, or in the fuburbs thereof, paying fcot and lot, and not receiving alms or charity.

That the whole parifhes of St. Chad, St. Mary, St. Alkmond, St. Julian, the Holy Crofs, and St. Giles, and the feveral vills of Hadnal, Acta, Reynold, Meriden, Hanwood, Grimfell, Ollerton, Onflow, Prefton, Gubald Pimley, and Merival, are not within the borough of Shrewfbury, or the fuburbs thereof.

That the feveral vills of Birton, Betton, Alkmear, Lengwar, Calcot, Whitley, Welbeck, Upper and Lower Roffal, Shelton, Oxon, Woodcot, Horton,

Horton, Munkmeal, and Goosehill, in the parish
of St. Chad; Great and Little Berwick, Almond
Park, Newton Albright Husley, Cotton Hill,
Leaton, Asley, Merrington, Wollascot, Sansaw,
and Clive, in the parish of St. Mary; Hencot,
Albright Lee, Preston Montford, Dintle, and
Arlescot, in the parish of St. Alkmond; and
Pully and Shelton, in the parish of St. Julian;
are not part of the ancient borough of Shrews-
bury, or the suburbs thereof.

That the parish of Holy Cross and St. Giles,
is no part of the ancient borough of Shrewsbury,
or the suburbs thereof.

 Number of Voters—About 600.

 Returning Officer—The mayor.

BRIDGENORTH.

 Political Character.—The family of Whitmore, of Apley, a seat in the neighbourhood of
this borough, have represented it in different parliaments ever since the 18th of James I. and the
attachment of the people to the present representative of his ancestors' independence, is not
diminished at this day.

 His interest with the electors is permanent;
but is neither established by undue means, nor
exercised by compulsory ones. The town gave

a proof of its independence, when they difplaced their old favourite reprefentative, admiral Pigot, 1784, for voting in fupport of the coalition, and electing in his room a gentleman, whofe political fentiments were congenial with their own.

The right of election in this town is in the freemen, refident and non-refident, the majority of whom are of the latter defcription. Voters are therefore brought from every part of the kingdom to an election, at a moſt enormous expence, and carried home again at the charge of the candidates. This is an imperfection in our reprefentative fyftem, that can only be cured by a radical reform. The ruinous expences attending the removal of electors, from the moſt remote parts of the country to the place of election, is deftructive of the freedom of choice, and precludes any but a corrupt, or a very rich man, from offering his fervices to the people.

Bridgenorth had feveral privileges granted it, by charters from Henry II. and King John. The greateſt part of it ſtands upon a rock, on the weſtern bank of the Severn, which has here a very great fall. Thefe two parts are called the Upper and Lower towns, which are feparated by
the

the river Severn, but united by a stone bridge of seven arches, upon which is a gate and gate-house, with several other houses.

CORPORATION.—It is governed by two bailiffs, annually elected out of twenty-four aldermen, by a jury of fourteen men, together with a recorder, forty-eight common-councilmen, a town-clerk, and other officers.

RIGHT OF ELECTION—In the burgesses and freemen, within and without the borough.

NUMBER OF VOTERS—About 700.

RETURNING OFFICERS—The bailiffs.

LUDLOW.

POLITICAL CHARACTER.—This town is not under the absolute controul of a patron; but Lord Clive has the Corporation attached to him, and possesses an interest sufficiently powerful to secure the election of one of its members, cemented to that of Mr. Knight, the other member, who originally became a candidate on the independent interest of the town, that they might assume the dictatorial influence of patrons; but as the burgesses are sufficiently numerous to assert their own independence, this place cannot be ranked amongst those boroughs which are at the private disposal of an individual.

CORPORATION.—By charter, anno 3 Charles I. confists of 2 bailiffs, 20 aldermen, and 48 common councilmen; but by charter of James II. it confists of 2 bailiffs, 12 aldermen, 25 common councilmen, a recorder, town clerk, steward, chamberlain, and other officers, under which it now acts.

RIGHT OF ELECTION.—1661, 26 February. Is in all the refident common burgesses, as well as the twelve and twenty-five.

1690, 22 December. The new charter, granted to the town of Ludlow by the late King James, whereby the antient method of electing burgesses for parliament is altered, is illegal and void.

1698, 1 March. The fons of burgesses of Ludlow, and thofe that marry the daughters of burgesses, have a right to be made burgesses of the faid borough.

Every perfon having a right to be made a burgefs of the borough of Ludlow, ought to demand fuch his right by petition, figned by the petitioner, according to the bye-law made in the year 1663, and not otherwife.

NUMBER OF INHABITANTS—6000.
NUMBER OF VOTERS—Nearly 500.
RETURNING OFFICERS—The two bailiffs.
PATRON—Lord Clive, partially.

WENLOCK.

WENLOCK.

POLITICAL CHARACTER.—This town is also called Much-Wenlock; but from its being an ill-built, dirty little place, consisting only of two ordinary streets, it is called *Muck*-Wenlock, by way of derision.

The villages of Little Wenlock and Broseley are within the limits of this borough, the whole of which are the property of Sir Henry Bridgman, Bart. and Mr. Forrester, the present members. The advowson of the living belongs to Sir Watkin Williams Wynne.

This insignificant borough is the first that ever sent members to parliament, by virtue of a charter from the crown, which was granted by king Edward IV. 29th November, 1478, who, by his authority, delegated to them the power of sending *one* member to parliament.

This monarch was seated upon a throne, tottering with the uncertainty of its possessor, who had been obliged, in his passage to it, to wade through a sea of blood. An act committed in that day of danger and perplexity, could not be a precedent sufficiently respectable to vest future kings with an authority to grant the same privileges, when and where it should seem expedient

dient to them, and particularly when no such power was committed to them by the constitution of this country. The act of union having limited the number of members of parliament for England to five hundred and thirteen, and that of Scotland to forty-five, has now prevented the future exercise of this extraordinary prerogative.

The buildings in this borough are small, mostly raised with limestone, and covered with thatch. The members are chosen by the resident burgesses, who are between fifty and sixty in number, and are all tenants of the patrons. Mr. Forrester, who owns the greatest part of the borough, has a seat in the neighbourhood, where the electors often repair to exchange their birthright for a mess of porridge.

CORPORATION.—By charter, anno 7 Char. I. consists of a bailiff, recorder, two other justices, and twelve bailiff peers, or capital burgesses.

RIGHT OF ELECTION—In the burgesses.

NUMBER OF VOTERS—About 60.

RETURNING OFFICER—The bailiff.

PATRONS—Sir Henry Bridgman, bart. and Cecil Forrester, esq.

BISHOP'S CASTLE.

POLITICAL CHARACTER.—This borough is entirely under the direction of lord Clive, who is proprietor of the greatest part of it. The right of voting is in the burgesses who are inhabitants.

WENLOCK and this are the only two places which come under the description of proprietory boroughs in this county. The rights are nearly the same in each, only that residence is not a requisite qualification in a burgess of Wenlock.

The general part of the inhabitants of this borough are very poor, having no manufactory or trade, except that of electioneering, which is equally profitable here as in all the other sources of legislative authority.

CORPORATION—Consists of a bailiff, recorder, and fifteen aldermen, out of whom the bailiff is annually chosen, and is justice of the peace and quorum for that and the ensuing year.

RIGHT OF ELECTION—In the bailiff and all the burgesses within the said borough.

NUMBER OF VOTERS—About 50.

RETURNING OFFICER—The bailiff.

PATRON—Lord Clive.

SOMERSETSHIRE.

Political Character.

THE freeholders of this county have, in their political character of electing their representatives, held out to all the people of England an example the most worthy of their imitation. At a county meeting, convened for the purpose of nominating the members, previous to the day of election, they resolved, and agreed unanimously, not to give their votes either to the brother or son of a peer of the realm, nor to any candidate supported by such an interest. By this conduct they have manifested their knowledge of the constitution of their country, and their zeal for its prosperity, in keeping the democratic part independent of, and unmixed, as it certainly ought to be, with the aristocratic. If this doctrine was universally understood, and generally practised, our representatives would be elected by, and out of, ourselves, who are better acquainted with our own interests, and necessarily more anxious to promote it, than those who are constitutionally separated from us; and who, from that and other circumstances,

circumstances, consider the people as an order of beings distinct from themselves, and value them only in proportion as they are serviceable or instrumental to their own consequence, pride, and ambition.

This county, which is seated in the province of Canterbury, and diocese of Bath and Wells, is divided into forty-two hundreds, containing three cities, thirty-two market towns, and three hundred and eighty-five parishes. It sends eighteen members to parliment, viz. two knights of the shire for the county, two citizens for each of the cities of Bristol, Bath, and Wells, and two burgesses for each of the following boroughs, viz. Taunton, Ilchester, Milbourne-port, and Minehead.

BRISTOL CITY.

POLITICAL CHARACTER.—This city was formerly considered a part of Gloucestershire. The return of its members to serve in parliament was made by the sheriff of that county; but afterwards, to dignify the county of Somerset with three cities, it was placed there before Bath and Wells, as the first of the three. In the 47th of Edward III. it was dissevered from Gloucester and Somerset, and made a county of itself. This city

city is certainly the second in England, with respect to the number and riches of its merchants. It is entirely free from aristocratic and ministerial controul; but it is at present represented by a coalition formed by the leaders of the two contending parties. One of its representatives votes uniformly with administration, and the other with opposition; so that the six thousand persons, to whom the right of election is supposed to be confined, have virtually no representation at all.

This city also labours under the intolerable grievance of having its right of election so complicated, and so exposed to fraud and imposition, as to render it absolutely impossible for them to accomplish a fair choice of their representatives. This right being in the freeholders and freemen; and the latter qualification extending to freemens' sons, and to the husbands of freemens' daughters, it is not unusual for a number of persons to be brought here at an election to personate the sons of freemen, whose absence may afford an opportunity of substituting a proxy; and others, to swear themselves the sons of parents to whom they have no other affinity than that of recording their names on the same parchment in the indenture of admission. Freemen's

men's daughters have also been married for the
express purpose of qualifying their husbands to
vote, and the husband selected for the occasion,
after fulfilling the purpose of the marriage, appears to have provided by anticipation against
the evils that might arise from the inconvenience of a bad partner, by discovering that the
marriage has no validity, from the circumstance
of his having a *former wife* living.

These, and innumerable other impositions,
have been known to have been practised at elections for this city, and we may defy the ingenuity of law to prevent them till one system of
right is established, and that system the constitutional one of extending the election franchise
to every housekeeper in the kingdom.

The tradesmen of this city are incorporated
into several companies, each of which has a hall,
or a large room hired for their meeting; and
by a charter of queen Elizabeth, every man that
marries the daughter of a citizen of Bristol becomes free of the city. Here is a Guildhall, in
which are held the assizes and sessions, with the
mayor's and sheriffs courts; and adjoining to it
is a spacious lofty room, called St. George's Cha-
pel, in which the mayor and sheriffs are annually
chosen. Here is also a large council-room, in
which

which the mayor and some of the aldermen meet every day, except Sundays, for the administration of justice. The Royal Exchange is a fine structure, built in the manner of that at London, and is about two-thirds as large. It is all of freestone, and the ground upon which it stands, cost the chamber of the city 20,000 l. It has four entrances to the square within, and above are rooms for shops. Behind the building is an extensive piece of ground laid out for the markets. In Wine-street is a large structure, called the Corn-market; adjoining to which is a guard-room, with barracks for soldiers.

This place, which was made a mayor town at the beginning of the reign of Hen. III. was, anno 1452, 34 Hen. VIII. made a bishop's see and city.

CORPORATION—Consists of a mayor, recorder, eleven aldermen, two sheriffs, and forty-eight common-councilmen.

RIGHT OF ELECTION—In the freeholders, having freeholds of forty shillings a year, and the free burgesses.

NUMBER OF INHABITANTS—60,000.

NUMBER OF VOTERS—Near 6000.

RETURNING OFFICERS—The sheriffs.

BATH.

BATH.

POLITICAL CHARACTER.—This city, which is the moſt elegant, and one of the firſt with reſpect to population in the kingdom, is under the ſame political excluſion, as the inhabitants of Shoreham and Cricklade, who have been convicted of the groſſeſt venality, corruption, and bribery; a crime, which the late Sir John Cuſt, when ſpeaker of the houſe of commons, in reprimanding the mayor and aldermen of Oxford, calls the moſt enormous that men can well commit. The puniſhment inflicted by the houſe of commons on ſuch as they have deemed it expedient to make examples of their juſtice, has been *diſqualification from voting in the election of members of parliament.* All the inhabitants of Bath, the corporation only excepted, are exactly in the ſame ſituation, with only the mental conſolation, of not having committed a ſimilar offence againſt the liberty of their country to deſerve it.

The repreſentation of this city is as complete a political farce as that of Old Sarum; for if thirty-two individuals are to elect two repreſentatives for the people of England, it is of very little conſequence whether they are choſen by that number of burgage-holders, or by the ſame number of aldermen and common-council. We, however, trust, that we may hail them with the prospect of a speedy reform, which will restore men to their rights, and the nation to its true dignity and independence.

Corporation—Consists of a mayor, nine aldermen, a recorder, two bailiffs, and twenty common-councilmen.

Right of election—1706, 26th January. In the mayor, aldermen, and common-councilmen only.

Number of inhabitants—30,000.

Number of voters—22.

Patrons—Marquis of Bath, and earl Camden.

WELLS CITY.

Political character.—The influence prevailing in this city, is that of Clement Tudway, Esq. one of its present representatives. This gentleman has a sufficient interest always to procure a return for himself without expence; and the corporation, &c. compliment some particular friend, or neighbouring gentleman with the other seat. There have been several resolutions of the house of commons respecting the right of election in this city.

In

In one resolution, it is agreed to be in the mayor, masters, and burgesses, and in such persons as are, by *consent* of the mayor, admitted to their freedom; this would have left the election of members, in a great measure, in the corporation; as the mayor, with such a discretionary power, would admit only those who were of his own party; the last resolution has, however, determined it to be in the mayor, masters, burgesses, and freemen, without the word *consent* being included in it.

Wells was first made a free borough in the reign of Hen. II. by the interest of Fitz-Joceline, its bishop. It afterwards received a charter from king John, by which it was made a market-town, and was raised into a city by queen Elizabeth. In 1738, a dreadful fire broke out, which consumed above a hundred dwelling-houses, in six hours time; so that very few had time to save their goods.

This is a very neat city, consisting of broad streets with handsome buildings. It has a cathedral, and only one parish church. The cathedral is said to have been first built by king Ina, about the year 704, but was afterwards so effectually repaired by bishop Fitz-Joceline, that it was considered as a new work. The front, which has been built upwards of five hundred years, is admired for its imagery and carved work in stone, and particularly for a window most curiously painted. Adjoining to the church are spacious cloysters, and a chapter-house of a circular form, supported by one pillar in the middle.

This city sent to parliament *ab origine*.

CORPORATION.—By charter, anno 16 Eliz. it consists of a mayor, recorder, seven masters, and sixteen common-councilmen.

RIGHT OF ELECTION—1695, 18 Feb. Is only in the mayor, masters, and burgesses of the said city, and in such persons, as are (by consent of the mayor and common-council of the said city) admitted to their freedom in any of the seven trading companies of the said city, on account of birth, servitude, or marriage.

1723, May 2. } Is in the mayor, masters,
1729, Apr. 18. } burgesses, and freemen of the said city, who are admitted to their freedom in any of the seven companies within the said city, being thereunto entitled by birth, servitude, or marriage.

NUMBER OF VOTERS—About 500.

RETURNING OFFICER—The mayor.

PATRON—Clement Tudway, esq. partially.

TAUNTON.

TAUNTON.

POLITICAL CHARACTER.—The borough of Taunton does not comprehend the whole of the town of that name, only part of the parish of St. Mary Magdalen being within its limits. The right of election, according to the last resolution of the house of commons, is in the inhabitants, *pot-wallers*, not receiving alms or charity. This qualification is defined to mean, all the resident male inhabitants, who have obtained a parochial settlement, whether they are occupiers of a house, or lodgers; and gives occasion to such innumerable objections at an election, as to leave in the returning officer, who is umpire between the parties, the power of deciding in favour of whichever he pleases.

A parochial settlement being acquired, and forfeited by such a variety of legal methods, witnesses to qualify and disqualify every person voting under that claim, are produced, and a decision is made in a court which has no authority, and before a returning officer who has not a power to examine on oath. The ministerial duties of his office, are thereby exercised judicially, and he admits or rejects votes at his own discretion.

The want of an univerfally eftablifhed right of election, muft ever be productive of thefe imperfections in a popular inftitution; exclufive rights, and local qualifications, have ever been the caufe of difpute and litigation, of which the numerous petitions from the corporation and burgage-tenure boroughs, bear a difgraceful teftimony: even the peerage of Scotland, where the election is vefted in not more than eighty individuals, is expofed to the fame inconvenience. Two years out of the feven for which they are elected, are now nearly elapfed, and yet only thirteen out of fixteen, which is the number of their reprefentatives, can take their feats in the houfe of lords, owing to the length of time occupied in the inveftigation of partial rights; and a committee of the houfe of commons is fometimes engaged ten times as long in afcertaining the right of franchife in a rotten borough, as they would be in digefting and eftablifhing a form for a fair, equal, and univerfal reprefentation of the people.

The influence of this borough is at prefent difputed between Sir Benjamin Hamet, one of its members, and Mr. Morland, the banker. The corporation, which, according to its charter, fhould confift of a mayor, recorder, two aldermen,

men, and twenty common-council, has at present twelve vacancies; but, as a majority of those which remain are in the interest of Mr. Morland, it is probable they will soon be filled with that gentleman's friends.

Sir Benjamin Hamet has founded a very powerful interest in this place, by building a new street, and purchasing the castle in which the county assizes are held. The latter will enable him, in case a spirit of *disobedience* should manifest itself amongst the electors, to refuse the use of it to the public, and, of course, to remove the assizes to some other place in the county.

A petition of Alexander Popham, Esq. and John Halliday, Esq. was tried on the 24th of February, 1775, against the return of the Hon. Edward Stafford, and Nathaniel Webb, Esq. complaining of the partiality of the returning officer, in protracting the poll, by unnecessary adjournments, from the 10th of October, when it began, to the 18th of the same month, and, that he had rejected many legal votes which were tendered for the petitioners, Popham and Halliday, and admitted many illegal votes for the sitting members.

That the sitting members, previous to, and during the poll, were guilty of divers acts of bribery and corruption by themselves and agents.

One hundred and sixteen voters were objected to as having received charity: the words "alms," and "charity," in this borough are admitted not to be synominous; the resolution of the house of commons having rendered all those receiving benefit, in either way, incapable of voting. There are a great many charitable funds in this place, such as the Town charity, Saunders's charity, Meridith's charity, &c.

Three Chelsea pensioners were objected to on the part of the petitioners;

Nineteen, as not having parochial settlements;

Sixteen, as not answering the description of potwallers;

Two, as certificate-men; and

Two, as bribery agents.

The counsel for the sitting members thought, that gentlemen of fortune were not under the necessity of gaining a legal parochial settlement to intitle them to vote; but this was over-ruled, there not appearing to be any principle upon which such a distinction could be supported.

They likewise contended, that the journals of the house have recognized, that apprentices cannot

not be potwallers qualified to vote; but of this question Mr. Douglas makes a query.

It was determined, that Chelsea pensioners had a right to vote.

That, by the *lex loci*, certificate men cannot vote for this borough.

That those who had received *charity* had no right to vote.

The counsel for the petitioners undertook to prove the charge of bribery so directly and palpably, as to disqualify the sitting members.

On Thursday the 16th of March, the committee determined,

That the petitioners were duly elected.

State of the poll at the last election:

  Sir Benjamin Hamet, - - 291
  Alexander Popham, esq. - - 257
  John Halliday, esq. - - - 239
  John Morland, esq. - - - 183

This town suffered greatly by the cruelty of major general Kirk, immediately after the duke of Monmouth's defeat, in the year 1685, who being sent hither, caused nineteen persons, by his own authority, without any trial or process, and without suffering their wives or children to speak with them, to be hanged, with pipes playing,
          drums

drums beating, and trumpets founding. The fame inhuman monſter, having invited his officers to dinner, ordered thirty perſons, condemned here by Jeffries, to be hanged while they were at table; namely, ten, in a health to the king; ten, while the health went round to the queen; and ten, while the health paſſed to Jeffries.

This borough ſent to parliament 23 Edw. I.

CORPORATION.—By charter of Cha. II. it conſiſts of a mayor, recorder, two aldermen, and twenty capital burgeſſes. The mayor and aldermen are annually choſen out of the burgeſſes.

It is remarkable, that the mayor's officers have no power to arreſt, and that there is no priſon here, except a Bridewell for vagrants; debtors and criminals being ſent to the county jail at Ilcheſter. Though this is one of the moſt flouriſhing towns in the county, it is the meaneſt corporation, having neither lands, houſes, nor joint-ſtock of money.

RIGHT OF ELECTION—1715, 28 July. Is in the inhabitants within the ſaid borough, being potwallers, and not receiving alms or charity.

NUMBER OF VOTERS—At a poll taken in the year 1722, was 727; but at a poll taken in 1774, the number was only 456.

RETURNING

RETURNING OFFICER—The mayor.
PATRON—Sir Benjamin Hamet.

BRIDGWATER.

POLITICAL CHARACTER.—This borough formerly acknowledged the patronage of the famous Bubb Doddington, of political memory, who was opposed by the late earl of Egmont, when they were leaders of the tory faction of the late reign. Earl Poulett had then the lead of the ministerial party in this place, and by coalescing with lord Egmont, contrived at last to possess himself of the controling influence. It has since been contested with earl Poulett, by the late Mr. Allen, member for this town, by Mr. Fox, and, at the last general election, by lord Percival, son of the present earl of Egmont. Earl Poulett's interest, however, had the superiority, the numbers on the poll being,

    For the Hon. Vere Poulett - 186
        John Langton, esq. - - 161
        Lord Percival - - - 87

This town was made a free borough by king John, a mayor town by Henry IV. and sent to parliament 23 Edw. I.; and is said to have been re-incorporated by queen Eliz. in the 29th year of her reign.

CORPORATION

CORPORATION—Confifts of a mayor, recorder, two aldermen, who are juftices of the peace, and twenty-four common-councilmen.

There are annually chofen out of the common-council, two bailiffs, who are invefted with a power equal to that of a fheriff; for the fheriffs of the county cannot fend any procefs into the borough. A receiver is alfo annually chofen out of the common-council, to collect the town rents, and make payments.

The revenues of the corporation, confifting of the manor of the borough, the great and fmall tithes, and fome eftates in Dorfetfhire, are valued at 10,000l. a year; and the freemen are free of all the ports in England and Ireland, except London and Dublin.

RIGHT OF ELECTION—1669, 7th Dec. Is in the majority of the corporation, confifting of a mayor, aldermen, and twenty-four capital burgeffes, being inhabitants of that divifion of the faid parifh of Bridgwater, which is commonly called the borough, paying fcot and lot within the faid divifion; and in them only.

1692, 10th Dec. Agreed to be in thofe that pay fcot and lot, inhabiting in the faid borough.

1769, 9th March. If the mayor, aldermen, and capital burgeffes, are not inhabitants, though

they

they pay scot and lot, yet they have no right to vote.

1769, 14th March. The inhabitants of the eastern and western division of the parish of Bridgwater have no right to vote for representatives; but the right of election is in the inhabitants of that division of the said parish, which is commonly called the borough, paying scot and lot within the said division, and in them only.

NUMBER OF VOTERS—300.

RETURNING OFFICER—The mayor.

PATRON—Earl Poulett.

MINEHEAD.

POLITICAL CHARACTER.—This borough was originally a feudal tenure, annexed to the castle of Dunster, which was given by William the Conqueror to William de Mohun, in whose family it continued till Sir John de Mohun, one of the first knights of the garter, having no male issue, conveyed it to trustees, for the use of his wife, who, after his decease, sold it, in the reign of king Edward III. to the lady Elizabeth Luttrell, daughter of Hugh Courtenay, earl of Devonshire, and widow of Sir Andrew Luttrell, Knt. Her son, Sir Henry Luttrell, Knt. who was lieutenant of Harfleur, and steward of the houshold to
Henry

Henry V's queen, added several buildings, now standing, and left the castle and honour to his posterity, by whom it is still possessed, and who is the present owner and patron of this borough, and at whose court-leet the returning officers are chosen.

The right of election is in the parishioners of Dunster and Minehead, *being housekeepers in the borough of Minehead*.

This borough has been lately nearly destroyed by fire, together with most of the property of the unhappy sufferers. A very liberal subscription has been made for the relief of the late occupiers, which does honour to the liberality and philanthropy of its promoters; and will, we hope, be equivalent to the heavy losses which they have sustained.

The brother of the patron, Mr. Luttrell, is a commissioner of the tax office.

This borough was imprivileged to return members to parliament, anno 1 Eliz.

RIGHT OF ELECTION—1717, 24th Feb. Is in the parishioners of Minehead and Dunster, being housekeepers in the borough of Minehead, and not receiving alms.

RETURNING OFFICERS—1717, 13 June. The precept

precept to be directed to the two constables, and they to make the return.

NUMBER OF VOTERS—160.

PATRON—John Fownes Luttrell, Esq.

ILCHESTER.

POLITICAL CHARACTER.—This borough lately came under the patronage of John Harcourt, esq. of this place, one of its present members, by the purchase of a majority of its houses, which we understand he has since disposed of to Mr. Troward, the attorney of Norfolk-street. Previous to its becoming the property of Mr. Harcourt, it was under the control of the late Mr. Peregrine Cust, who represented it many years. It was then, however, subject to continual contests and petitions.

The first, under the Grenville act, came before a committee of the house of commons, on Saturday the 25th of November 1775, when the petitioners were Richard Brown, Esq. and Inigo William Jones, Esq. and the sitting members were Peregrine Cust, Esq. and William Innes, Esq. The petition stated,

That Mr. Christopher Lockyer, bailiff, and returning officer of the borough of Ivelchester, being a known friend to the sitting members, had

had shewn great partiality in their favour, and had admitted many persons to poll for them who had no right to vote, and rejected several persons who had a right to vote, and had tendered their votes for the petitioners; that the fitting members, by themselves, their friends, and agents, were guilty of bribing and treating; and that the petitioners had a majority of legal votes, and ought to have been returned.

There is no last determination of the right of election in Ilchester. The constitution of the place is as follows: it is a borough by prescription; and, according to Willis, sent members to parliament from the time of Edward I. till 34 Edward III. From which time it did not choose representatives till 12 Edward IV. nor after that year till 12 Jac. I. when it was restored to its ancient privileges. By a charter granted 3 and 4 Phil. and Mary, the inhabitants were incorporated, by the name of the bailiff and burgesses of Ilchester. There were to be a bailiff and twelve capital burgesses, who were to choose annually, on the Monday before Michaelmas, one of themselves to be bailiff for the ensuing year; on the death of any of the capital burgesses, his or their place to be supplied out of the common burgesses, by the election of the remaining capital

pital burgesses. The charter says nothing of the qualification necessary to common burgesses; nor of the mode of electing the members of parliament.

The numbers on the poll were,

  For Mr. Innes 103
    Mr. Cust   102
    Mr. Brown 53
    Mr. Jones   53

The counsel for the petitioners undertook to prove, that such number of the votes for Cust and Innes had been bribed, as, when deducted from the poll, would leave the majority of legal votes in favour of Brown and Jones, so as to entitle them to be declared duly elected. And, if they should not succeed in affecting a sufficient number of the votes for the sitting members to answer that end, still, they said, they would prove acts of bribery, by them or their agents, so as to avoid the election, by rendering them incapable of retaining their seats.

The counsel for the sitting members, after attempting, by evidence and argument, to overturn the case which had been made against them, endeavoured to prove, that Brown and Jones, by bribery, or promises, had disqualified themselves,

themselves, even if the majority of legal votes had been in their favour; and consequently, that at all events they could not be declared duly elected.

All the acts of bribery, and the corrupt promises charged on the two fitting members, were, by the intervention of agents, and long before the *teste* of the writ. It appeared, that when the gifts and promises were made, Mr. Cust and " *his partner*" were mentioned to the voters, but Mr. Innes's name was not specified, and was not at all known in the borough till a few days before the election, when he canvassed along with Mr. Cust and his friends. All those who had engaged their votes for Cust and " *his partner*," voted for Innes as the partner.

The promises, imputed by some of the witnesses, called on the part of the fitting members, to Brown and Jones, were said to have been made directly by themselves, during their canvas on the election week.

1st. The counsel for the petitioners having began to examine John Lloyd, concerning a conversation with certain voters, in which the voters had acknowledged that they had been bribed in order to vote for the fitting members;

the

the counsel on the other side objected to their pursuing their questions, so as to charge the sitting members themselves with bribery, by such evidence. After some argument, the counsel for the petitioners agreed, that evidence of the declarations of the voters could only be admitted to affect the voters themselves, and not third persons.—The question first put, objected to, and given up, was, " Whose money did you " understand it to be, which the voters said they " had received?" The question, which it was agreed might be put, and which was put, in lieu of the other, was, " Did the voters when they " said they had received the election money, say " in whose interest they were to vote, in conse- " quence of their taking this money?"

2. One William Handover, a witness called on the part of the petitioners, was going to relate a conversation which passed between him and one James Pitman, alledged to be an agent for the sitting members, and dead since the election.

This was objected to.

It was contended, that evidence of any acts of a supposed agent could not be admitted, until proof of his being an agent had been previously

produced

produced to the committee; that the propriety of such a rule is obvious, because, otherwise, many days might be employed in hearing evidence against a person, who might appear afterwards to have no connection with the cause; that, by the printed history of the two cases of Hindon and Shaftesbury, it appeared that such a rule had been laid down in both those cases.

On the other side the counsel insisted,

That it would be found impracticable to adhere to this rule; for that the circumstances which were to prove that a person had bribed, and that, in so doing, he had acted as the agent of another, were very often the same, or, at least, so complicated together, that they could not be separated; and that the committee, in the case of Bristol, had, on that account, over-ruled an objection like the present.

When the counsel had argued the point, the chairman said, That he had enquired into what had been done by the committee in the case of Shaftesbury; and that he had been informed by the gentlemen who had sat in that committee, as well as by some of the counsel in the cause, that, although on the first day of the trial, a resolution had been come to, agreeable to what is stated in the printed report of the case, yet they had afterwards found such inconvenience attending the rule, that it was agreed on all hands not to abide by it; that, accordingly, in the course of the trial, it was not adhered to after the first day.

Upon this observation from the chairman, the counsel for the sitting members desisted from the objection.

3. One John Tiptree, a witness called on the part of the sitting members, swore, That some days before the election, Mr. Jones asked him for his vote, and said, that if he would vote for him, he would give him fifty guineas after the election: That, until he came to town in consequence of the speaker's warrant, he had never mentioned this circumstance, but to one Target, a person who had been a witness in the beginning of the cause, but who had died pending the trial, and before this evidence was given by Tiptree: That since he had been in town, and before Target died, he had mentioned it to several persons, of whom he named three.

4. James Corry being called, was rejected, because he was one of the two persons who had signed the petition on behalf of the electors.

His inadmiffibility was on all hands agreed on. Similar inftances have occurred before feveral other committees, during this and the laft feffions.

5. One Charles Gillet was proved to have received ten guineas, in order to vote for the fitting members, and it was admitted on the part of the fitting members, that by this act, his vote was deftroyed.

The committee, after hearing the evidence of one James Rogers, and fome other witneffes, having cleared the court, refolved,

" That the chairman do report to the houfe,
" that James Rogers being called as a witnefs
" before the committee, has grofsly prevaricat-
" ed in giving his evidence."

And, accordingly, on the fame day, Monday 27 November, 1775, agreeably to the 26th fection of 10 George III. cap 16, the chairman did report to that effect; and the houfe being moved, that the entry in the journal of the houfe, of the 11th May 1772, of the proceedings of the houfe, in relation to Mary Hoffe, might be read; and the fame being read, the following orders were made:

Ordered, " That the faid James Rogers,
" having

"having grofsly prevaricated in giving his evi-
"dence before the felect committee, appointed
"to try and determine the merits of the petition
"of Richard Brown, and Inigo William Jones,
"Efqrs. and alfo the petition of James Corry
"and John Cox, on behalf of themfelves and
"others, being inhabitant houfeholders, parifhi-
"oners, and others, within the borough of
"Ivelchefter in the county of Somerfet, feve-
"rally complaining of an undue election and
"return for the faid borough, be, for his faid
"offence, committed to his majefty's gaol of
"Newgate.

Ordered, "That Mr. Speaker do iffue his
"warrant accordingly."

On Friday the 1ft of December following, the chairman prefented to the houfe, in confequence of a motion for that purpofe, a petition of Rogers, fetting forth, " That he was extremely
"forry for having incurred the difpleafure of
"the houfe, by prevaricating in his evidence
"before the committee; that he was fenfible of
"his great offence, and of the juftice of the
"houfe; and hoping, as his farther confinement
"would be prejudicial to his health, that the
"houfe would order him to be releafed."

On this petition it was ordered,

That he should be brought to the bar of the house, on the Monday morning following, in order that he should be discharged, and that the speaker should issue his warrant accordingly.

On Monday, December 4, he was, according to order, brought to the bar; where he received a reprimand from the speaker, and was ordered to be discharged out of custody, paying his fees.

During the whole course of this cause, the committee made it a rule, to order the clerk to read over to every witness the minutes of his evidence, that he might set right any mistakes made in setting it down.

They also made it a rule, where one witness directly contradicted what another had sworn, to call in such other witness, and confront them together.

On Monday, December 4, the committee, by their chairman, informed the house, that they had determined,

That none of the four candidates were duly elected;

And that the last election for the borough of Ilchester, was a void election.

On

On which a warrant for a new writ was immediately ordered.

This town having sent to parliament in the reign of Edward I. Edward II. and to 34 Edward III. ceased sending till 12 Edward IV. when it again intermitted sending till 18 James I. at which time it was restored to this privilege.

CORPORATION.—Consists of a bailiff and 12 burgesses.

RIGHT OF ELECTION—1689, 7 May. Alledged to be in the inhabitants of the said town, paying scot and lot, which the town called Potwallers.

1702, 28 January. Agreed to be in the bailiff, capital burgesses, and inhabitants not receiving alms.

NUMBER OF VOTERS—155.

RETURNING OFFICER—The bailiff.

PATRON—Mr. Troward.

MILBORNE PORT.

POLITICAL CHARACTER.—This borough, which consists of nine parcels of burgage lands, each of which gives a right of voting at elections for members of parliament, is the sole property of Mr.

Mr. Medlycott and the Earl of Uxbridge. In the year 1747, Michael Harvey and Jeffry Finch, Efqrs. and Thomas Medlycott and Charles Churchill, Efqrs. were returned. This being a borough by prefcription, there have always been in it nine capital bailiffs, who hold their refpective offices by virtue of deputations, granted by the proprietors of nine ancient parcels of borough lands. Two of them prefide yearly, by rotation, as head officers; and thefe two prefiding capital bailiffs may, if they pleafe (at a court-leet held in October yearly) appoint fubftitutes to execute the menial offices of the borough, who are called fub-bailiffs. This borough difcontinued fending members to parliament for many years; but was reftored to its ancient privileges in the 4th of Charles I. fince which time it has continued to fend two members to every parliament; and the fheriffs precept for chufing members is always directed to the bailiffs thereof.

For feveral years after the borough was reftored to its privileges, the two prefiding capital bailiffs, when prefent, or one of them when the other was abfent, enjoyed the fole

right

right of making the return to the sheriff's precept, that is to say, of returning the members they thought legally chosen.

But since the restoration these nine ancient parcels of borough lands having been all engrossed, and become the property of two neighbouring gentlemen, by agreement between themselves, they, or some of their friends, were generally chosen, and returned without opposition; and, as it often happened, that neither of the capital presiding bailiffs were present, the return was often made by their substitutes or sub-bailiffs, but sometimes by the capital bailiff or bailiffs, and most frequently by the bailiffs and burgesses of the said borough. This was the constitution of the borough at an election, when Thomas Medlycott, Esq. and William Bishop, were the presiding bailiffs, and one Arthur Ansty, said to be a common day-labourer, and servant to the said Thomas Medlycott, was the sub-bailiff, appointed by the said Medlycott. The candidates were, Michael Harvey, and Jeffry Finch, Esqrs. on one side, and the said Thomas Medlycott and Charles Churchill, Esqrs. on the other side; and when the election was over, the return of the two former were

made

made to the sheriff by the said William Bishop, which he accepted and annexed to his precept; but some days after, another return of the two latter was made to the sheriff by the said Arthur Ansty, which he likewise accepted and annexed to his precept; so that his writ was returned with a double return for the said borough. Which was the legal return, was the question; and the only question that by order came to be determined on Thursday the 1st of December last.

As to the return made by William Bishop, it was objected, first, that the sub-bailiffs, and not the capital bailiffs, were, by the custom of that borough, the returning officers; and secondly, that the said William Bishop was not properly qualified to act, because he had not previously taken an oath of office. To the first objection it was answered, that by the custom of the borough, the sub-bailiffs never acted but in the absence, or by the order or permission of their principals; and when either of the capital bailiffs was present, neither of the sub-bailiffs could act as a principal, the capital bailiffs being then sole presiding officers. To the second objection it was answered, that William Bishop

Bishop had taken all the oaths requisite by law; but that an oath of office was not requisite either by law, or the custom of that borough, as had been admitted by the said Thomas Medlycott himself. Then, as to the return made by the said Arthur Ansty, it was objected, first, That as he was only a sub-bailiff, and both the capital presiding bailiffs not only present, but acting as presiding officers, he could not act as a presiding officer, in any case whatsoever, much less in such a principal one as that of returning members to parliament; and secondly, That the return made by the said Arthur Ansty was void, by virtue of a resolution of that house, of the 2d of June 1685; by which it was resolved, That no mayor, bailiff, or other officer to whom the precept ought to be directed, is capable of being elected to serve in parliament for the same borough, of which he is mayor, bailiff, or other officer, at the time of election. And as the return made by the said Arthur Ansty, must be supposed to be a return made by the said Thomas Medlycott, whose substitute and servant he was, according to the axiom in law, *qui fecit per alium, fecit per se*; therefore, by this resolution it ought to be void. To the first objection

it

it was anſwered, That by the cuſtom of the borough, the ſub-bailiffs were the only proper returning officers, conſequently the return made by Arthur Anſty was the only legal return; and to the ſecond it was anſwered, That if the axiom of law were to be applied to the election for this borough, neither of the two proprietors of the nine ancient parcels of borough lands, could ever be choſen or returned as repreſentatives for this borough; becauſe, both the capital and ſub-bailiffs are but their deputies; and as this would be inconſiſtent with common law, as well as contrary to the cuſtom of the borough ever ſince the above-mentioned reſolution, it could not be ſuppoſed, that the houſe thereby intended to render the ſub-bailiffs of this borough incapable of returning, either their immediate principals, the capital bailiffs, or their remote principals, the proprietors of theſe ancient parcels of borough lands. Upon the whole, the houſe, after having ſpent two days in hearing counſel, reading former returns, &c. and examining witneſſes, came to a reſolution, That the execution of a precept for electing burgeſſes to ſerve in parliament for the borough of Milborne Port, and the making the return thereof, are

only

only in the two fub-bailiffs of the faid borough, or in one fub-bailiff, if there are not two, (one *fub-bailiff* is undoubtedly more likely to be bribed than *two capital bailiffs*,) in confequence of which, the clerk of the crown, by order, took off the file the return made by *William Bifhop*; and the faid *Thomas Medlycott*, and *Charles Churchill*, Efqrs. became thereby the only fitting members.

ANOTHER CASE.

On the 20th of January, 1775, the petition of Edward Walter, Efq. and Ifaac Hawkins Browne, Efq. againft the return of the Hon. Temple Luttrell, and Charles Wolfely, Efq. came on to be tried by a committee of the houfe of commons.

There were three petitions read; when it appeared, that there were, in this cafe, three returns made by different perfons claiming to be returning officers, all of which had been annexed to the writ by the fheriff, and returned into the office of the clerk of the crown; by one, Walter and Browne, by the other two, Luttrell and Wolfely, were returned.

The petitions likewife contained a claim made

by

by each party, of the majority of legal votes, and mutual allegations of bribery. In the petition of Walter and Browne, it was also alledged, that Luttrell, at the time of his election and return, " had by himself, or some person in trust " for him, an office, place, or employment, " touching or concerning the farming, collect- " ing, or managing his Majesty's customs," whereby he was incapable of being elected. It was agreed first, to proceed upon the legality of the different returns, separately from the other questions; and the return of *Walter* and *Browne*, being *immediately* annexed to the precept, their counsel began:

Mr. Medlycott's property is so intermixed with Mr. Walter's, that, in following the established rotation, in some years one of the reigning bailiffs is in the appointment of Medlycott, and the other in the appointment of Walter; in some years they are both appointed by Medlycott, and in others, both by Walter. In 1773, one of them was appointed by Medlycott, who nominated one Elias Oliver to be his sub-bailiff; the other by Walter, who nominated one Robert Baunton to be his sub-bailiff. In 1774, it was Mr. Medlycott's turn to appoint both the reigning bailiffs. The sub-bailiffs have always been appointed at a court-leet after Michaelmas-day, holden by a steward, named by the former sub-bailiff. Since the interests have been divided, there have been two stewards, who have holden separate courts, but always on the same day. It appeared by the witnesses, that the court-leet for appointing sub-bailiffs had always been holden, before and since the style was altered, on the first Tuesday after a fair at Sherborne, called Pack-Monday fair; and that there were entries to this purpose in the minute book of the steward of the court; but in none of the court-books or rolls, was there any entry referring the holding of the court to the Tuesday after Sherborne fair; it only appeared to have been always holden on the first Tuesday of October, before the change of the style took place.

On the third of October, 1774, the precept for the election was delivered to Robert Baunton, who gave his receipt for it; and having communicated with the other sub-bailiff (Oliver), they concurred in appointing the day of election to be on the tenth, (the fourth being the first Tuesday in October, N.S.). Oliver, together with Medlycott and others, broke open the Town-hall, the person who had the key not being found; and Mr. Medlycott having nominated his brother, the Rev. George Hutching, and Robert Curtis, to be the reigning capital bailiffs for the year ensuing, they came into the court-leet (which was opened according to form), and appointed John Newton, jun. and John Peckham, to be their sub-bailiffs. The reigning bailiffs and the sub-bailiffs, enter on their offices immediately after their appointment. At the same court, Oliver was appointed a constable by the jury, and sworn into that office. On the 10th, the election came on, and there were three polls taken; one by Baunton, who declared the majority of legal votes to be in favour of Walter and Browne, and accordingly annexed a return of them to the precept; one by Oliver, and a third by Newton and Peckham. By each of the two last, Luttrell and Wolseley had the majority of votes; and accordingly there were two returns made of them. Counter parts of all the three were executed by the under sheriff, and they were all annexed to the writ. If Newton and Peckham were the legal bailiffs at the time of election, their return only was valid; if they were not, it was void; and in such case, the question would be, Whether the return of Baunton, or of Oliver, was the legal return? or whether

they

they were both void? If the court-leet, holden on the 4th of October, was the legal court for the appointment of the annual fub-bailiffs, Newton and Peckham were the legal fub-bailiffs and returning officers on the 10th. The queftion concerning the legality of the court-leet turned chiefly upon the ftatute for altering the ftyle.

The counfel for Walter and Browne contended, That the court in queftion, was " *a court ufu-* " *ally holden with a fair,* and to be holden on the " fame natural day as formerly, that is, according " to the Old Style." That this was evident from the conftant practice fince the change of the ftyle, and the general fenfe of the place, and from the fteward's book.

That if it were not fo, yet the holding it laft year according to the New Style, for the firft time, immediately on the eve of the election, contrary to the ufage ever fince the ftatute of 24 George II. without any notice being given of fuch an intended innovation, till the precept for the election came to the borough, fhewed, that the intention of holding it then was occafional, and evidently only taken up on account of the diffolution of the parliament, which brought on the election before Mr. Medlycott's two fub-bailiffs could have come into office, if he had waited till the ufual time; confequently, that on this ground, the appointment of Newton and Peckham was fraudulent and void.

That if they were legally appointed, ftill the former fub-bailiffs, being the returning officers at the time when the precept was delivered, and one of them having received, and given his receipt for it, they were the only perfons competent to make the return, according to the 7th and 8th of William III. cap. 25.

That if the queftion came to be argued between the returns made by Baunton and Oliver, it was clear that Oliver, by accepting the office of conftable at the court-leet, holden on the 4th of October, had abdicated his former office, and could not afterwards pretend to exercife it; fo that Baunton was the only fub-bailiff at the time of election, and muft of courfe be the only legal returning officer.

The counfel for Luttrell and Wolfeley argued, That though it did appear that the Michaelmas court-leet had ufually been holden on the Tuefday after Sherborne, or Pack-Monday fair, yet *that* was merely *accidental;* becaufe it happens, that the firft Tuefday in October muft of neceffity be the day immediately following the firft Monday after Michaelmas.—That the entries in

the

the minute or memorandum book of the steward, prove only that he assisted his memory in recollecting the time of holding the court, by referring it to Pack-Monday.—That it was natural, from this *accidental* connection between the two days, for the people of Milborne Port to call the court-day Pack-Tuesday.—That if they had any *necessary* connection, it would have appeared by entries in the court books, in some such terms as these: " At a court holden on the first Tuesday after Pack-Monday, or Sherborne fair;" but no such entry could be found.

That it did not appear, that the office of constable and that of sub-bailiff were incompatible.

The counsel for Walter and Browne, in reply, insisted, that there was nothing absurd in supposing an original connection between Sherborne fair and the court-leet at Milborne Port, although the two places are in different counties.—That, in former times, the grants of the crown used to extend very commonly into different counties, and the fair and court, at first, might have made part of the same grant.—That it is not true, that if a fair were forfeited, a court *usually holden with it*, but belonging to another person, would be so likewise.—That the old prescriptive day for holding the fair would still continue to be the guide for fixing the prescriptive day for the court-leet.

The committee having cleared the court, deliberated among themselves; and the counsel being again called in, the chairman acquainted them, that the committee had resolved,

" That the return made by John Newton, jun. and John Peckham, of Mr. Luttrell and Mr. Wolseley, was an illegal return.

" And that the other two returns appeared to the committee to be so complicated together, that they thought it their duty to go upon the merits of the election, without previously deciding between them."

The counsel for Walter and Browne now went into the whole that remained of their part, the bribery by Luttrell and Wolseley, or their agents, and Luttrell's ineligibility. When they had finished and summed up their evidence, the counsel on the other side proceeded to remove the imputation of bribery from Luttrell and Wolseley, and to fix bribery on the other two candidates. Lastly, they answered the objections to Luttrell's eligibility; and after they had summed up their case, the counsel on the other side replied.

During

During the trial of this petition, the committee thought fit to propose, that the following question should be urged by the counsel, viz.

" Whether persons rateable, and having paid to the rate, though that rate was made and collected by officers illegal and doubtful, may vote as inhabitants paying scot and lot."

The counsel for Walter and Browne contended, that they might. They said that scot and lot existed long before overseers of the poor, or poor rates, were known in England, and for this they appealed to the definitions in Spelman's Glossary.—That the poor-rate indeed was, in common cases, very properly taken to be the rule for discovering who are to be considered as persons paying scot and lot, but that the right of such persons to vote is so far from being created by the poor-rate, that it is neither necessarily connected with, nor altered by it.

The committee, after hearing the counsel on the other side, cleared the court, and resolved,

" That persons *rateable*, and *having paid* to the *rate*, though that rate be made by officers illegal or doubtful, have a right to vote, as inhabitants paying scot and lot."

On the head of Mr. Luttrell's ineligibility, it appeared, from the evidence of Mr. Charles Hartford,

Hartford, the perfon who executes the office he was fuppofed to hold as deputy, that it is the place of *Cuftomer inwards in the port of Briftol.*—That it ftands in the name of one Mr. Smith, who refides in Ireland, and the accounts are always made out in his name. He faid, he paid profits (amounting to between three and four hundred pounds a year) to Luttrell, confidering him as agent for Smith. That he had feen a power of attorney from Smith to Luttrell, authorizing him to appoint a deputy for him; and that he had received a deputation from Luttrell, as attorney for Smith, but that afterwards, that deputation being found to be improper, he had deftroyed it, and had received his deputation (which was produced and read) directly from Smith. That he thought, from this tranfaction, that there was fuch a connection between Smith and Luttrell, as made it fafe for him to pay the money to Luttrell; but that he never had confidered, whether the payments he had made to Luttrell were ftrictly legal, and he thought, that if Smith were to die, he would be liable to pay the arrears of the profits to his executors.—He faid he was appointed by Mr. Luttrell's intereft.

On the part of Walter and Browne it was contended,

tended, that Smith's holding the office was merely colourable.—That Luttrell received the profits, and was in fubftance the perfon who poffeffed the office; and that he was thereby incapable of being elected, fince the ftatute of the 12th and 13th of William III.

Mr. Luttrell's counfel contended, it was unneceffary to urge this point, as no evidence had been given to fhew that he had any beneficial intereft in the place. John Coxe Hippefley, Efq. barrifter, being called on the fubject of Mr. Luttrell's office, refufed to anfwer any queftions which might affect him, as he had conftantly acted as his confidential advifer and counfel.

The committee took feveral days to confider of the merits of this election, after the counfel had clofed their evidence and their arguments.

On Friday, the 10th of February, their chairman informed the houfe, that the committee had determined,

" That Edward Walter, Efq. is not duly elected a burgefs to ferve in this prefent parliament, for the borough of Milborne Port, in the county of Somerfet.

" That Ifaac Hawkins Browne, Efq. is not duly elected.

" That

" That the honourable Temple Luttrell, and Charles Wolfeley, Efq. are duly returned burgeffes to ferve in this prefent parliament, by the return executed by *Elias Oliver.*"

There was alfo a petition, in 1772, of George Prefcot, Efq. againft Richard Combe, Efq. the fitting member, when the petitioner was declared duly elected; but as there is nothing in that cafe but what is reported in the above, we fhall not trouble our readers with a repetition of it.

A very ferious charge of corruption was brought againft lord North, in the houfe of commons, during his adminiftration, by the honourable Temple Luttrell, for *inducing* Thomas Hutchins Medlycott, Efq. one of the proprietors of this borough, to oppofe the re-election of Mr. Luttrell at the enfuing diffolution of parliament, in 1780; when, after a full hearing, the houfe got rid of the bufinefs in a manner nearly fimilar to that of Mr. Rofe's, in Weftminfter.

The property of Mr. Walter has been fome time fince purchafed by Lord Uxbridge, who is now joint proprietor of this borough.

This borough having fent, anno 26, 28, 33, 35 Edward I. ceafed fending till 15 Charles I. when it was fummoned to return members to parliament.

CORPORATION

Corporation—It is governed by two bailiffs and two sub-bailiffs.

Right of election—1702, 8th Dec.—Is only in the capital bailiffs and their deputies, in the commonalty stewards, and inhabitants thereof, paying scot and lot.

Number of actual voters—9. Nominally—114.

Returning officers—The two sub-bailiffs.

Patrons—William Coles Medlycott, Esq. and the Earl of Uxbridge.

STAFFORDSHIRE.

Political Character.

THIS county is completely under the direction of aristocratic influence. The marquis of Stafford and lord Bagot, have the commanding interest. The marquis of Bath, earl of Stamford, earl of Uxbridge, earl Talbot, the earl of Dartmouth, and lord Vernon, have also a powerful weight in this county; but the arrangement of parties, always throwing the preponderance of it into the scale of the two first, they have generally the dictation in the choice of the representatives.

It is seated in the province of Canterbury, and diocese of Litchfield and Coventry, and has one hundred and fifty parishes. It is divided into five hundreds, containing the city of Litchfield, and seventeen market-towns; and sends ten members to parliament, viz. two knights of the shire for the county, two citizens for the city of Litchfield, and two representatives for each of the following boroughs, Stafford, Tamworth, and Newcastle under Line.

STAFFROD TOWN.

POLITICAL CHARACTER.—This town acknowledges no patron; but how far it may stand clear of corruption, we do not take upon us to determine. As there has been no public accusation of that crime before the house of commons, or any other tribunal, it is far from our purpose to step out of our way to explore its recesses. We confine ourselves to acts of notoriety, and such as have provoked the interposition of the legislature, or incurred the chastisement of national justice. The electors have at present the honour of giving a seat to one of the most shining ornaments of the British senate, who possesses those genuine principles of liberty which have ever distinguished his great political

leader,

leader, Mr. Fox, and which were never displayed to greater advantage, than when his eloquence dispelled the cloud of prejudice, which was artfully and malignantly intended to envelop the lustre of the French revolution. The family of lord viscount Chetwynd, of Ingestre, in this county, had formerly a considerable interest in this town; but that has ceased since the estates became the property of earl Talbot, the present possessor.

The ancient custom, called Borough English, prevails here, by which, if the father dies intestate, the youngest son inherits the lands lying within the liberties of the town.

This borough sent anno 23 Edward I. and was incorporated anno 3 Edward VI.

CORPORATION—It is governed by a mayor, a recorder, ten aldermen, and twenty common-councilmen. Here the county assizes and quarter-sessions are always kept.

RIGHT OF ELECTION—1710, 25th Jan.—The sons of burgesses, and those who have served apprentices seven years in the borough, have a right (upon demand thereof) to be made burgesses of the said borough.

1722, 27th Nov.—Is in the mayor, aldermen, and burgesses, resident within the said borough.

1724,

1724, 4th Feb.—Perſons made burgeſſes of the ſaid borough, ſince the death of John Dolphin, Eſq. late member of parliament for the ſaid borough, (not being ſons of burgeſſes, or not having ſerved ſeven years apprenticeſhip within the ſaid borough) had not a right to vote in the late election of a burgeſs to ſerve in this preſent parliament for the ſaid borough.

NUMBER OF VOTERS—About 400.

RETURNING OFFICER—The mayor.

LITCHFIELD.

POLITICAL CHARACTER.—This city, which in conjunction with Coventry, is a biſhop's fee, is under the moſt dictatorial influence in the election of its members of parliament. The right of election is of a very complex kind, being in the bailiff, magiſtrates, freeholders of forty ſhillings a year, and all that hold by burgage tenure, together with ſuch freemen only as are inrolled, and pay ſcot and lot. It is a county of itſelf, and contains a juriſdiction of about ten or twelve miles in compaſs; on which account the ſheriff, on the 19th of September, rides round the bounds, and gives a feaſt to the corporation and neighbouring gentry.

That part of the town which is on the ſouth
ſide

side of a stream that falls into the river Trent, is termed the City, and that on the north side is called the Close, from its being encompassed with a wall and dry ditch on every side, except that next the City, which is much the largest part, and is joined to the Close by two bridges. The Close is not included in the jurisdiction or privilege of the City, and is consequently deprived of all share in the elective franchise.

This City was made a metropolitan see by king Offa; and, together with Coventry, is the see of a bishop. About the year 789, king Offa, by the favour of pope Adrian, constituted it an archi-episcopal see; but Litchfield, about ten years after, lost this honour, and its church and diocese were again rendered subject to the metropolitan see of Canterbury. In 1075, this see was translated to Chester, and from thence, in 1102, to Coventry; but soon after the bishops settled here again.

The right of election here being in *freeholders* of forty shillings per annum, as well as in the *burgage-holders* and *enrolled freemen*. The marquis of Stafford, and Thomas Anson, Esq. of Shugborough, the patrons of this City, have contrived by the most admirable finesse to make the burgage-

holds,

holds, which they have been careful to purchase up at an immoderate expence, give *two votes* each, or in the election phrase *to carry double*. The mode by which this master-piece of craft has been effected is as follows: The marquis of Stafford, and Mr. Anson, possessing the fee simple of the burgage-holds, convey them to certain friends and dependents on the eve of an election, by which they create as many electors as they have burgage tenures to qualify. They then cause an *annuity* of forty shillings per annum to be granted upon each tenement, by which means they establish just the same number of freeholders. These surrepticious electors out number the enrolled freemen, and forming a majority, depute two delegates to the British Senate.

Corporation—It is governed by a high and low bailiff, a recorder, sheriff, and twenty-four burgesses.

Right of election—1701, 10 Mar.—The bailiff, magistrates, freeholders of forty shillings a year, and all that hold by burgage tenure, have a right to vote.

Such freemen only of the said city as are inrolled, and pay scot and lot, have a right to vote.

Such freemen of the taylors company as are
enrolled

enrolled in the old book of the conftitutions of the taylors company, in the faid city, have not a right to vote.

Such freemen only of the taylors company as are enrolled in the new book of the conftitutions of the taylors company, in the city of Litchfield, have a right to vote.

To thefe refolutions the houfe agreed.

1718, 10 Dec. Is in the bailiff, magiftrates, freeholders of forty fhillings per annum, and all that hold by burgage tenure, and in fuch freemen only of the faid city as are enrolled, paying fcot and lot there.

NUMBER OF VOTERS—600.

RETURNING OFFICERS—The fheriff and bailiffs.

PATRONS—Marquis of Stafford and Thomas Anfon, Efq.

NEWCASTLE UNDER LINE.

POLITICAL CHARACTER—The right of election in this borough has been attended with that fingularity which diftinguifhes the abfurdity and folly of the prefent deranged fyftem of partial reprefentation.

This right has three times been the fubject of parlia-

parliamentary inveſtigation; viz. in 1624, 1705, and, laſtly, in 1792; the firſt determination was in favour of ancient cuſtom, which was that of the freemen reſidents, who did not forfeit their claim till a year and a day after they had left the town; the ſecond, and laſt, have been confined to the queſtion of reſidence for the year and day that they had actually ceaſed to reſide; which, in both caſes, was decided againſt this ridiculous claim.

In the trial of the laſt petition, which was that of Thomas Fletcher, Eſq. and Clement Kynnerſley, Eſq. againſt Sir Archibald Macdonald and the Hon. John Leveſon Gower, the ſitting members, it appeared in evidence, that a great part of this borough was the property of the marquis of Stafford, whoſe influence directs the choice of the electors; and that it is very cuſtomary for the burgeſſes, who are the electors, to live ten, fifteen, and twenty years, in their houſes, *without paying any rent.*

Upon the trial of the above petition, the counſel for the petitioners ſtated the right of election to be in the mayor, bailiffs, and burgeſſes or freemen, whoſe place of reſidence, at the time of their giving their votes, was in the
said

said borough; or who, at such time, have no place of residence elsewhere; and who have never been absent from the borough for the space of a year and a day, without interruption, since they were admitted to the freedom thereof; or whose families (if they were masters of families) have not been absent for the space of time aforesaid, without interruption, after the time of the admission of such burgesses or freemen, having families, to the freedom of the said borough.

The counsel for the sitting members, stated the right of election to be in the freemen residing in the borough of Newcastle, and not receiving alms or church-bread; and that persons living a year and a day out of the borough lost their freedom.

The committee determined, that neither of the statements delivered in by the petitioners, or sitting members, were the specific right of voting for this borough; but that the right was, "In "the freemen residing in the borough of New- "castle under Line."

Admiral Gower dying in 1792, Mr. Fletcher was again invited, by the independent part of the electors, to assert the independence of the town a second time, in opposition to the aristocratic influence of the marquis of Stafford; at the clofe of the poll the caufe of the people was fuccefsful, the numbers being,

> For Mr. Fletcher, 256
> Mr. Egerton, 254

A fcrutiny being demanded by Mr. Egerton, and the returning officer being in that gentleman's intereft, Mr. Fletcher's majority was foon reduced to a minority, when he declined proceeding any further before thofe judges; but declared his determination of making a fecond appeal to the houfe of commons.

This borough was incorporated by king Henry I. and again, by queen Elizabeth and king Charles II. and began to fend members anno 27 Edward III.

CORPORATION—It is governed by a mayor, two bailiffs, and twenty-four common-councilmen.

The corporation has a court for holding pleas, for any fum under 40l.

RIGHT OF ELECTION—1624, 9 April. Was (before the charter) in the mayor, bailiffs, and common-councilmen; and it was refolved, That the late conftitution altered not the former cuftom.

1705, 27 February. The right was agreed to
be

be in the mayor, burgeffes, and freemen, refident within the borough.

1792, March 21. In the freemen refiding in the borough of Newcaftle under Line.

NUMBER OF VOTERS—664.
RETURNING OFFICER—The mayor.
PATRON—Marquis of Stafford.

TAMWORTH.

POLITICAL CHARACTER—This borough was the joint property of the marquis Townfhend, and the marquis of Bath; but the latter having fold his fhare to Mr. Peel, the banker, that gentleman has eftablifhed a confiderable manufactory here, and is one of its prefent members.

The freeholders had formerly votes, in common with the inhabitant houfeholders; but they loft that privilege by a refolution of the houfe of commons, 1722.

This town appears to have been incorporated by queen Elizabeth, and firft fent to parliament in the fifth year of her reign.

CORPORATION—Confifts of two bailiffs, a recorder, and twenty-four principal burgeffes.

The corporation have power to keep a three-weeks court of record, and a court-leet twice a year; they have alfo a jail, and a common feal.

RIGHT OF ELECTION—1698, 17 March. Is in the inhabitants paying fcot and lot, and in fuch perfons as have freeholds within the faid borough, whether refident in the faid borough or not.

1722, 23 January. Is in the inhabitants being houfeholders, paying fcot and lot, and not receiving alms.

NUMBER OF VOTERS—About 250.

RETURNING OFFICERS—The two bailiffs.

PATRONS—Marquis Townfhend and Robert Peel, Efq.

SUFFOLK.

POLITICAL CHARACTER.

THIS county poffeffes much independent fpirit, which it never fails to exert when called forth into action. In 1784, the people, in confequence of the connections of Sir T. C. Bunbury, Bart. with the coalition formed by lord North and Mr. Fox, propofed, as a candidate for their reprefentation, Jofhua Grigby, Efq. with whofe attachment to the caufe of liberty in all its branches, and averfion to ariftocratic influence, they were well acquainted: and their exertions in his favour were

finally

finally fuccefsful. At the laft election, in 1790, Mr. Grigby declined the honour that was intended him, when Sir Gerard Vanneck was thought the beft fubftitute to fupply the place of that gentleman. The fuccefs of the independent yeomanry would in this inftance, as well as the former one, have been certain, but for the union of fo many heterogeneous fubftances, as adminiftration, oppofition, and ariftocracy. The junction of all thefe parties, and the intereft arifing from it, was hardly fufficient to overthrow and fubdue the laudable efforts which were ufed againft it, as appears by the poll; when the numbers were,

  For Sir T. C. Bunbury, Bart,   3065
  Sir J. Rous, Bart.   2755
  Sir Gerard Vanneck, Bart.   2047

This county is divided into two parts; the firft, called the franchife or liberty of St. Edmund, which contains the weftern part of the county; and the fecond, called the geldable land, contains the eaftern part. Each of thefe furnifhes a diftinct grand jury at the county affizes. In the franchifes, the iffues and forfeitures are paid to the lords of the liberties, and in the geldable part, they are paid to the king. There are likewife two other general divifions of this county, into High Suffolk and Low Suffolk, which is subdivided into twenty-two hundreds. It is situated in the province of Canterbury and diocese of Norwich; has 575 parishes, 29 market towns, and sends sixteen members to parliament.

IPSWICH.

POLITICAL CHARACTER—This borough is independent of influence, except what may be corruptly established by the candidates, or their agents, at the time of election, as the following case, which was tried before a committee of the house of commons, in 1780, will explain: the petition of Charles Alexander Crickitt, Esq. stated, that Mr. Cator, the sitting member, had, by himself or his agents, after the teste of the writ, been guilty of a most notorious and flagrant attempt to bribe the corporation of Ipswich to elect him, by offering a large sum of money to them for that purpose; that he had, in the same manner, been guilty of bribing the electors of the borough, by promises of presents, and by treating; that one of the returning officers was an avowed agent of Mr. Cator, and did, by his direction, corrupt the electors to vote for him; in consequence whereof, many of them did vote for him; that by these means Mr. Cator had procured an illegal majority of votes over the petitioner,

tioner, who would otherwife have been elected and returned.

No objection was made to the election of Mr. Middleton. By the opening of the cafe it appeared, that the petitioner endeavoured to avoid the election of Mr. Cator, by proceeding upon all the charges in the petition; and accordingly evidence was produced upon all of them.

Upon the firft point, the following facts were given in evidence:

The electors of this borough are, two bailiffs, ten portmen, twenty-four common-council men, and an indefinite number of freemen; they have been for a long time divided into two parties, diftinguifhed by the names of *Blues* and *Yellows;* at the head of the former are the common-councilmen; the latter is headed by the portmen. The Yellows had been predominant at the late elections; Mr. Wollafton, one of the late members, had been fupported by them, and being abroad at the time of the late election, his brother, the Rev. Dr. Wollafton, propofed him as a candidate upon that intereft. Mr. Staunton, the other late member, declined this election. Mr. Middleton was fupported by the Blues, on which intereft he had failed in the laft conteft.

The laft election happened on Saturday, the 3d
of

of April: in the preceding week, the Blues had propofed to the Yellows to fupport Wollafton, if the Yellows would fupport Middleton, and thus fettle their differences; but this was rejected by the Yellows, who then had hopes of carrying both members; and they perfuaded Dr. Wollafton, againft his own inclination, to join with Cator, whom they had invited to ftand: about the fame time, the portmen, who were told by Dr. Wollafton that he would fpend no money in the election, afked him to withdraw his brother; which he refufed. Cator was at this time a ftranger to the borough. On the Monday before the election, Dr. Wollafton, by appointment, met Mr. Cator at the houfe of Mr. Cornwall, a banker in Ipfwich, and partner in that bufinefs with the bailiff Spooner. Here thefe three held a converfation about the election: Cornwall, who had before been told by Dr. Wollafton, that he would not fpend more than 300l. on the election, and had communicated this to Mr. Cator, in this converfation faid to Dr. Wollafton, " he had eftimat-
" ed the expence at about 2000l.; that Cator
" was willing to advance 1700l. of this fum, if
" Wollafton would anfwer for the remaining
" 300l." This being agreed to by the latter, Cornwall faid, " if the expences were to be paid at
" his

" his bank, he should expect a deposit of the mo-
" ney before hand." This was likewise agreed
to, and then they went about the town on a joint
canvas for Wollaston and Cator. On the same
day Cator paid 1700l. into Cornwall's banking-
house; on the next day, at Cator's desire, the
above agreement was put in writing and signed;
it is as follows:

" Mr. Wollaston, by Dr. Wollaston, deposits
" 300l. in the hands of Messrs. Alexander, Corn-
" wall, and Spooner; and John Cator having
" deposited 1700l. in the same hands, for the pur-
" pose of paying the expences already incurred,
" and which may be incurred, for their election;
" and it is agreed, if the expence is less than
" 2000l. all the money remaining shall be return-
" ed to John Cator; and if the expences exceed
" 2000l. all above that sum is to be paid in equal
" portions by Dr. Wollaston and John Cator.
" In witness whereof, they have set their names
" this 30th March, 1784.

" FRED. WOLLASTON.
" JOHN CATOR.

" N. B. If the expence does not amount to
" 1200l. Dr. Wollaston is to have returned the
" proportion of one to four."

Dr. Wollaston in his evidence said, he had no
knowledge

knowledge of election matters, nor of the particular expences, or the manner in which they were incurred, in an election at Ipswich; he had heard that a great deal was incurred on account of the out-voters; and being told by Cornwall, that the expences of the former election had exceeded the above sum, he relied on his estimate, as he made it, without knowing how, in particular, the money was to be applied; but he understood it was for necessary joint expences of the election, and not to be used for any purposes in which both parties were not concerned; and that no unlawful use would be made of it. Cornwall was to disburse the money, and to return the remainder, if any, with an account. He wished the transaction to have been kept secret, though not from any notion of its being wrong; but found it was known to all his principal friends in the corporation.

In the course of the canvas, he perceived his brother's interest to have declined considerably, and hereupon determined, after consulting one or two private friends, to withdraw his name, on being indemnified the expences at that time incurred. On the Thursday before the election, at Cornwall's house, in the presence of Cator, Cornwall, Spooner, Notcote the town clerk, and

one

one or two more of the corporation, he faid, he feared his brother might fail, and afked them, " If Middleton fhould be at the head of the poll, " whom they would defert, Cator or his bro- " ther?" To this queftion no anfwer was made; upon which he faid to them, " I now fee you " would defert my brother and fupport Cator;" hereupon Notcote came forward and faid, " What would our enemies fay of us if we " fhould not, as he pays fo much more than " you." No more was faid on the fubject. In the afternoon of that day, Dr. Wollafton offered to withdraw his brother, according to his firft re- folution, and Mr. Cator agreed to repay him what he had laid out upon his canvas: as to the 300l. he had not paid it into the bank.

Mr. Cornwall in his evidence faid, that he had known Mr. Cator before, and would have trufted him with any fum, but would not have given credit to the parties jointly; for which rea- fon he defired a depofit, as he had before found difficulties in getting the money advanced; that he believed the 1700l. was intended for the com- mon expences of the election, jointly with the 300l. but that it was liable to fuch ufes as Cator might think proper, and he might have drawn for it without defraying the expences. On being
afked,

asked, "Where then was the security of the deposit?" he said, it was so, notwithstanding, in his mind. Being asked if he did not know, before the meeting of Cator and Wollaston, that the former was to make a deposit? he said, he could not recollect this with certainty; he was not sure, but believed not. He delivered in an account current of his house with Cator for the 1700l. of which, about 1100l. was spent, the rest was repaid to him on a draught of the 24th of May; the disbursement of the money was made under the direction of Spooner. Mr. Cornwall said, he himself was no corporator.

All the expences were paid out of his fund.

In order to shew that the lawful expences of the election, particularly the travelling charges of the out-voters, could not require such a sum as Mr. Cator placed in Cornwall's hands, the counsel for the petitioner gave in evidence the following account of the situation of the voters for him, which had been examined with the poll, and the distances proved:

LIST

LIST of the OUT-VOTERS for Cator, and of the distances of their residence from Ipswich.

	Miles.	Voters.
Resident at Harwich, distant	11	37
Ditto, within	5	8
Ditto, between	5 & 10	13
Ditto	10 & 15	12
Ditto	15 & 20	12
Ditto	20 & 30	10
Ditto	30 & 40	5
Ditto	40 & 50	4
Ditto	50 & 60	1
Ditto (including London and its environs)	60 & 70	39
Ditto, between	70 & 80	17
		158
Voters for Cator resident at Ipswich		139
	Total	297

Upon the charge of corrupting the electors, the facts proved were as follow:

An extensive distribution of money was made, after the election, to many of the out-voters for loss of time, with the approbation of Mr. Cator, out of the sum in the bankers hands; thirteen voters, resident in London or its neighbourhood, who

who were examined before the committee, were paid three guineas each, immediately after the election; they had all their travelling expences paid befides; this fum was given without enquiry into their circumftances, or the profits of their feveral employments, which were various; fome being capable of earning five or feven fhillings a day, and others two fhillings; they were abfent from their bufinefs, fome four days, fome five; to none of them was any direct expectation given of a reward for their votes; two or three were told, when canvaffed by Cator's agent, Prigg, whom he had employed to canvas and convey voters to Ipfwich, that "they fhould be fatisfied "for lofs of time." Some of them had voted at former elections, and had received a fimilar gratuity, and faid they expected it at this. One man faid to the committee, "he could not tell "what the three guineas were for, unlefs for his vote." One, when canvaffed by Cator's agent, bargained that his fon fhould go and take up his freedom, and was afterwards paid five guineas by the fame perfon, for himfelf and his fon, though his fon did not vote.

The greater number of thefe thirteen did not promife their votes to Cator before they went to Ipfwich,

Ipswich, though they travelled there at his expence. They voted for Middleton and Cator.

Five voters, resident at Harwich, likewise gave their evidence to the committee: these men, in the same circumstances as the others from London, had in the same manner received a guinea and a half a-piece; and it appeared that the same sum was given to most of the Harwich voters. Harwich is eleven miles distant from Ipswich, and the passage by water (their usual way of going thither) costs sixpence: they were absent on Saturday and Sunday. To all these Cator was a stranger at the time of the election, and some of them came to Ipswich intending to vote for Wollaston.

It was admitted by the counsel on both sides, that Middleton and Cator had no joint expences in the election. And it was either proved or admitted, that all the London voters generally received three guineas a-piece after the election, out of the money deposited.

Upon the charge against Spooner, these facts appeared in evidence:

That he had a very extensive influence in Ipswich; that he canvassed the town for Wollaston and Cator, and afterwards for Cator singly; wrote letters soliciting votes for him, and in particular

ticular to Prigg, before-mentioned, in London, to canvas for him and Wollaston, whose bills of expences he paid, and to whom he gave, or sent money to pay some of the London voters the three guineas; he likewise told Prigg, that he had given one Burney one hundred and fifty guineas for paying expences. In Cator's presence he sent an agent to London, in order to accompany the freemen to Ipswich, and afterwards paid him for his trouble. He gave orders at two inns for entertaining some of the London voters, and afterwards paid the bills. He paid some of the Harwich voters a guinea and a half for loss of time; in Cator's presence he told one who had voted, that he should have three guineas when he came to London; and paid several bills of the election expences.

Being examined himself, he said he had done every thing in the election which one friend does for another; had voted for Cator, and, as a banker, paid his draughts for the expences.

The following evidence was given of one particular charge of bribery by Spooner.

One Reynolds, who had voted in the election in 1780, for Staunton and Wollaston, had been employed at the same time in some election business for that party, upon whom he now had a demand

mand of 4 l. 16 s. for expences then incurred, and not paid. He met Spooner at Ipſwich at this laſt election, and aſked him, why this demand had not been paid according to his (Spooner's) promiſe? Spooner told him, " it ſhould be ſettled; " that Wollaſton had declined, Cator was in his intereſt:" whereupon he went to the poll, and voted for Cator and Middleton. Reynolds ſaid in his evidence, he ſhould not have voted for the Yellows, if he had not been eaſy on this demand. This man went to Ipſwich on the part of Middleton, and was paid three guineas by his agent after the election.

Upon theſe facts, the counſel for the petitioner agreed, That the election of Mr. Cator had been obtained by corrupt influence, and muſt be declared void.

June 18. The committee determined, " That " neither the ſitting member nor the petitioner " were duly elected, and that the laſt election " was void as to Mr. Cator."

A new writ was accordingly iſſued, and Mr. Crickitt was unanimouſly elected.

At the laſt general election in 1790. Mr. Middleton and Mr. Crickitt were oppoſed by Sir John Hadley D'Oyley and major Rochfort. At the cloſe of the poll the numbers were, for

Sir John Hadley D'Oyley 323
C. A. Crickitt, Efq. 312
William Middleton, Efq. 299
Major Rochfort 243

By the event of this poll, the borough loft, in Mr. Middleton, a reprefentative, whofe independence was an ornament to the Britifh fenate.

CORPORATION—By charter of Charles II. it is governed by two bailiffs, a recorder, ten portmen, and twenty-four common-councilmen.

RIGHT OF ELECTION—1710, 3d February. Is in the bailiffs, portmen, common-councilmen, and freemen at large, not receiving alms.

1714, 31ft March. Portmen are an effential conftituent part of the great court for making freemen of the faid borough; without fome of which portmen being prefent, the faid court cannot be held.

1714, 1ft April. A motion being made, and the queftion being put, that the perfons voted freemen at the pretended great courts, held in the corporation of Ipfwich, 15 June, 7 Auguft, 25 and 28 September, 1711, without any legal portmen then prefent, were duly made, and have a right to vote for members to ferve in parliament for the borough of Ipfwich; it paffed in the negative.

Number of voters—623.
Returning officers—The two bailiffs.

DUNWICH.

Political character—This town, which was formerly the most considerable in the county of Suffolk, and the see of a bishop, is now reduced to a mean village of about thirty houses, with only one church left, and that in part demolished. It still, however, retains *the name* of a corporation, having two bailiffs, and twelve capital burgesses, all of whom reside in other parishes, and never assemble here but upon election purposes, for the choice of bailiffs, or members of parliament.

The destruction of this borough was occasioned by the incursion of the sea, seven of its parishes out of eight having been destroyed: and the encroachment that is still making, will probably, in a few years, oblige the constituent body to betake themselves to a boat, whenever the king's writ shall summon them to the exercise of their elective functions; as the necessity of adhering to *forms*, in the farcical solemnity of borough elections, is not to be dispensed with.

This is one of those places which, with Orford, in this county; Castle Rising, in Norfolk; Gatton, in Surrey; Old Sarum, in Wiltshire; with many others, which have scarcely the appearance of having ever been the seat of population, elect a majority of the house of commons, while the towns of Birmingham, Manchester, Sheffield, Leeds, Halifax, and Wolverhampton, which are the first in opulence, manufacture, and population, are as much excluded from all share in the legislature of their country as Pekin or Constantinople.

The right of election in this borough (if we may be allowed to call it by such a name) is in the freemen, inhabiting within the remains of the borough, and not receiving alms.

CORPORATION—Consists of two bailiffs, and twelve capital burgesses.

RIGHT OF ELECTION—1691, 8th and 22d December. Is not in the freemen of the said borough, commonly called out-fitters, as well as in the freemen inhabiting within the said borough.

Is only in the freemen inhabiting within the said borough.

1795, 25th November. Is in the freemen of the said borough, commonly called out-fitters, as well as in the freemen inhabiting within the said borough.

1708, 5th February. Is only in the freemen
inhabiting

inhabiting within the said borough, not receiving alms.

NUMBER OF VOTERS—About 14.

RETURNING OFFICERS—The bailiffs.

PATRONS—Sir Joshua Vanneck and Mr. Barne.

ORFORD.

POLITICAL CHARACTER—The corporation of this borough consists of a mayor, recorder, eight portmen, and twelve capital burgesses, in all twenty-two, in whom the right of election is vested. The number is seldom complete, there being scarcely ever more than ten or twelve, who are chiefly composed of the sons and relations of the earl of Hertford. It was formerly a town of great commerce, but it is now only a decayed village, owing to the sea having for some time past, withdrawn itself from it. The constituent and representative body being made up of this nobleman's family, the usual mode of canvassing is laid aside, and the election made among themselves without trouble or expence.

The earliest account we hear of this borough is in the reign of Hen. I. when Bartholomew Glanville was governor. It was once the capital

tal seat of Peter de la Valoines, and was lately in the possession of Price Devereux, lord viscount Hereford, whose executors sold it to the right honourable the earl of Hertford, who now possesses it. It had a charter, with great privileges, granted to it by Rich. III. and was certainly a much larger place formerly than it is at present, as it sent three ships, and sixty-two men, to the siege of Calais, in the year 1359.

This town having sent to all the parliaments in the reign of Edward I. discontinued sending till the reign of Hen. VIII.

CORPORATION—Consists of a mayor, eight portmen, and twelve capital burgesses.

RIGHT OF ELECTION—1699, 10th Feb. Is in the mayor, portmen, capital burgesses, and freemen, of the said borough.

1708, 29th Jan. Is in the mayor, portmen, capital burgesses and freemen, not receiving alms.

NUMBER OF VOTERS—12

RETURNING OFFICER—The mayor.

PATRON—Earl of Hertford.

ALDBOROUGH.

ALDBOROUGH.

POLITICAL CHARACTER—The right of election was anciently in the inhabitants paying scot and lot within this borough; but, by the resolution of 1709, it is confined to the bailiffs, burgesses, and freemen, not receiving alms; which right is again further limited, by a subsequent resolution of 1715, omitting the word *freemen*, and adding that of *resident*, by which it is now understood to be in the bailiffs and burgesses, resident within the said borough, and not receiving alms.

The corporation consists of twenty-two burgesses, and two bailiffs, who are the returning officers. Mr. Crespigny, who has the influence of the corporation of Sudbury, is also patron of this borough.

CORPORATION—Consists of twelve superior, and twelve inferior burgesses.

RIGHT OF ELECTION—1709, 23d Dec. Is in the bailiffs, burgesses, and freemen not receiving alms.

1715, 16th June. Is in the bailiffs and burgesses resident within the said borough, and not receiving alms; to which the house disagreed.

NUMBER OF VOTERS—24.

SUDBURY.

RETURNING OFFICERS—The two bailiffs,
PATRON—P. C. Crespigny, Esq.

SUDBURY.

POLITICAL CHARACTER—This borough has been for many years under the influence of the Crespigny family, of Hontlesham-hall, in this county, although their interest in the borough is not deemed by any means secure; it having been defeated in 1774, by Sir Walden Hanmer and Sir Patrick Blake, baronets; and again, in 1784, by William Smith, Esq. of Pardon-hall, in Essex, and John Langston, Esq. a banker in London.

Mr. Smith petitioned against the return of Thomas Champion Crespigny, Esq. and John Coxe Hippesley, Esq. the present sitting members, which was decided in their favour.

In the year 1774, a petition was presented by Sir Walden Hanmer, and Sir Patrick Blake, against the return of Philip Champion Crespigny, and Thomas Fonnereau, Esqrs. The petition complained, that a great many legal voters, who tendered their voices for Hanmer and Blake, had been rejected, although they had been for many years in possession and exercise of their rights, to the knowledge of the mayor,

and

and of Fonnereau, one of the fitting members; that others, who were not legally qualified, had also been admitted to vote for them; that the fair majority of legal votes was in favour of the petitioners; but that William Strutt, the mayor and returning officer, had acted partially and corruptly, before and during the poll, and had declared the fitting members duly elected, and had returned them; and that money was given by the fitting members, or their agents, by way of bribe or reward, to perfons who voted for them at the election.

Upon the hearing of the petition, it appeared, that the corporation confifts of a mayor, recorder, fix aldermen, twenty-four capital burgeffes, and an indefinite number of freemen. The freedom in this borough is acquired by birth, fervitude, or redemption. There have been a few inftances of making what are called honorary freemen, or faggots; but they have never been allowed to exercife any franchife, as members of the body corporate.

The point upon which the petition turned was, the partiality of the corporation, who were in the intereft of Mr. Crefpigny, in refufing freemen, duly qualified by the cuftom of the borough, to their admiffion and enrollment.

The

The decision of the committee, according to Douglas, was,

"That persons who derived their claim to their freedom, from the antecedent title of birth, who had exercised all the rights of freemen, and that of voting for members of parliament among the rest, for twenty years and upwards, before the last election, who had demanded to be enrolled (and offered to prove, that at their birth, their fathers exercised and enjoyed the rights and franchises of freemen) but were refused, had a right to vote, though they could not produce evidence of their admission, enrolled upon stamps."

And they afterwards informed the house, that they had determined, "That Sir Walden Hanmer, Bart. and Sir Patrick Blake, Bart. were duly elected, and ought to have been returned."

The duke of Grafton takes the title of baron from this place.

This being made a mayor town, and incorporated by queen Mary, first began to return members to parliament, anno 1559, 1 Eliz.

CORPORATION—It is governed by a mayor, recorder, six aldermen, and twenty-four capital burgesses, or common-councilmen.

RIGHT OF ELECTION—1702, 19th Jan.—The

sons of freemen born after their fathers were made free, and those that have served apprenticeships in the said borough, have a right to vote, without an admission in form to their freedom, or taking the oath of freemen.

1703, 6th Dec. Is only in the sons of freemen, born after their fathers were made free, and in such as have served seven years apprenticeship, or are made freemen by redemption.

RETURNING OFFICER—The mayor.

NUMBER OF VOTERS—725.

PATRON—T. C. Crespigny, Esq.

EYE.

POLITICAL CHARACTER—The right of election in this borough extends to the corporation, consisting of two bailiffs, a recorder, ten superior and twenty-four inferior burgesses, and to the inhabitants paying scot and lot.

The greatest part of the town is the property of marquis Cornwallis, who is also lord of the manor, and possesses the parliamentary influence.

CORPORATION—Consists of two bailiffs, a recorder, ten principal or superior, and twenty-four inferior burgesses.

RIGHT OF ELECTION—Is in the free burgesses and

and corporation, together with the inhabitants paying fcot and lot.

Number of voters—About 200.
Returning officer—The bailiff.
Patron—Marquis Cornwallis.

St. EDMUNDSBURY.

Political character—Although this town is the principal one in the county, both in extent, antiquity, and number of inhabitants, yet the right of voting, as in the cities of Bath, Winchefter, and Salifbury, and in the towns of Andover, Banbury, Tiverton, and Dartmouth, is confined to the corporation only. That the privilege of returning the members fhould be placed in this fmall body of men, to the exclufion of the reft of the inhabitants, is as unjuft as it is deftructive of that adequate reprefentation, which the conftitution fuppofes the people to poffefs.

The influence prevailing here, is that of the duke of Grafton, whofe fervices in the caufe of religion and liberty, as well as his known attachment to a parliamentary reform, merit the thanks of his fellow-citizens.

This place was firft imprivileged to fend members to parliament by king James I. who

incorporated

incorporated it in the fourth year of his reign, and by two other charters in the fixth and twelfth years of his reign.

CORPORATION—Confifts of an alderman, recorder, twelve capital burgeffes, and twenty-four common-councilmen.

RIGHT OF ELECTION—Is in the alderman, burgeffes, and common-councilmen.

NUMBER OF VOTERS—37.

RETURNING OFFICER—The alderman.

PATRON—Duke of Grafton.

SURREY.

POLITICAL CHARACTER.

THIS county is independent of abfolute controul; and, although it is at prefent reprefented by the brothers of peers, it is not under the immediate influence of either. In the year 1775, Sir Jofeph Mawbey, bart. upon the death of Mr. Scawen, one of their reprefentatives, became a candidate, in the intereft of the yeomenry. He was oppofed by the late Sir Francis Vincent, who had the fupport of the ariftocracy, and

and by the Hon. William Norton, now Lord Grantley, who had the countenance of the administration of that day; but, notwithstanding these powerful exertions, which were used against him, he was finally victorious. The next instance that the freeholders gave of their independance, was, in the contest between Admiral Keppel and the Hon. Thomas Onslow, when the former gentleman was returned by a majority of six hundred. Upon the admiral's being called up to the house of lords, lord Althorp, now earl Spencer, was chosen in his stead. The death of this nobleman's father occasioned another vacancy for this county, when Sir Robert Clayton was elected. This gentleman however gave so much umbrage to the people, and became so unpopular, from the support which he gave the coalition, that in the year 1784 the Hon. William Norton was the object of their choice, and Sir Robert was thrown out. At the last election there was a cross poll; the three candidates opposed each other; when lord William Russell and captain Finch were elected by a considerable majority.

Surrey is divided into thirteen hundreds. It lies in the province of Canterbury, and diocese of Winchester, and has one hundred and forty

parishes;

parishes, in which are thirteen market-towns; viz. Chertsey, Croydon, Dorking, Epsom, Ewel, Farnham, Godalming, Guildford, Haslemere, Kingston, Ryegate, Southwark, and Woking, besides two ancient boroughs, which have no markets; viz. Bletchingly and Gatton. It sends fourteen members to parliament; viz. two knights of the shire for the county, and two members for each of the following boroughs; Southwark, Guildford, Ryegate, Haslemere, Bletchingly, and Gatton.

SOUTHWARK.

POLITICAL CHARACTER—This borough is not under influence in any degree, or of any kind, owing to its great population and opulence, and the right of election being vested in the inhabitants, housekeepers, paying scot and lot.— It consists of five parishes, St. John's, St. Olave's, St. Thomas's, St. George's, and St. Saviour's. Christ-church parish formed a part of this borough by the charter of Edward VI. but owing to disuse it has lost the privilege of voting, as well as great part of the parish of St. Saviour, which is called the Clink Liberty. The parish of Christ-church is on the south-side of Blackfriars-bridge, and was formerly part of the parish of St. Saviour, but has been separated by act of parliament. This parish, in conjunction with the Clink Liberty, has undoubtedly a right to suffrages, in common with the other parishes of the borough; and it is in agitation to petition parliament, at a future election, for a re-establishment of those rights which have been lost for want of usage. Southwark is one of the twenty-six wards of the city of London, and is called in the city records, the ward of Bridge Without, though it has not, in common with the other wards of the city, the election either of an alderman, or common council; the former being chosen by the court of aldermen, from amongst such of that body as have served the office of lord-mayor; and the choice usually falls upon the senior.

The inhabitants have lately petitioned the corporation of London, for the same liberty which is exercised by all the other wards, of electing their own aldermen and common-council; and as the city of London have lately obtained a decision, in the court of Common Pleas, which confirms to them the privilege of an exclusive jurisdiction over this borough, it is presumed that this ancient right will be extended to them: a right which has its foun-

.. dation

dation in juſtice, and which ought to be a leading feature in every conſtitution which has for its objeƈt the liberty, ſecurity, and proſperity of the community at large.

The borough of Southwark was governed by its own bailiff, till the year 1327, when the city of London finding great inconvenience from the eſcape of the malefaƈtors thither, out of the reach and cognizance of the city magiſtrates, obtained a grant, by which the mayor of London was conſtituted bailiff of Southwark, and impowered to govern it by his deputy. However, the inhabitants, ſome time after, recovered their former privileges, which they enjoyed till King Edward VI. granted Southwark to the city of London, for the ſum of 647l. 2s. 1d.; and about a month after the paſſing of this patent, Southwark was made one of the city wards, named Bridge Ward Without, in conſideration of the city's paying to the crown an additional ſum of 500 marks; upon which, the number of aldermen was increaſed from twenty-five to twenty-ſix, a new one being choſen to govern that borough. Hence Southwark has ever ſince been conſidered as ſubjeƈt to the lord-mayor, who has under him a ſteward and bailiff, the former of whom regularly holds a court of record, in the hall, on St. Margaret's Hill, for all debts, damages, and trefpaffes within his limits; and the lord-mayor proclaims a fair, held at Southwark, on the 19th of September.

It is divided into two parts; the Borough Liberty, in which the lord-mayor's fteward or bailiff holds the above courts; and the Clink, or Manor of Southwark, which is fubdivided into the Great Liberty, the Guildhall, and the King's Manor; for each of which fubdivifions a court-leet is held, where the conftables, aleconners, and flefh-tafters, are chofen, and other bufinefs tranfacted. The Clink Liberty is under the jurifdiction of the bifhop of Winchefter, who, befides a court-leet, keeps a court of record here, by his fteward and bailiff, for pleas of debt, damages, and trefpaffes. Court-leets are alfo kept at Bermondfey and Rotherhithe.

The military government of Southwark is under the lord-lieutenant of the county of Surrey, and eleven deputy-lieutenants.

Oppofite the weft end of St. George's church was anciently a magnificent ftructure, belonging to the duke of Suffolk, which coming to Henry VIII. he erected a mint in it for the coining of money; it being afterwards pulled down and converted

verted into streets, they still retained the name; and it being a privileged place, it became a harbour for bankrupts and debtors, to which they fled, in order to defraud their creditors.

Though the privilege of this place was taken away in the reign of William III. they still kept their station, in defiance of the laws, and of the civil power, till an act of parliament was made, in the latter end of the reign of king George I. which obliged them to disperse.

In this borough were anciently a number of brothels, called the Stews, situated on the Bankside, Southwark, and licensed by the bishop of Winchester. At first there were eighteen of these houses, but afterwards twelve were only allowed. They stood in a row, and had signs on their fronts facing the Thames, which were not hung out, but painted on the walls; as the Cardinal's Hat, the Cross Keys, the Bell, the Castle, the Swan, the Boar's Head, &c. These houses were under very strict regulations, confirmed by act of parliament in the reign of Henry II. which were to be observed, under the penalty of suffering great pains and punishments. No single woman, desirous of forsaking her sins, was to be kept against her will; and every lewd woman was forbidden the rites of the church, and deni-

ed

ed Chriftian burial, if fhe was not reconciled to the church before her death. Hence there was a plot of ground, termed the fingle woman's church-yard, appointed for thefe lewd women, at a diftance from the parifh-church. Thefe lewd houfes were put down by order of King Henry VIII. in the year 1546, when it was proclaimed, by found of trumpet, that the ftews fhould be no longer privileged and ufed as common brothels.

Corporation—It is under the jurifdiction of the corporation of London.

Right of election—1702, 10 Nov. Is only in the inhabitants thereof paying fcot and lot.

1714, 29 June. " That the perfons inhabiting in the Mint, or rules of the Queen's-Bench, in the borough of Southwark, and paying a rent of ten pounds per annum, or upwards, have not a right to vote, though they do pay fcot and lot within the faid borough."

It paffed in the negative.

Returning officer—The bailiff,

Number of voters—1900.

BLETCHINGLY.

Political character—This borough, which confifts of about fixty fmall houfes, is a proper companion to Gatton, from which it is not more than

than three miles diftant. The right of voting is burgage-tenure, and the lord of the manor's bailiff was the returning officer; but by the laft refolution of the houfe of commons, in 1723, he was deprived of that office; and the borough has now the fingularity of fending two members to parliament, without a mayor, conftable, or any other legal officer, who can claim the exclufive exercife of that authority. We have feveral inftances of boroughs without electors, but this is the only one that prefents itfelf without a returning officer.

Sir Robert Clayton is fole proprietor of the majority of burgage-tenures, and of courfe has the appointment of the reprefentatives.

RIGHT OF ELECTION—Is in the borough-holders only, without the bailiff.

RETURNING OFFICER—None.

NUMBER OF VOTERS.

The number of burgage-holds are 90, but are all the property of an individual.

PROPRIETOR—Sir Robert Clayton.

RYEGATE.

POLITICAL CHARACTER—The right of voting is in the freeholders of the borough. The earl of Hardwicke and lord Somers have bought up all the freeholds in it, each of whom appoints an attorney in the town as their agents, as well in elections as other bufinefs. The property being nearly equally divided between thefe two noblemen, each procures the return of one member for a near relation or a particular friend. The former nobleman's brother, the Hon. Jofeph Sydney Yorke, and the latter's fon, the Hon. John Somers Cocks, are the prefent members. This circumftance alone is fufficient to prove where, and in what degree, influence and authority prevail here, and how far the electors are fuffered to exercife their judgment and their choice in the election of their reprefentatives.

RIGHT OF ELECTION—In the freeholders.

RETURNING OFFICER—The bailiff.

NUMBER OF VOTERS—About 200 freeholds; now the property of the earl of Hardwicke and lord Somers.

PROPRIETORS—Earl of Hardwicke and lord Somers.

GUILDFORD.

POLITICAL CHARACTER—The right of election in this borough is of a very peculiar kind, and differs from all others in the kingdom, being in

the

the freemen and freeholders paying scot and lot, and resident in the town.

The majority of the freeholds are the property of lord Onslow and lord Grantley, and the number of voters not exceeding one hundred. They have been considered for some years past to have had the nomination of its members, until the last general election, when Mr. Sumner opposed the brother of the latter, and was successful only by a majority of three votes; but it is supposed that, at a future election, lord Grantley will regain his former interest. The corporation of this town, which consists of a mayor, recorder, seven aldermen, and an indefinite number of bailiffs, is in the interest of lord Onslow, who has very liberally provided for several of them in different departments under government. This place, like Cirencester, Shrewsbury, Lewes, &c. &c. is not more than half of it within the limits of the borough.

This being the county-town, the assizes are frequently held here, and always the election for knights of the shire.

This borough sent members to parliament anno 23 Ed. I.

CORPORATION—By charter of Henry VIII. it
is

is governed by a mayor, seven magistrates, and sixteen bailiffs.

Right of election—1699, 24 April. Is only in the freemen and freeholders paying scot and lot, and resident in the town.

1710, 3 Feb. It was agreed that one who had served seven years to a freeman, was, *ipso facto*, a freeman.

Returning officer—The mayor.

Number of voters—About 120.

Patrons—Lord Onslow and lord Grantley.

GATTON.

Political character—This borough, which now consists only of two houses, was the property of the unfortunate Sir George Colebrooke: at the time of his failure, it was sold by the assignees, under his commission, to lord Newhaven, who afterwards disposed of it to Messrs. Percy and Graham. Since the year 1786, it has been purchased and re-purchased by three or four different persons, and is now the property of William Currie, Esq. one of its present members, and Robert Ladbroke, Esq. who obtained possession of it, at an expence of seventy-four thousand pounds. The returning officer

officer is the constable appointed at the court-leet of the two proprietors. In this case, the constituent and representative body, who are the same in number, may also possibly be the same persons, as they would have the power to elect each other. This, among many others, is a striking instance of the present fallacious and inadequate state of representation, and shews the indispensable necessity of applying some immediate remedy to an evil of such an enormous magnitude.

Right of election—1628, 26 March. Is in the inhabitants; and the return made by them being adjudged good, was (by the then petitioner) insisted to be in the inhabitants not receiving alms, and in the freeholders having such freehold in their own occupation.

1696, December 15. Was (by the then sitting member) insisted to be in the freeholders and inhabitants paying scot and lot; and he was adjudged duly elected.

Returning officer—The lord's constable.

Number of voters—2.

Proprietors—Robert Ladbroke, Esq. and William Currie, Esq.

HASLEMERE.

HASLEMERE.

POLITICAL CHARACTER—The right of election here is in the freeholders of messuages, lands, or tenements, lying within the borough and manor of Haslemere. These freeholds, in which the right is vested, were formerly the property of the families of Oglethorpe and Molyneux; of whom they were purchased by Mr. Chandler, an attorney of Guildford, who sold them to the earl of Lonsdale, the present proprietor of the borough.

There exists however here, as in most other boroughs, a disputed right, between what is called the short, and long poll. The first consists of fifty-two votes, and the latter of sixty-two. The last ten votes arose originally from splitting one or two freeholds into twelve, and are deemed doubtful votes.

The right of election is not in such freeholds as vote at a county election, but in such as pay a part of the sum of *twelve shillings and one penny three farthings* burgage rent, per annum, to the earl of Lonsdale, lord of the manor and borough. This arbitrary and ridiculous limitation of right, has been the cause of litigation,

and

and produced the resolution of April 24, 1755.

A second petition of William Burke, Esq. and Henry Kelly, Esq. was tried by a committee of the house of commons, in 1775, against the return of Thomas More Molyneux, Esq. and Sir Merrick Burrel, bart. The complaint was then against *splitting* and *dividing* freeholds, when the committee determined in favour of the sitting members.

Lord Lonsdale has, however, prevented the necessity of future litigation, by a purchase of the whole, and attaching this borough to his parliamentary interest.

RIGHT OF ELECTION—1661, May 20. The inhabitant freeholders in the borough have only votes in elections.

1698, Feb. 9. Was agreed to be in the freeholders resident within the borough.

1755, April 24. In the determination of 1661, by the word "*freeholders*" is meant only freeholders of messuages, lands, or tenements, lying within the borough and manor of Haslemere, whether the same pay to the lord of the said borough and manor or not, exclusive of any lands or tenements which are, or have been, parcel of the waste ground of the said borough

borough and manor, or any messuages or buildings, which are or shall be standing, or being thereon.

1713, March 3 and 4. Petition of Mr. Oglethorpe rejected, for not being signed by himself. The like relating to Wigan.

Returning Officer—The bailiff, who is annually chosen at the lord's leet.

Number of Voters—52.

Proprietor—Earl of Lonsdale.

SUSSEX.

Political Character.

THIS county was considered formerly as entirely under the influence of aristocracy; but the contrary to this was evinced in 1774. The independent part of the county, being at that time much dissatisfied with the conduct of administration, in attempting to procure a return for a candidate of their own nomination, contrary to the wishes of the people, exerted themselves in such a manner as convinced them that their unanimity and abilities, when called forth into action, would, when similar encroachments were made

made upon their rights, be equally certain, as well as deserving, of similar success.

They entered into voluntary subscriptions, for the support of their cause, and proposed Sir Thomas Spencer Wilson, Bart. in opposition to Sir James Peachy, the court candidate. The contest was carried on with unabating diligence and vigour on both sides, for a continuation of twenty-eight days; when a great majority was declared in favour of Sir Thomas Spencer Wilson, in whose person the honest and independent yeomen of the county obtained an entire and complete victory over the mandates of ministerial despotism. There is, however, much aristocratical influence prevailing here, arising from the residencies and estates of the duke of Richmond and duke of Dorset, the earl of Ashburnham, earl of Abergavenny, the earl of Egremont, and lord Pelham. There has been no contested election for this county since 1774. The representation at present is divided; the Right Hon. Thomas Pelham voting uniformly with the opposition, and Charles Lenox, Esq. with administration.

Sussex is divided into six rapes, which are general divisions peculiar to this county; and each of these rapes is said to have anciently had

its

its particular river, foreft, and caftle. Thefe rapes are fubdivided into fixty-five hundreds; in which are contained one city, fixteen market-towns, and two ancient boroughs, which are ancient corporations, but have no market. Thefe are the city of Chichefter, with the market-towns of Arundel, Battel, Brighthelmftone, Cuckfield, Eaft Grinftead, Haftings, Hailfham, Horfham, Lewes, Midhurft, Petworth, Rye, New Shoreham, Steyning, Terring, and Winchelfea, with the boroughs of Bramber and Seaford, that have no markets. It is feated in the province of Canterbury, and diocefe of Chichefter, contains three hundred and forty-two parifhes, and fends twenty-eight members to parliament; namely, two reprefentatives for the county, two citizens for the city of Chichefter, two burgeffes for each of the following boroughs, Lewes, Horfham, New Shoreham, Midhurft, Arundel, Eaft Grinftead, Steyning, Bramber, and two barons for each of the cinque-ports of Rye, Haftings, Winchelfea, and Seaford.

CHICHESTER.

CHICHESTER.

POLITICAL CHARACTER—This city was many years under the dictation of the duke of Richmond, whose political interference was submitted to with much reluctance by the electors. Upon the death of General Keppel, in 1782, an attempt was made to oppose the duke's nomination of the Hon. Percy Windham, brother to the earl of Egremont, but without success. Mr. Brian Edwards, who was the candidate in opposition to Mr. Windham, however, lost his election, by being in a minority of only eight votes. At the ensuing general election of 1784, the independent electors triumphed in the choice of George White Thomas, Esq. one of the present representatives; and, at the last dissolution of parliament, in 1790, they became powerful enough to carry both the members. Mr. Steele, the representative of the duke of Richmond's interest, attempted to divide the phalanx of uninfluenced electors, by canvassing upon *his own interest*, without the appearance of aristocratical support; but this was found to be too insignificant, even to countenance the manœuvre. The friends of Mr. Thomas, who were now become a decisive majority of the inhabitants,

habitants, for the sake of preserving the peace and harmony of the city, and to avoid those ruinous expences which generally attend a contest with influence and power, made a voluntary offer of admitting the duke of Richmond to recommend one of the members, if he would engage to leave the other to their own choice. This offer was accepted by his grace: and Mr. Steele published a letter disclaiming all pretensions to the honour he aspired at, upon the foundation of his own merits, and modestly acknowledged his gratitude to those of a superior source.

The corporation are all in the interest of the duke of Richmond, who is high steward; and his brother, lord George Henry Lenox, is one of the aldermen.

CORPORATION—By charter of king James II. it is governed by a mayor, recorder, and 38 common-councilmen.

RIGHT OF ELECTION—In the inhabitants paying scot and lot.

RETURNING OFFICER—The mayor.

NUMBER OF VOTERS—620.

PATRON—Duke of Richmond, partially.

HORSHAM.

HORSHAM.

POLITICAL CHARACTER—This town is among the firſt in the county in trade and number of inhabitants; but the right of election here, as in many other towns of much larger extent in this country, is excluſively in the burgage-holders. The number of theſe burgage-holds is twenty-five, fourteen of which are the property of lady Irvine, and eleven are the duke of Norfolk's. At the laſt general election, Timothy Shelley, Eſq. and Wilſon Braddyll, Eſq. were candidates in the duke's intereſt, and lord William Gordon, and James Baillie, Eſq. were ſupported by lady Irvine. The numbers on the poll were,

For Timothy Shelley, Eſq.   25
     Wilſon Braddyll, Eſq.   24
     Lord William Gordon   20
     James Baillie, Eſq.   9

In conſequence of which the two former were returned.

Lord William Gordon and Mr. Baillie preſented a petition to the houſe of commons; the merits of which being tried in the late ſeſſion, before a committee of the whole houſe, the petitioners were declared to be duly elected, and ought to have been returned; and they accordingly took their seats.

The votes allowed to be legal by the committee were,

>   For Lord William Gordon   15
>   James Baillie, Esq.   14
>   Timothy Shelley, Esq.   10
>   Wilson Braddyll, Esq.   9

The two bailiffs, who are the returning officers, are annually chosen at the court-leet of the duke of Norfolk, who is lord of the manor.

RIGHT OF ELECTION—1715, 16 June. Is in all such persons as have an estate of inheritance, or for life, in burgage-houses or burgage-lands, lying within the said borough.

RETURNING OFFICERS—The bailiffs.

NUMBER OF VOTERS—Twenty-five.

PROPRIETORS—Duke of Norfolk, and lady viscountess Irvine.

MIDHURST.

POLITICAL CHARACTER—This is a borough, which has the privilege of sending two members to parliament, although there is not a single house standing within the limits of it. The right of election is in one hundred and twenty burgage-holds, the situation of which is distinctly marked at present by the position of a large stone upon each of them. There is no part of the town of Midhurst built upon these tenures; they were the property of the late lord viscount Montagu, who made, at the time of an election, a temporary assignment of a part of them, either to some of his domestics or particular friends, for the purpose of having those members returned that he should nominate. The trustees of the estates of the present lord sold these burgage-holds to the earl of Egremont, for forty thousand guineas; whose brothers were returned for this borough at the last general election. How can these gentlemen be called representatives, when there is not so much as one solitary individual existing within the precincts of the place, to make a constituent body? If the voice of the nation is only to be heard in the house of commons, how can that possibly happen, unless it be its real representatives? And whether we are governed contrary to our inclinations, or by persons to whom we have given no such commission, we are equally an enslaved people. The above instance is a sufficient conviction of the mockery of our representation, and of the want of some immediate radical cure for so great an evil.

RIGHT OF ELECTION—In the burgage-holders.

RETURNING OFFICERS—The steward and bailiff.

NUMBER OF VOTERS—One.

PROPRIETOR—The earl of Egremont.

LEWES.

POLITICAL CHARACTER—This town was never incorporated; and the right of voting here is in the inhabitants housekeepers paying scot and lot. This borough was formerly under the absolute controul of the late duke of Newcastle. This influence his grace acquired from the weight of property which he possessed here, and from the distribution of employments under government, of which he was at that time sole manager. In 1768, the late Colonel Hay, of Glynde Bourne, near this town, was recommended by the duke, as one of the candidates for its representation; in consequence of which he obtained from the voters a promise of their suffrages. Immediately after this transaction, the duke thought proper to countermand his former recommendation, and accordingly withdrew his sanction from Colonel Hay, and gave it to Sir Thomas Miller. The people however thought themselves bound in honour to abide by their promises; and Colonel

Hay,

Hay, conceiving himself ill treated in the business, resolved to stand the poll. Upon the day of election, he was firmly supported by his friends, who gave him sixty single votes, and obtained for him so great a majority over his opponent, as to make him finally succefsful. In 1780 there was a crofs poll, when the Hon. Henry Pelham, Colonel Hay, and Thomas Kemp, Esq. of this borough, were candidates, each of whom stood upon his own separate interest. In this contest Mr. Hay was unfuccefsful; and Mr. Kemp was returned by the interest which had always shewn itself hostile to that of Lord Pelham. In 1784 Sir Henry Blackman, Knt. was put in nomination, to represent this town, by the famous Mr. Harben, of upstart notoriety, who, notwithstanding this profefsion of friendship, on the day of election deserted and cruelly betrayed him: upon which Sir Henry reprefented to the people the situation into which he had been led by the artifices of this man, in so pathetic and convincing a manner, that Mr. Harben was obliged instantly to quit the hall, amidst the hifses and execrations of his fellow townsmen.

At the last general election there was an union between the leading men in the independent party, and those in the interest of Lord Pelham, which Mr. Shelly, who was countenanced by administration, oppofed.

At the clofe of the poll the numbers were,

For the Hon. Henry Pelham — 154
Thomas Kemp, Efq. — 149
Henry Shelly, jun. Efq.— 88

Mr. Kemp, when he firft offered himfelf a candidate, agreeable to the principles of the conftitution, pledged himfelf to the electors, as the late alderman Bull did to the city of London, that he would accept of neither place, penfion, gratuity, nor reward of any kind from any adminiftration, while he fhould have the honour of reprefenting them in parliament.

RIGHT OF ELECTION—1735, 8 May. Is in the inhabitants, being houfeholders, paying fcot and lot.

Agreed to by the houfe, *nem. con.*

RETURNING OFFICERS—The conftables.

NUMBER OF VOTERS—About two hundred and forty.

PATRON—Lord Pelham, partially.

SHOREHAM.

POLITICAL CHARACTER—This borough has rendered itfelf more confpicuous than moft others, by a remarkable fcene of corruption, which

which was brought to light before a committee in the houfe of commons, in the year 1771. The returning officer had returned a candidate with only 37 votes, in prejudice to another who had 87; of which he had queried 76, and made his return without examining the validity of the votes he had fo queried.

It appeared, from the defence made by the officer, that a majority of freemen of that borough had formed themfelves into a fociety, under the name of the Chriftian Club; the apparent ends of which inftitution were to promote acts of charity and benevolence, and to anfwer fuch other purpofes as were fuitable to the import of its name. Under this fanction of piety and religion, and the cover of occafional acts of charity, they profaned that facred name, by making it a cloak for carrying on the worft purpofes; making a traffic of their oaths and confciences, and fetting their borough to fale to the higheft bidder; while the reft of the freemen were deprived of every legal benefit from their votes.

The members of this fociety were bound to fecrecy, and to each other, by oaths, writings, bonds with large penalties, and all the ties that could ftrengthen their compact; and carried on this traffic by the means of a felect committee, who,

who, under pretence of scruples of conscience, never appeared or voted at any elections themselves; but, having notwithstanding sold the borough, and received the stipulated price, they gave directions to the rest how to vote; and by this complicated evasion, the employers and their agents, having fully satisfied their consciences, shared the money as soon as the election was over, without any scruple.

The returning officer had belonged to this society; and having taken some disgust to his associates, he quitted the party. The majority of legal voters which he objected to, was, he said, in part owing to his experimental knowledge of their corruption, and partly founded upon several improper acts which had come within his knowledge as magistrate upon the late election; particularly an affidavit of a very considerable sum of money which had been distributed among them. Upon these grounds, though they had the hardiness to take the oath against bribery and corruption, he looked upon them as disqualified; and having, besides, taken the opinion of counsel, which, it seems, coincided with his own, he returned the candidate who had the smaller number of votes, as they were free from these objections.

Upon these principles, and his not acting intentionally

tentionally wrong, the officer rested his plea of
justification for the illegality of his conduct. As
the assumption of such an act of power by a returning officer, upon whatever principle it was
founded, would, however, have been a precedent
of the most dangerous tendency, he was accordingly taken into custody; but, in consideration
of the circumstances in his favour, and of his
bringing so infamous a combination to light, he
was discharged, after receiving a reprimand, upon his knees, from the speaker, in the presence of
the house.

As this combination was of too flagrant a nature to be overlooked, and the select committee
had not power to proceed any further in it, they
reported the whole matter to the house, and moved, that they would make a further inquiry into
it. Though this met with an opposition from
some of those who, having no good wishes for the
late act for regulating the trial of controverted
elections, were glad of so early an opportunity to
point out its inefficacy, and depreciate its merits;
yet the general excellency of that law, notwithstanding any of its present deficiencies, which
every day's experience would give new opportu-
nities of supplying, carried with it such conviction
as to be already well understood; and the motion

on for an inquiry was carried through without a division.

The allegations made by the returning officer having been as fully proved, in the courſe of this inquiry, as the nature of the caſe would admit, and entirely to the ſatisfaction of the houſe, a bill was at length brought in, to incapacitate 81 freemen of Shoreham, by name, from voting at elections of members to ſerve in parliament, and for the preventing bribery and corruption in that borough; and at the ſame time an addreſs was ordered, for the attorney-general to proſecute the five members of the Chriſtian Club who compoſed the committee which tranſacted the bargain, as to the ſale of the borough at the laſt election.

The different tranſactions, however, conſequent of this ſubject, ran through the whole ſeſſion; and it was not till the laſt day of it that the bill received the royal aſſent. The members of the club were heard by counſel againſt it. Many doubts alſo aroſe as to the mode of puniſhment. It was propoſed to disfranchiſe the borough; this, however, was thought too dangerous a precedent: others thought that the culprits ſhould be left to the puniſhment of the law; but, though there was a clear conviction of their guilt,

it

it was a matter of such a nature, as made the establishments of legal evidence very difficult; and if they escaped without some signal mark of reprobation, it would be an encouragement to the most barefaced corruption, when the whole kingdom saw that it could be done with impunity.

The 11th Geo. III. cap. 55, recites, in the preamble, that, " Whereas a wicked and corrupt society, calling itself the Christian Society, hath, for several years, subsisted in the borough of New Shoreham, in the county of Sussex, and consisted of a great majority of persons having a right to vote at elections of members to serve in parliament for the said borough; and whereas it appears, that the chief end of the institution of the said society, was for the purpose of selling, from time to time, the seat or seats in parliament for the said borough: and whereas John Burnett, Charles Hannington, Thomas Haselgrove, Ralph Moor, Thomas Parsons, Thomas Snook, junior, Thomas Hannington, John Hannington, John Robinson, William Cheesman, George Browne, John Parsons, John Curl, Frederick Dean, William Dean, Samuel Tuppen, John Sawyers, Thomas Crowter, Thomas Pockney, Joseph Dedman, John Dean, John Whiting, William Stevens, John Bawcomb, Robert Parker, John Hogsflesh,

John Purſe, John Dean, Thomas Jennings, John Snook, junior, Richard Tilſtone, William Turner, Walter Sawyers, Charles Mitchell, John Jarmand, John Wood, Friend Daniel, William Gratwick, Nathaniel Hillman, Thomas Roberts, John Aſhman, William Cooter. Thomas Froſt, Michael Smith, Richard Carver, Michael Durrant, Emery Churcher, Walter Broad, Richard Stoneham, James Bennett, Clement Freeman, William Jupp, Thomas Crowter, John Barnard, James Mitchell, James Millar, otherwiſe Miller, William Newnham, Jeffery Carver, Randall Button, James Carver, John Martin, John Dedman, ſenior, William Jennings, William Hards, Thomas Gear, William Ruſbridge, Henry Robinſon, and Henry Hannington, were members of the ſaid ſociety: in order therefore, to prevent ſuch unlawful practices for the future, and that the ſaid borough from henceforth be duly repreſented in parliament, be it enacted, that the ſaid parties ſhall be, and by virtue of this act are, from henceforth, incapacitated, and diſabled from giving any vote at any election for chooſing a member or members to ſerve in parliament. It is alſo enacted, That from henceforth it ſhall and may be lawful to and for every freeholder, being above the age of one-and-twenty years, who ſhall have, within

the

the rape of Bramber, in the said county of Sussex, a freehold of the clear yearly value of forty shillings, to give his vote at every election of a burgess or burgesses to serve in parliament for the said borough of New Shoreham.

"And it is further enacted, That the right of election of a member or members to serve in parliament for the said borough of New Shoreham shall be, and is hereby declared to be, in such freeholders as aforesaid, and in the persons who, by the custom and usage of the said borough, have, or shall hereafter have, a right to vote at such election; those whose names are mentioned herein, and incapacitated and disabled by this act, only excepted: and the constable, or other proper officer for the time being, to whom the return of such writ or precept does belong, is hereby required to return the person or persons, to serve in parliament for the said borough, who shall have the major number of votes of such freeholders and other persons having a right to vote at such election (except such persons as are herein before excepted); any law or usage to the contrary notwithstanding."

The right of election being now extended by the above act to about twelve hundred freeholders of the rape of Bramber, the arts of corruption

tion have been defeated; the borough has since
been represented by independent country gentlemen, and every election has been conducted with
constitutional decorum. The practical experiment that has been tried here, and at Cricklade,
of the advantages which would attend a parliamentary reform, or even a similar disfranchisement of the corrupt and decayed boroughs, is a
complete refutation of every objection that has
been urged against that important measure.

Right of election—11 Geo. III. c. 3, § 6.
(To be publicly read before they proceed to election)
Is in such freeholders, and in the persons who,
by the custom and usage of the said borough, had
a right to vote at such election (sixty-nine persons in this act particularly named, freeholders
of the said borough, always and only excepted).

Returning officers—The constables.

Number of voters—1200.

BRAMBER.

Political character—This borough, which
consists of six-and-thirty miserable thatched cottages, is composed of two intersections of a street,
the upper and middle parts of which constitute
the borough of Steyning. The Duke of Norfolk
is lord of the manor in both places; and the constables,

stables, who are the returning officers in each borough, are chosen at his courts-leet; but the six-and-thirty cottages, which are burgage-holds, and give the right of voting to the tenants, are one half of them the property of the duke of Rutland, and the other of Sir Henry Gough Calthorpe, Bart. who, since the year 1786, have each agreed to send one member.

In 1786 there was a contest between the two proprietors of this borough; when a tenant of one of these miserable cottages had the fortitude and integrity to resist the offer of a thousand pounds to influence his apostasy; and we are happy to have it in our power to add, that this fact is authenticated by unimpeachable authority.

From the year 1298 to 1472 this borough was joined with Steyning in the writs for electing burgesses to serve in parliament; since which time they have elected as different boroughs.

RIGHT OF ELECTION—1703, 18 Jan. 10 Mar. 1715, 1 June. Is in the persons inhabiting houses built on ancient foundations, paying scot and lot.

RETURNING OFFICER—The constable.

NUMBER OF VOTERS—36.

PROPRIETORS—Duke of Rutland, and Sir Henry Gough Calthorpe, Bart.

STEYNING.

Political character—This borough, together with that of Bramber, confifts of one ftreet, not more than two thirds as large as Grub-ftreet in London; but conftituting *two boroughs*, with a right of fending *four members to parliament!!!* They formerly elected in conjunction, and intermitted till 31 Henry VI. One part of Bramber is in the centre of the borough of Steyning, and a part of Steyning interfects Bramber in like manner. Inveloped in the dark cloud of legal quibble and intricacy, they prefent us, like all the rotten boroughs, with a finifhed picture of political deformity; irregular in their diftricts, unintelligible in their conftitutions, indefinite in their rights, corrupt in the exercife of their functions, contradictory in their refpective organizations, and adverfe to the ancient eftablifhed principles of the conftitution, and the rights of men.

The right of election has been the fubject of litigation in this place for near a century, and has lately received a final decifion from a committee conftituted under the authority of 28 Geo. III. to determine the fame, upon an appeal from a contrary determination the preceding year.

In 1701 the right was determined to be in the
inhabitants

inhabitants paying scot and lot, and not receiving alms;

In 1710, to be in the conftables and houfeholders (inhabitants) paying scot and lot;

In 1791, to be in the inhabitants of ancient houfes, and houfes built on the fcites of ancient foundations, within the borough of Steyning, being houfeholders, paying scot and lot, and not receiving alms.

In 1792, the felect committee appointed to try and determine the merits of the petition of James Martin Lloyd, Efq. and others, refolved,

That no perfon has a right to vote at an election for members to ferve in parliament for the borough of Steyning, in refpect of any houfes within the borough of Bramber, the tything of Bidlington, or the manors of Charlton or King's Barns.

The faid felect committee, at the fame time, alfo determined,

That the right of election of members to ferve in parliament for the borough of Steyning, in the county of Suffex, is in the conftable and houfeholders, inhabitants within the faid borough, paying scot and lot, and not receiving alms.

The houfes built on ancient foundations are all the property of Sir John Honeywood; the reft belong to the duke of Norfolk: and as thofe of a general defcription are more numerous, the refolution of 1792, repealing that of 1791, changes the patron, and gives that influence to the duke of Norfolk, which the former gave to Sir John Honeywood.

The refolution of 1791 oufted Henry Howard, Efq. the prefent member for Arundel, who had a majority of the houfeholders paying fcot and lot, and declared John Curtis, Efq. who had only the votes of thofe perfons who inhabited houfes built on ancient foundations, duly elected.

The refolution of 1792 eftablifhed the right of the houfeholders, and confequently repealed the refolution of the former year.

Thefe contradictory refolutions have been productive of the fame parliamentary inconfiftency which diftinguifhed the borough of Saltafh in the laft parliament. Mr. Ambler obtained his feat for that place by the decifion of a committee in 1785, againft the petition of lord Strathaven, and the fame Mr. Curtis, who has now fucceeded at Steyning, on the right of the corporation to elect the members for that borough. In 1787, Mr. Lemon, the petitioner, by the determination of a fecond committee, appointed to try the fame queftion, fucceeded

on

on the votes of the burgage-holders, and ousted the earl of Mornington, the sitting member, who had been elected by the corporation.

" Thus two members were sitting in the
" house of commons, at the same time, and for
" the same borough, upon the right of different
" descriptions of electors, who had each of
" them been deemed ineligible in the same par-
" liament."

This is exactly the case with the representatives of this borough. The inhabitants of houses built on ancient foundations, and the inhabitants in general, have each been declared to have the right of election; and a member, chosen by each description of voters, has been seated and ousted in the present parliament.

This place first sent to parliament 4 Edw. II. and after intermitted sending (as Bramber had done before) till 31 Hen. VI.

RETURNING OFFICER—The constable.

NUMBER OF VOTERS—About 100.

PROPRIETORS—Duke of Norfolk, and Sir John Honeywood.

EAST GRINSTEAD.

POLITICAL CHARACTER—The right of voting formerly was allowed to be, by a resolution of the house of commons, in the inhabitants as well as burgage-holders; but by a subsequent one it is confined to the latter description of persons only. The burgage-holds here are in number thirty-six; twenty-nine of which are the property of the duke of Dorset; and the remaining seven belong to persons residing in the place. This minority is so inconsiderable, that no opposition can be made to the duke's interest. If indeed the last resolution of the house of commons was rescinded, and the right of election left where it was, previous to that determination, an attempt to shake off the aristocratic yoke might then be as successful as it would be commendable; but it would be, in the present state of things, both ridiculous and impolitic to attempt it.

The county assizes are generally held here. John Sackville, earl of Dorset, in the reign of king James I. built an hospital here, and endowed it with 33ol. a year, for the support of thirty-one poor persons of this town.

The firſt return of this borough is anno 1 Edward II.

Right of Election—1679, April 7. Being an ancient borough by preſcription, the inhabitants, as well as the burgage-holders of the ſaid borough, have a right to vote in elections.

1695, Feb. 9. Is not in the burgage-holders and inhabitants of the ſaid borough:

Is in the burgage-holders only.

Number of Voters—36.

Returning Officer—The bailiff, choſen at the duke of Dorſet's court-leet.

Proprietor—Duke of Dorſet.

ARUNDEL.

Political Character—This borough was under the influence of Sir George Colebrooke, in the days of his affluence; ſince which time its repreſentation has been an object of conteſt, till 1784, when an agreement took place between the electors and the duke of Norfolk, whoſe ancient and venerable caſtle is near the town, that each party ſhould name one of its members. The corporation are in the intereſt of the duke, who has likewiſe built a magnificent

cent inn, and has a confiderable property in this borough and its neighbourhood.

In 1780, a petition being prefented to the houfe of commons by the Hon. Percy Charles Wyndham, complaining of the undue election and return of Sir Patrick Crauford, Knt. and Thomas Fitzherbert, Efq. a committee was appointed on the 6th of March, 1781, to try the merits of the fame; when it appeared in evidence, that a fociety exifted in this borough, under the name of the Malt-houfe Club, fimilar, in its inftitution and practices, to the Chriftian Club at Shoreham; and that the perfons who compofed this club had actually received thirty guineas a man for giving their votes at the preceding election. The evidence did not extend to the incapacitation of both the members. Mr. Fitzherbert was included in the allegations of the petition, but not in the decifion of the committee, who reported to the houfe, on the 12th of March, 1781,

That Thomas Fitzherbert, Efq. was duly elected.

That Sir Patrick Crauford, Knt. was *not* duly elected.

That the Hon. Percy Charles Wyndham, the petitioner, was *not* duly elected.

A new

ARUNDEL.

A new writ was accordingly issued, when Peter William Baker, Esq. was unanimously chosen to supply the vacancy.

The present members are, Henry Howard, Esq. a relation to the duke of Norfolk, and Sir George Thomas, Bart. of Dale-Park, near this borough.

CORPORATION—It is governed, under a charter of queen Elizabeth, by a mayor, and twelve burgesses. The mayor is annually chosen, and is judge at a court-leet of the lord of the manor, held every three weeks. He has the authority of a justice of the peace, though he seldom executes the office; he appoints collectors of the package and stallage, ale-conners, and flesh-tasters; no writ can be executed within the borough without his permission.

RIGHT OF ELECTION—1693, Feb. 22. Is only in the inhabitants of the said borough paying scot and lot.

NUMBER OF VOTERS—About 190.

RETURNING OFFICER—The mayor.

PATRON—The duke of Norfolk, partially.

WARWICK

WARWICK COUNTY.

Political Character.

THIS county, from the opulence and extent of its manufactories, is independent, in a great degree, of aristocratic controul; but it has been the last in the kingdom to emancipate itself from high-church bigotry, and that spirit of persecution, which, in proportion to the increase of learning and science, is now becoming exploded in every part of Europe.

The late disgraceful riots in this county, and those of June 1780, is a humiliating proof, to the people of this country, that they do not take the lead in the extinction of prejudice, or in the advancement of literature, the inseparable companions of each other's progress.

The town of Birmingham, from its extent and population, has sufficient weight to return one of the county representatives, which the people of that place never fail to avail themselves of, notwithstanding the indifference that is affected to be shewn by some leading individuals, to the advantages they would derive from a perfect representation.

Warwickſhire is divided into five hundreds, containing one city, and thirteen market-towns, viz. the city of Coventry, Atherſton, Aulceſter, Birmingham, Bitford, Coleſhill, Henley, Kineton, Nuneaton, Rugby, Southam, Stratford, Sutton-Cofield, and Warwick. It lies in the province of Canterbury, partly in the dioceſe of Litchfield and Coventry, and partly in that of Worceſter; and has one hundred and fifty-eight pariſhes. It ſends ſix members to parliament, namely, two knights of the ſhire for the county, two citizens for the city of Coventry, and two burgeſſes for the town of Warwick.

WARWICK TOWN.

POLITICAL CHARACTER—The right of election in this borough, according to the firſt reſolution of the houſe of commons, was in the commonalty, which in the caſes of Colcheſter, Boſton, Bridport, and this place, has been explained to be houſekeepers paying ſcot and lot; though, in the caſe of Pool, the ſame word was defined to be the ſelect burgeſſes only. There have been frequent ſtruggles here for ſuperiority between the earl of Warwick, of Warwick-caſtle, adjoining to this town, and the independent party. In 1780, and in 1784, the Hon.

C. F.

C. F. Greville, and Robert Ladbroke, Efq. were returned to reprefent this town in parliament, in oppofition to his lordfhip's intereft. At the laft general election, however, in 1790, thofe gentlemen conceived that the earl of Warwick's influence had increafed to a great degree; in confequence of which they were induced to decline an oppofition to it, which would have been attended with the certainty of much expence, and the uncertainty of being finally fuccefsful. Lord Arden, and Henry Gage, Efq. now lord vifcount Gage, both in the earl's intereft, were returned without a conteft. Upon Mr. Gage's fucceeding to his uncle's title, the Hon. Mr. Villiers was propofed by his lordfhip's friends; and Mr. Knight, by the independent party. Mr. Villiers obtained a majority on the poll, over Mr. Knight, of nearly two to one. The latter gentleman petitioned parliament, in which he complained of the undue influence which had been ufed againft him at the time of election, &c. but upon a trial before a committee the former eftablifhed his feat.

CORPORATION—This is a very ancient corporation, being made a mayor town by Queen Mary, in the year 1554, and re-incorporated by King

King Charles II. under whose charter it is at present governed by a mayor, a recorder, twelve aldermen or brethren, and twenty-four burgesses or common-councilmen.

The county assizes and general quarter-sessions are held in this town.

RIGHT OF ELECTION—1628, 3 May. Is in the commonalty of the said town.

1722, 31 Jan. Is in such persons only as pay to church and poor of the said borough.

NUMBER OF VOTERS—391.

RETURNING OFFICER—The mayor.

PATRON—The earl of Warwick.

COVENTRY.

POLITICAL CHARACTER—A singular case occurred at the election for this city in 1780. Mr. Roe Yeo and Mr. Holroyd were candidates in the interest of administration; and Sir Thomas Halifax and Thomas Rogers, Esq. were supported by the corporation of Coventry, in opposition to those gentlemen. On the 9th day of September the election commenced, and the poll was opened and conducted in a peaceable and orderly manner for about the space of half an hour, when upwards of five hundred persons, who

who were not freemen or inhabitants of this city, tumultuously assembled together at the place of election, with a blue flag carried before them, and having blue and white cockades in their hats, the badges by which the party of Roe Yeo and Holroyd were distinguished, and there beat and ill treated all the electors who came to vote for Halifax and Rogers, and so impeded and obstructed the voters, that the sheriffs adjourned the poll to the Monday following, being the eleventh of the said month of September, and continued the same, by divers adjournments, from day to day, to the 18th of the said month, in order that the election might be made; but the poll was impeded, from time to time, by like tumults and assaults; and though the magistrates had appointed two hundred and thirty additional constables to preserve the peace, and to open a free accefs for the voters on both sides to come and poll, yet no more than eighty-three, out of two thousand could give their votes: for which reason the sheriffs could not cause to be elected two citizens, according to the form and effect of the writ.

The sheriffs having certified the above to the house of commons, on the sixth day of November following, they were ordered to attend the house on the 23d of the same month.

A petition of Sir Thomas Halifax, and Thomas Rogers, Esq. of similar import, was presented to the house on the 20th of the same month; which was ordered to be taken into consideration on the same day that the sheriffs were to attend; as was another petition of certain electors in the interest of Sir Thomas Halifax and Mr. Rogers.

A petition of Edward Roe Yeo, Esq. and John Baker Holroyd, Esq. was also presented on the same day, stating, that the sheriffs, who are chosen by the mayor and aldermen, and were the declared friends and partisans of their opponents, Sir Thomas Halifax, and Thomas Rogers, Esq. had shewn the most flagrant partiality to those gentlemen, by constructing the poll-booth in such a manner as to allow a commodious access, through the mayor's parlour, to the voters in the interest of Halifax and Rogers, while the agents and friends of the petitioner were obliged to ascend by a ladder; and enumerating a variety of other charges, to shew the gross partiality and illegal conduct of the sheriffs.

This petition was also ordered to be taken
into

into confideration with all the former. A new writ having been iffued on the 21ft Nov. following, petitions were again prefented from Mr. Roe Yeo, and Mr. Holroyd, complaining, that in the interval of time between the general election and the 29th day of November, when a fecond election was had in purfuance of the above writ, a great number of freemen were illegally admitted to the freedom of the faid city, who had no right to fuch freedom, and without paying the ufual fees on admiffion, on condition of their undertaking to vote, at the faid election, for Sir Thomas Halifax, and Thomas Rogers, Efq. and that a great number of perfons duly intitled to be admitted to the freedom of the faid city, demanded in the ufual manner to be fo admitted, being ready to produce the evidence of their titles, and to pay the ufual fees, but were refufed to be admitted, becaufe they were believed to be in the intereft of the petitioners; and that, at the faid laft election, after the poll had lafted near three weeks, almoft all the legal freemen having then voted, and when it was known that there would be a large majority of votes in favour of the petitioners, a great number of perfons were, on Monday the 18th, and Wednefday the 20th of December

laft,

last, in a fraudulent and clandestine manner, admitted to the freedom of the said city, although the said persons had no title to such freedom, and were known, by the members of the corporation, who composed the council-chambers at which they were admitted, to have no title; and without paying the accustomed fees, or any fees, on condition of their voting for the said Sir Thomas Halifax, and Thomas Rogers, Esq.

The above petition also contained the usual allegations, of the returning officers admitting these freemen to poll who were not duly qualified, and rejecting others who were so qualified; and of the said candidates, Sir Thomas Halifax, and Thomas Rogers, Esq. having, by themselves, or agents, been guilty of bribery, &c.

A similar petition was presented from several of the freemen in the interest of Mr. Roe Yeo and Mr. Holroyd, which were both ordered to be taken into consideration on Thursday the 15th day of February, 1781.

On the 31st of January, 1781, Thomas Noxon and Thomas Butler, late sheriffs of Coventry, were brought to the bar of the house of commons,

mons, and had leave to be heard by counſel in their juſtification.

A petition of Edward Roe Yeo, Eſq. and John Baker Holroyd (now lord Sheffield, of the kingdom of Ireland), and alſo of ſeveral freemen of the city of Coventry, on behalf of themſelves and others, complaining of the conduct of the ſaid ſheriffs, being read to the ſaid Thomas Noxon and Thomas Butler, leave was given them to be heard by counſel againſt the charges in the ſaid petition, and the counſel for the petitioners ordered to proceed in ſupport of the allegations of their petition.

Orders were made for ſixty-nine witneſſes to attend in ſupport of the charges againſt the ſheriffs; and the matter had a full inveſtigation, after various adjournments, on the 15th of March, 1781; when the order of the day being read for the attendance of Mr. Thomas Noxon and Mr. Thomas Butler, late ſheriffs of the city of Coventry, and for taking into further conſideration the ſeveral petitions preſented to this houſe upon the 20th day of November laſt, relating to the return made by the ſaid ſheriffs at the laſt general election;

The ſaid ſheriffs, and the counſel for lord Sheffield and Mr. Roe Yeo, and for the ſeveral freemen

freemen of the city of Coventry, who have petitioned this houfe, complaining of the conduct of the faid fheriffs, were called in;

And the fheriffs acquainted the houfe, That the counfel they had applied to had not time to prepare himfelf to undertake their defence.

Then one of the counfel for lord Sheffield and Mr. Roe Yeo, and for the feveral freemen of the city of Coventry, who have petitioned this houfe, complaining of the conduct of the faid fheriffs, fummed up their evidence:

And the fheriffs being afked by Mr. Speaker, what they had to fay in juftification of their not having made any return of members to ferve in parliament, at the laft general election; and in anfwer to the matters charged againft them in the petitions of lord Sheffield and Mr. Roe Yeo, and of the feveral freemen of the city of Coventry, who have petitioned this houfe, complaining of their conduct:

The faid fheriffs were heard; and, having defired that their under-fheriff, who attended as their agent, might examine the witneffes who had been ordered to attend this houfe on their behalf;

The faid agent was called in; and, at the bar, examined the feveral witneffes who were attending,

attending, in juſtification of the conduct of the ſheriffs.

And the ſaid agent having ſubmitted to the houſe, That the ſaid ſheriffs had ſtill ſeveral other witneſſes, but that they were now at Coventry, and that they therefore deſired further time, in order to have an opportunity to ſummon the ſaid witneſſes;

The ſaid ſheriffs and their agent, and the ſaid counſel, were directed to withdraw.

And a motion being made, and the queſtion being put, " That the further attendance of the
" ſaid ſheriffs, and the further conſideration of
" the ſeveral petitions relative to the return made
" by them for the city of Coventry, at the laſt
" general election, be adjourned till this day
" ſe'nnight;"

It paſſed in the negative.

Then the ſaid ſheriffs and their agent, and the ſaid counſel, were again called in;

And the ſheriffs having acquainted the houſe, that they had not any other witneſſes to produce,

The ſaid ſheriffs and their agent, and the ſaid counſel, were again directed to withdraw.

Reſolved, " That it appears to this houſe, that
　" at the laſt general election of citizens to
　" ſerve in parliament for the city of Coven-
　　　　　　　　　　　　　　　　　" try,

"try, Thomas Noxon and Thomas Butler,
"the sheriffs, who were the returning offi-
"cers at the said election, were not prevent-
"ed, by riots or otherwise, from making a
"return of members to serve in parliament
"for the said city:"

Resolved, nem. con. " That the said Thomas
"Noxon and Thomas Butler, late sheriffs of
"the said city of Coventry, not having made
"any return of members to serve in parlia-
"ment, at the late general election, for the
"said city, are thereby guilty of a high vio-
"lation of the law, and a gross breach of
"the privileges of this house."

A motion was made, and the question being proposed, " That the said Thomas Noxon and
"Thomas Butler be, for their said offence, com-
"mitted to his majesty's gaol of Newgate, and
"that Mr. Speaker do issue his warrants accord-
"ingly;"

An amendment was proposed to be made to the question, by leaving out the words, " his
"majesty's gaol of Newgate," and inserting the words, " the custody of the serjeant at arms at-
"tending this house," instead thereof.

And the question being put, that the words,
"his

" his majesty's gaol of Newgate," stand part of the question;

It was resolved in the affirmative.

Then the main question being put;

Ordered, " That the said Thomas Noxon and
" Thomas Butler be, for their said offence,
" committed to his majesty's gaol of New-
" gate; and that Mr. Speaker do issue his
" warrants accordingly."

On the 26th day of March the said sheriffs presented a petition to the house, setting forth, that they had been found guilty of a high violation of the law, and a gross breach of the privileges of the house, for not having made any return of members to serve in parliament at the last general election for the city of Coventry; and that they were thoroughly sensible of the great offence they had been guilty of, and humbly begged pardon of the house for the same.

They were accordingly ordered to be brought up to the bar, the next day, when they were reprimanded by the speaker, and discharged.

A committee was appointed, on the 15th of February, to try the merits of the petition of Mr. Roe Yeo and lord Sheffield, against the return of Sir Thomas Halifax, and Thomas Rogers, Esq.

Esq. who reported, on the 27th of the said month, that the petitioners were duly elected.

Mr. Elwes, the chairman of the committee, also reported, " That it appeared, that much parti-
" ality and fraud was used in the admission of
" persons to the freedom of the city of Coventry,
" during the last election in that city. The com-
" mittee are of opinion, that it would be expe-
" dient, in order to prevent the like fraudulent
" practice for the future, that a bill should be
" brought in for that purpose."

A bill was accordingly brought in, on the 12th of March, for better regulating elections of citizens to sit in parliament for the city of Coventry; which was passed into a law on the 14th of May, and received the royal assent on the 5th of July following.

This city is not under immediate influence, and might be perfectly independent in the choice of its members, if the present destructive mode of treating was abolished.

It is worthy of remark, that the case of Hindon affords us the only instance, in the present reign, of a prosecution being ordered by the house of commons against any candidate for bribery; and that the Coventry case is the only one which occurs, in the same period of time, of a returning officer being punished for partiality. In both cases the parties were in opposition to government.

This city, which was made a mayor-town by Edward III. and a county of itself by Henry VI. having returned to the four first parliaments of Edward I. intermitted sending members, except 8 Edward II. and 20, 25, Edward III. till 31 Henry VI.

CORPORATION—By charter of James I. it is governed by a mayor, recorder, two sheriffs, ten aldermen, thirty-one superior, and twenty-five inferior common-councilmen.

RIGHT OF ELECTION—1701, February 24. The freemen of Coventry receiving alms or charity, have no right to vote.

1708, March 1. Is in such persons who have served apprenticeships for seven years within the city, to one and the same trade, not receiving alms or constant charities.

Persons receiving Sir Thomas White's gift, are thereby disabled from giving their votes.

It passed in the negative.

1708, March 3. Persons receiving Mr. Wheatley's gift not disabled.

1711, March 13. The members of the Fullers company have a right to vote, being freemen,

men, and not receiving alms or weekly charity; and all such freemen as do not receive alms, and have served seven years apprenticeship in the city or suburbs, who do not receive alms or weekly charity.

1722, November 20. In such freemen as have served seven years apprenticeship to one and the same trade, in the same city or the suburbs thereof, and do not receive alms or weekly charity; such freemen being duly sworn and enrolled.

NUMBER OF VOTERS—2400.
RETURNING OFFICERS—The sheriffs.

WESTMORELAND.

POLITICAL CHARACTER.

THIS small county is as much under the command of an individual, as the most rotten borough in the kingdom. The great estates which the earl of Lonsdale possesses, are sufficient to procure a passive obedience to dictatorial authority of his lordship. The most spirited efforts of the few independent freeholders, in support of their rights, would here be inefficient;

nor

nor can any oppofition to the above nobleman's nomination of members to reprefent it in parliament, be productive even of a probability of fuccefs.

This county confifts of two divifions; the barony of Weftmoreland, fometimes called the Bottom, and the barony of Kendal. The barony of Weftmoreland, which includes the north part of the county, is an open, champaign country, twenty miles long and fourteen broad, confifting of arable and pafture land. The barony of Kendal, which is fo called from the town of that name, comprehends the fouth part of that county, and is very mountainous: it has, however, fruitful vallies; and even many of the mountains yield pafture for fheep and cattle, while others are not only barren, but feem formed of rocks, thrown together by the hand of difcord, and frightful deferts, laid wafte by the piercing ftorms of the north.

With refpect to the civil and ecclefiaftical divifions, each of them are divided into two wards, and each ward into conftablewicks, the number of which does not appear. It is remarkable, that it was never divided, either into hundreds, wapentakes, or rapes, like other counties; the reafon of which is fuppofed to be,

becaufe

because the inhabitants paid no fubfidies, they having been thought fufficiently charged, in being obliged to defend that part of the kingdom againſt the Scots. It is feated in the province of York: that part which is called the barony of Weſtmoreland, is comprehended in the dioceſe of Carliſle; and the other part, called the barony of Kendal, in the dioceſe of Cheſter; both baronies containing thirty-two large pariſhes. It has no city, and only contains eight market-towns, viz. Ambleſide, Appleby, Brough, Burton, Kendal, Kirkby-Lonſdale, Kirkby-Steven, and Orton. It ſends only four members to parliament, two knights of the ſhire for the county, and two burgeſſes for the borough of Appleby.

APPLEBY.

POLITICAL CHARACTER—The right of voting in this borough, although there is no ſpecial reſolution of the houſe of commons concerning it, is admitted to be in burgage-tenure. Theſe burgage-holds are now the property of the earl of Lonſdale and the earl of Thanet. Hog-ſties have been deemed freeholds here, and purchaſed by the Thanet and Lonſdale families, at a price exceeding all belief. The contention

tion between thefe two families has given the borough its only confequence; but they have now agreed, that each fhall fend one member. The electors of this place, therefore, fit down quietly, to be reprefented by a hog or a horfe, as its noble proprietors fhall think moft proper.

Corporation—It is governed by a mayor, recorder, twelve aldermen, two bailiffs, and fixteen capital burgeffes.

Right of election—Is in the burgage-holders.

Number of voters—Nominally, in about one hundred burgage-tenures, which are now the property of two individuals.

Returning officer—The mayor.

Proprietors—The earl of Thanet and the earl of Lonfdale.

WILTSHIRE.

Political Character.

THIS county poffeffes all that fpirit of independence for which the neighbouring county of Somerfet is fo remarkably eminent. The freeholders and yeomen are as independent in their minds as in their fortunes; and a combination

of

of those, who call themselves the great men of the county, to deprive them of their constitutional privileges of electing their own representatives, will only tend to expose the inability and arbitrary principles of the one party, and the manly exertions and ability of the other, when exercised in supporting their rights. About twenty years ago, Mr. Herbert, now earl of Carnarvon, was proposed as one of the candidates to represent this county in parliament; in which he was supported by the whole aristocracy in it. The independent freeholders could not help feeling an honourable resentment at such an arbitrary measure, the intention of which was to render their suffrages of no effect; they therefore immediately opposed to that candidate Ambrose Goddard, Esq. one of their own body; and, after a poll of several days, victory was declared for them in his favour.

This county, which consists of two parts, north and south, is divided into twenty-nine hundreds, containing three hundred and four parishes, the city of Salisbury, and twenty-three market-towns. It sends thirty-four members to parliament, viz. two knights of the shire, two citizens for Salisbury, and two burgesses for each of the following places; Chippenham, Calne,

Calne, Cricklade, Devizes, Heytesbury, Hindon, Downton, Great Bedwin, Marlborough, Malmesbury, Luggershal, Westbury, Wilton, Wotton Basset, and Old Sarum.

SALISBURY.

POLITICAL CHARACTER—It is equal in population to Winchester; but, like that city, Bath, Portsmouth, Plymouth, Andover, Poole, Tiverton, Banbury, and many other large towns, has no share in electing the democratic branch of the legislature, but what is exercised by its corporation, consisting of a mayor, twenty-three aldermen, and thirty common-council. This exclusion from constitutional rights, places the inhabitants of these towns, in common with all the unrepresented part of the kingdom, in a situation not to be envied by the subjects of any other nation. If freedom consists in electing our own legislators, and in delegating to them the authority by which we are to be governed, those persons who are not allowed the exercise of this privilege, taste as little of the sweets of liberty, as where the will of mankind is subject to an absolute monarch, or an unlimitted aristocracy.

The earl of Radnor, who is recorder of this city,

city, has the principal intereſt with the corporation, who uſually elect one of his lordſhip's relations for their repreſentative.

Corporation—It was firſt incorporated by King Henry III. and afterwards by Queen Anne, and conſiſts of a mayor, recorder, twenty-three aldermen, and thirty common-council-men.

Right of election—1689, April 1. Is in the mayor and corporation.

Number of voters—54.

Patron—Earl of Radnor, partially.

WILTON.

Political character—This borough, on account of its vicinity to the ſeat of the earl of Pembroke, is entirely under his lordſhip's influence. The right of election is in the corporation, conſiſting of a mayor, recorder, five aldermen, three capital burgeſſes, and eleven common-councilmen. Theſe are all in the intereſt of his lordſhip; an oppoſition to which would be attended only with expence; ſo that his nomination of the members to repreſent it in parliament is final and commanding.

The county courts are uſually held here, and the knights of the ſhire choſen.

Corporation

Corporation—By charter of Henry VIII. it confifts of a mayor, recorder, five aldermen, three capital burgeffes, and eleven common-councilmen.

Right of election—1702, November 28. The election of any perfon to be a burgefs of Wilton, who has not taken the facrament of the Lord's-fupper, according to the rites of the church of England, within one year before fuch election, is a void election.

1710, March 17. Agreed to be in the mayor and burgeffes, who are to do all corporate acts, and receive the facrament.

Number of voters—24.
Returning officer—The mayor.
Patron—Earl of Pembroke.

DOWNTON.

Political character—The right of election in this borough is in the burgage-holders. The tenures, which give this privilege, are all the property of the families of the earl of Radnor, or of Robert Shaftoe, Efq. between whom an oppofition has fubfifted for many years.

This conteft has caufed a petition to parliament at every election fince the paffing of the Grenville act.

The

The first was tried in 1775, in which Sir Philip Hales, and John Cooper, Efq. were petitioners on the Shaftoe interest, against Thomas Duncombe, Efq. and Thomas Dummer, Efq. sitting members on the Radnor interest; in which the Shaftoe interest was succefsful.

The second was tried in February 1780, on the petition of Robert Shaftoe, Efq. on his own interest, against the Hon. Bartholomew Bouverie, on that of his brother the earl of Radnor; in which Mr. Shaftoe was succefsful.

The third was tried in March 1781, in which John Saunders, Efq. and Alexander Hume, Efq. were petitioners, and Robert Shaftoe, Efq. and the Hon. Henry Seymour Conway, Efq. were sitting members; when the Shaftoe interest was again succesful.

The fourth was tried in June and July 1784, when there was a double return; Mr. Shaftoe, and the Hon. H. S. Conway, upon the Shaftoe interest; and the Hon. Edward Bouverie, and the present Sir William Scott, on the Radnor interest; when Mr. Shaftoe was declared duly elected, and the election void with respect to a second member.

The fifth petition was in consequence of the above vacancy, when a double return again took place: the Hon. E. Bouverie, in the Radnor intereſt, and the Hon. H. S. Conway, in the Shaftoe intereſt; when the Shaftoe party was again ſuccefsful.

The ſixth petition was at the laſt general election, in 1790, which was tried the enſuing year, when Mr. Shaftoe and his colleague petitioned againſt the return of the Hon. Bartholomew Bouverie, and Sir William Scott, who had been returned on the Radnor intereſt; when that intereſt, for the ſecond time, became ſuccefsful.

The number of legal votes in this borough do not appear to be above twenty. Sir Philip Hales, and Mr. Cooper, in 1775, were declared duly elected with eleven, and ten votes; but they are ſometimes ſplit into four times that number.

The right is admitted to be in perſons having a freehold intereſt in burgage-tenements, holden by a certain rent, fealty, and ſuit of court of the Biſhop of Wincheſter, who is lord of the borough, and paying reliefs on deſcent, and fines on alienation.

The points at iſſue upon theſe ſeveral petitions were, ſplitting and occaſionality; and whether the returning officer was the deputy of the

biſhop

bifhop of Winchester's bailiff, or the deputy of the steward of the lessee of the manor; the said manor and borough having been leased out for lives from the reign of Elizabeth.

The late Anthony Duncombe, lord Feversham, was proprietor of the greater part of the burgages in Downton; to some of which he was entitled under a settlement of Sir Charles Duncombe, the rest he had purchased. Upon his death in 1763 with male issue, the settled estate descended to the late Mr. Duncombe; the remainder of his estates in Downton, he by will directed to be sold for the benefit of his two daughters, giving the refusal of them to the Duncombe family, in order to prevent disputes. The present earl of Radnor married one of the daughters, and Mr. Bowater the other. Mr. Duncombe also left a daughter, married to Mr. Shaftoe, to whom he bequeathed his Downton estate. The trusts of lord Feversham's will not having been carried into execution, the manner in which his trustees exerted the influence of his property, occasioned a new scheme of election in Downton, after the dissolution of the parliament in 1780; for, in the former elections, the opposition to Mr. Duncombe's family had not been maintained by the estate of lord

O 2   Feversham,

Feverfham, or by any other family intereſt, but by the legal objections before-mentioned; but, in the elections of 1784 and 1790, Mr. Shaftoe, having the ſtrength of Mr. Duncombe's property, was oppoſed by that of lord Feverſham's, which his truſtees employed for that purpoſe.

The Biſhop of Wincheſter's bailiff deputy, and Sir Philip Hales, the leſſee of the manor, ſteward's deputy, each taking upon them to act as returning officer.

The former admitted upon his poll.

  For Shaftoe, — 50
  Conway, — 49
  Bouverie, — 38
  Scott, — 37

The latter, upon his poll, made the numbers,

  For Bouverie, — 44
  Scott, — 43
  Shaftoe, — 2
  Conway, — 1

The committee determined, that the deputy ſteward of the leſſee, was the legal returning officer.

To follow this intricate **inveſtigation** of the right of twenty thatched cottages to return two members to parliament, would be a waſte of our time, and our readers' patience; nor would the

the volumes, to which we have limited our work, admit a report of all the fix cafes. Should not a reform of this fyftem of reprefentation render this reporting bufinefs premature, we fhall foon fee the cafes of boroughs without houfes, and reprefentatives without conftituents, exceed the voluminous bulk of the ftatutes at large.

RIGHT OF ELECTION—1775, Feb. 4. Was confidered, by the counfel on both fides, in their arguments, to be in perfons having a freehold intereft in burgage tenements, holden by a certain rent, fealty, and fuit of court, of the Bifhop of Winchefter, who is lord of the borough, and paying reliefs on defcent, and fines on alienation.

1 Dougl. El. 235. There is no determination on the right of election.

NUMBER OF VOTERS—About twenty; fometimes fplit into eighty.

RETURNING OFFICER—The deputy fteward of the leffee of the manor.

PROPRIETOR—Earl of Radnor.

HINDON.

POLITICAL CHARACTER—The right of election in this borough is in the bailiff and inhabitants

paying

paying scot and lot; the number of which is two hundred and ten. Shaftesbury, Arundel, Stockbridge, and this place, have exhibited the most flagrant acts of bribery and corruption, before committees of the house of commons, nearly similar in their circumstances, and equally injurious in their consequences, to those which we have reported of Shoreham and Cricklade; though the two last are the only places to which an effectual remedy has been applied, by carrying the right of suffrage to such an extent of district, as shall increase the number of voters to a limit that the purse of an individual cannot seduce.

The case of Hindon is the only one in the present reign, in which the house of commons have directed a prosecution against the sitting members, or petitioners; and in this instance it appears to have been attended with singular hardship, as the promises made to the electors, on behalf of the sitting members, were, by an imprudent and unpardonable officiousness of their agents, without either the authority or knowledge of their principals; and the petitioners upon their trial were acquitted.

The petition was heard before a committee of the house of commons, in the month of February, 1775.

1775. The fitting members were Thomas Brand Hollis, Efq. and General Smith; the petitioners, Richard Beckford, Efq. and James Calthorpe, Efq. Reciprocal charges of bribery were made by each party, and fubftantially proved againft the agents of both; whereupon the committee determined,

That Richard Smith, Efq. is not duly elected a burgefs to ferve in this prefent parliament for the borough of Hindon, in the county of Wilts;

That Thomas Brand Hollis, Efq. is not duly elected a burgefs to ferve in this prefent parliament for the faid borough of Hindon;

That James Calthorpe, Efq. one of the petitioners, is not duly elected a burgefs to ferve in this prefent parliament for the faid borough of Hindon;

That Richard Beckford, Efq. one of the petitioners, is not duly elected a burgefs to ferve in this prefent parliament for the faid borough of Hindon;

That the laft election of members to ferve in this prefent parliament for the faid borough, was a void election.

At the fame time Mr. Dundas acquainted the houfe, that in the courfe of the examination into the merits of the petition of James Calthorpe, Efq.

Esq. and Richard Beckford, Esq. it having appeared to the committee, that the moſt flagrant and notorious acts of bribery and corruption had been practiſed; and that a very confiderable majority of the electors of the borough of Hindon had been bribed and corrupted in a very groſs and extraordinary manner; and that ſeveral others of the ſaid electors had been concerned as agents for that purpoſe; the committee, defirous that the houſe might adopt ſuch meaſures as may diſcourage, and if poſſible put an end to a practice ſo ſubverſive of the freedom of elections, had directed him to lay before the houſe the whole of the evidence given before the ſaid committee, with their opinions thereupon. And he read the report in his place, and afterwards delivered it in at the table, where the ſame was read; and the reſolutions of the committee are as follow:

Reſolved, " That it appears to this committee,
   " That Richard Smith, Eſq. by his agents,
   " has been guilty of notorious bribery, in
   " endeavouring to procure himſelf to be
   " elected and returned a burgeſs to ſerve in
   " this preſent parliament for the borough of
   " Hindon, in the county of Wilts."

The like reſolution reſpecting Mr. Hollis.

Reſolved, " That it appears to this committee,
                                            " That

"That James Calthorpe, Efq. by his agents,
"has been guilty of notorious bribery, in
"endeavouring to procure himfelf to be
"elected and returned a burgefs, to ferve in
"this prefent parliament for the faid bo-
"rough of Hindon."

Refolved, "That it appears to this committee,
"That Richard Beckford, Efq. has, by his
"agent, endeavoured, by promife of money,
"to procure himfelf to be elected and re-
"turned a burgefs, to ferve in this prefent
"parliament, for the faid borough of Hin-
"don."

Refolved, "That it appears to this committee,
"That the Reverend John Nairn, of Hin-
"don; Fafham Nairn, Efq. late of Berry's-
"ftreet, St. James's; Francis Ward, of
"Sherborne-lane, London; Stevens, a but-
"cher, at Salifbury, commonly called Job-
"ber Stevens, &c. &c. (in all, thirteen,
"fpecified by name) have acted as agents,
"and have been acceffary to, and concern-
"ed in, notorious acts of bribery and cor-
"ruption, that have been practifed at the
"laft election for the faid borough of Hin-
"don."

Refolved, "That it is the opinion of this com-
                                           "mittee,

"mittee, that the house be moved for leave
"to bring in a bill, to disfranchise the said
"borough of Hindon, in the county of
"Wilts."

The consideration of this report was adjourned till the 23d of February; and in the mean time, an order was made, that the speaker should not issue his warrant for a new writ, till the house proceeded to such consideration.

On that day, it was *Ordered*, "That leave be
"given to bring in a bill, to incapacitate,
"from voting at elections of members of
"parliament, one hundred and ninety per-
"sons by name (including several of those
"mentioned in the fifth resolution of the
"committee), out of two hundred and ten
"who had polled at the election; and for
"the preventing bribery and corruption in
"the election of members to serve in par-
"liament for Hindon."

Mr. Dundas, Mr. Byng, Mr. Elwes, and the other members of the committee, were ordered to prepare and bring in this bill; and in the mean time, it was *Resolved*, "That the speaker
"should not issue his warrant to make out a new
"writ for a month longer."

On the 8th of March Mr. Dundas presented
the

the bill, which was read, and ordered to be read a fecond time on the 29th of that month. It was of courfe alfo ordered to be printed; and a printed copy of the bill, with the order for the fecond reading, was ordered to be ferved on all the perfons named in it; and it was *Refolved*, " That leaving them at their refpective abodes " fhould be good fervice."

The day following (the 29th of March) the order of the day being read, and the queftion being propofed, for reading the bill a fecond time, the meffenger, who had been charged with the fervice of the copies of it on the parties, was called to prove fuch fervice; and Thomas Spencer, one of the perfons named in the bill, was, at his own defire, heard on behalf of himfelf, againft the bill: then, in confequence of a motion for that purpofe, the entry on the journals of the houfe, of the 22d of March, 1722-23, and the 4th of April, 1723, of the proceedings of the houfe upon the bill for inflicting certain pains and penalties upon Francis, Lord Bifhop of Rochefter, was read; after which, the bill was read a fecond time; and it was

Refolved, " That it fhould be confidered in a
" committee of the whole houfe, on the 5th of
" April, and that the petitioners againft it fhould
" be

" be heard before that committee, by themselves
" or their counsel."

" That it be an instruction to the said commit-
" tee of the whole house, that they have power
" to receive a clause, or clauses, for inflicting a
" suitable punishment on the said Richard Smith,
" Esq. for his said offence."

" It passed in the negative."

And the second resolution being read, and a similar question put, respecting Mr. Hollis, that likewise passed in the negative; which being done, the house resolved itself into a committee of the whole house, on the bill.

In this committee, it being proposed to call certain persons named in the bill, and incapacitated by it, to prove the allegations it contained (for it had been debated and settled in the house, in some former stage of the business, that the evidence before the select committee, and reported by them, could not be admitted upon this occasion), it was objected, that they, being parties, and like defendants in an indictment, could not, without overturning the known rules of law and justice, be received as witnesses in this case. This objection produced a debate; and though it was treated as of no weight, by some gentlemen of the long robe, it was strenuously supported

ed by others, and proved fatal to the bill; for all the perfons who were capable of proving the facts, and who had proved them before the felect committee, were themfelves offenders, and named in the bill.

When the Speaker refumed the chair, on a motion of Mr. Dundas, leave was given to bring in a new bill, fimilar to the former, but leaving out the names of certain perfons, who were intended to be made ufe of as witneffes; and Mr. Solicitor-general, Sir George Hay, Mr. Grenville, and Lord George Germaine, together with the members of the felect committee, were ordered to prepare and bring it in.

On Wednefday, the 12th of April, Mr. Dundas prefented this new bill; which being received, and read the firft time, the houfe was moved, that the four firft refolutions of the felect committee fhould be read; and this being accordingly done, the 20th day of April was appointed for the fecond reading. A fimilar order to what had been made on the former occafion, was now made, relative to the ferving of the parties with copies; and orders were made, feverally, that Francis Mead, Thomas Spencer, John Becket, *(baker)*, John Becket, fon of William, John Baldwin, William Crabb, Thomas Penry,

Penry, Thomas Richardson, and Thomas More, persons named in the former, but omitted in this bill, should attend the house, at the time appointed for the second reading.

The order of the day being now read, the bill was ordered to be read a second time, and the counsel against it (Mr. Pepys, for the petitioners incapacitated by the bill; Mr. Bearcroft for the other petitioners, electors of Hindon; and Mr. Macdonald, for the Rev. Mr. Nairn) being called in, the bill was read a second time, and the petition of Thomas Howell and others was read, and counsel heard.

The bill was then committed to a committee of the whole house for the ensuing day; and the several petitions were referred to that committee, and the witnesses ordered to attend.

On Thursday the 27th of April, the petition of Thomas Howell and others, praying to be admitted witnesses, was referred to the committee of the whole house: and Mr. Elwes, chairman of that committee, reporting, that Thomas Howell, on being examined in relation to the non-attendance of Thomas Spencer and John Becket, two of the witnesses who had been summoned, had grosly prevaricated, he was ordered to be committed to Newgate; and afterwards, Mr. Elwes reporting,

reporting, that William Lucas, being examined before the committee, had grofsly prevaricated, and given falfe evidence, he was ordered to be committed to the Gate-Houfe.

A fimilar report, and the like order, were made, concerning Henry Chant; and Mr. Elwes reporting, that Spencer and Becket had attended the day before, in purfuance of the order of the houfe, but had purpofely kept out of the way, to avoid being ferved with the order for their attendance this day, they were ordered to be fent for in cuftody of the ferjeant at arms; and an order being made for the houfe to refolve itfelf again, on the Tuefday following, into a committee of the whole houfe, for the future confideration of the bill, the orders for the attendance of the witneffes were renewed.

On Monday the 1ft of May, Thomas Howell was ordered to be removed from Newgate to the Gate-Houfe, having petitioned the houfe for that purpofe.

On Tuefday the 2d of May, the ferjeant at arms being called upon to give an account of what had been done, in relation to the taking Thomas Spencer and John Becket; the meffengers who were fent in fearch of them, informed the houfe, that very ftrict inquiry had been made

after

after them, but that they were not as yet taken: upon which the committee of the whole houfe, for the confideration of the bill, was put off till the Monday following; the orders for the witneffes were renewed; and it being fufpected, from the teftimony given by the perfons who had been committed, that Mr. Smith and Mr. Fafham Nairn had been concerned in fecreting Spencer and Becket, they were ordered to attend on the Monday.

On Monday the 8th of May, petitions were prefented from Howell and Lucas, acknowledging their prevarications, which they faid were unintentional; but alledging they had declared all they knew concerning Spencer and Becket, and defiring, on account of their poverty, and their having families to maintain, that they might be admitted to afk pardon at the bar of the houfe, and be difcharged without the payment of fees.

Thefe petitions were ordered to lie on the table.

The like information as on the Tuefday preceding, was given by the meffengers who had been fent in fearch of them, concerning Spencer and Becket.

Mr. Smith and Captain Fafham Nairn were then

then examined, in relation to the non-attendance of Spencer and Becket; after which, the order of the day, for the committee of the whole houfe on this bufinefs being read, it was

Refolved, " That it appeared to the houfe, that,
" from the abfence of Spencer and Becket, two
" material witneffes in fupport of the bill, it
" would not be expedient to proceed in it in this
" feffion of parliament."

It was then feverally refolved, that the houfe would take the report of the felect committee who were appointed to try the petition of James Calthorpe and Richard Beckford, Efqrs. into further confideration as early as poffible the next feffion; that until then no warrant for a new writ fhould be ordered; and that an humble addrefs fhould be prefented to the king, to iffue a proclamation for apprehending Spencer and Becket, with the promife of a reward, fo that they might be delivered into the cuftody of the ferjeant at arms during this feffion of parliament; and this addrefs was ordered to be prefented by fuch members of the houfe as were members of the privy-council.

Then, upon motion for that purpofe, the firft refolution of the felect committee, as agreed to by the houfe on the 23d of February, was read;

and then, upon a motion for that purpose, the following entry in the votes of the house, of the 5th of December last, was read:

Resolved, " That if it shall appear that any per-
" son hath procured himself to be elected or
" returned a member of this house, or en-
" deavoured so to be, by bribery, or any
" other corrupt practices, this house will
" proceed with the utmost severity against
" such person."

And an order made,

" That the attorney-general do forthwith pro-
" secute Richard Smith, Esq. for the said of-
" fence."

The second resolution was read in like manner, and the like order made, that the attorney-general should prosecute Mr. Hollis.

The third resolution being also read, a motion made, and the question proposed, that the attorney-general should prosecute James Calthorpe, Esq. the previous question was put, and resolved in the affirmative; and then the like order was made for the prosecution of Mr. Calthorpe.

Lastly, the fourth resolution being read, it was ordered that the attorney-general should likewise forthwith prosecute Mr. Beckford.

The address for apprehending of Spencer and
Becket

Becket was prefented to the king, and the proclamation iffued; but on Thurfday the 11th of May, they furrendered themfelves; and, it being feverally refolved by the houfe, " That they " had purpofely abfconded, in order to avoid " being ferved with an order for their atten- " dance, as witneffes, on a committee of the " houfe," they were ordered to be committed to Newgate.

On the 8th of May, 1775, the houfe refolved to take the whole matter into their moft ferious confideration, as early as poffible in the next feffion of parliament, and that, in the mean time, no warrant fhould be ordered for a new writ.

On the 31ft of January, 1776, an order was made, that leave fhould be given to bring in a bill for the fame purpofes with the two which had been brought in during the former feffion.

Monday the 5th of February, the bill was brought in, and the fecond reading was fixed for the 19th.

Various petitions were prefented by interefted parties againft the bill, who were heard by counfel; and, after innumerable debates and adjournments, the houfe came to the following refolution,

Refolved, " That this houfe will, upon this day
" three

"three months, resolve itself into a committee of the whole house, to consider
further of the bill to incapacitate certain
persons therein mentioned, from voting
at elections of members to serve in parliament for the borough of Hindon, in the
county of Wilts."

The reader will perceive, that by this resolution the bill was virtually thrown out; it was
known that the session would be at an end, long
before the day appointed for taking it again into
consideration; and all bills depending at the end
of a session fall, of course, to the ground. If the
house had intended to take up the affair in the
succeeding session, they would have come to a
like resolution with that of the 8th of May, 1775;
but in truth there was no such design.

Mr. Douglas observes, that there would be
great difficulty in fixing on the new class of voters,
because the influence of different gentlemen of
property in the neighbourhood of the place would
have been more or less increased, or diminished,
according as the freeholders of one, two, or more
hundreds should have been admitted to a partici-
pation of the right of election. There was some
danger, therefore, that a law, which in its origin
was intended to be a public benefit, and to amend
the

the conſtitution, might, in the end, turn out a mere job, and become ſubſervient to the particular intereſt of certain individuals; in ſhort, many who had at firſt promoted and ſupported the bill, began in the courſe of the ſeſſion to alter their opinion with regard to it; or loſt at leaſt much of the zeal which they had formerly ſhewn for its ſucceſs. On the different occaſions when it was to be taken into conſideration, there was often other buſineſs more urgent, and more generally intereſting, to be diſcuſſed; and by the time that was finiſhed, and the order of the day for the houſe to reſolve itſelf into a committee on the Hindon bill called for, the greater number of members, already worn out by long attendance, were glad to leave the houſe: advantage was taken of this by ſome gentlemen, who, from the beginning, made no ſcruple of avowing their reſolution of employing every means and every ſtratagem which the forms of procedure in the houſe of commons ſhould furniſh, or authoriſe, in order to defeat the bill. Forty members are neceſſary to conſtitute a houſe; and if it appear that there is not that number preſent, an immediate adjournment muſt take place. Whenever thoſe gentlemen imagined the number preſent was under forty, they moved that the houſe

P 3　　　　　　　　ſhould

should be counted; and in this manner the proceedings were, at several times, suddenly stopped; viz. on Thursday the 7th of March, on Wednesday the 27th of that month, and on Tuesday the 7th of May. Another art was practised, with equal, or even greater success: every possible objection to the admissibility of evidence was either raised by some member of the house, or taken by the counsel, who attended at the bar on the part of the persons who had petitioned against the bill; almost every such objection produced an argument, a debate, a question, and a division. Thus the progress of the business was clogged and retarded so very effectually, as to make even those who continued the most anxious promoters of it, despair of ever bringing it to a conclusion; insomuch, that at length, by a sort of tacit agreement of all parties, the whole was dropped on the 8th of May 1776, and a new writ ordered to be issued for the electing of two burgesses to serve in parliament for the borough of Hindon; by which means the fate of Shoreham and Cricklade was avoided.

This borough is under the influence of Sir Henry Gough Calthorpe, Bart. and William Beckford, of Fonthill, Esq. The interest of the former is preserved by the property he possesses in the borough,

borough, and that of the latter by his refidence in the neighbourhood; but we have not yet learned that it is become more immaculate, notwithftanding the ordeal it has paffed.

RIGHT OF ELECTION—1701, April 3. Is in the bailiff, burgeffes, and fuch inhabitants only as pay fcot and lot.

1701, May 13. Is in the inhabitants of the faid borough not receiving alms.

Agreed to by the houfe.

1728, April 12. Is in the inhabitants of houfes within the faid borough, being houfekeepers and parifhioners, not receiving alms.

NUMBER OF VOTERS—Two hundred and ten.

RETURNING OFFICER—The bailiff.

PATRONS—William Beckford, Efq. and Sir Henry Gough Calthorpe, Bart.

HEYTESBURY.

POLITICAL CHARACTER—This place, as well as Weftbury, which are both but fmall villages, have a right to fend members to parliament; while Warminfter, which is one of the largeft towns in the county, has no fuch privilege; but, from their contiguity to it, being four miles diftant, it derives only the unpleafant reflection, that

advantages

advantages of such a superior tendency should be affixed to so much insignificance.

The right of election here is in the burgage-holds, which are about fifty in number, and are the property of the duke of Marlborough, and W. P. Ashe A'Court, Esq. each of whom returns a member. This town was entirely burned down in the year 1766; since which time it has been rebuilt to its former extent.

Right of election—In the burgage-holders.
Number of voters—Fifty.
Returning officer—The lord's bailiff.
Proprietors—Duke of Marlborough, and P. W. A. A'Court, Esq.

WESTBURY.

Political character—The right of election in this borough is of a particular nature, being in every tenant of any burgage tenement in fee, for lives, or ninety-nine years, determinable on lives, or by copy of court-roll, paying a burgage-rent of four-pence or two-pence yearly, being resident within the said borough, and not receiving alms. There are three kinds of burgage-holds; viz. freehold, copyhold, and leasehold. In some places the proprietor of the burgage-hold only has a right to vote; in others, it is the tenant or occupier

occupier of such a tenure; so that the same perplexities and doubts which arise, as to the right of voting, in scot and lot or corporation boroughs, happen also in places of this description.

These burgage tenures, which are twenty-four in number, compose a *long stone wall*; which, like the sheep at Old Sarum, and the posts at Midhurst, affords the only appearance of a constituent body that a stranger can discover; the inhabitants of the village of Westbury having no more concern in the election of its representatives than those of Constantinople.

CORPORATION—Consists of a mayor, recorder, and twelve burgesses.

RIGHT OF ELECTION—1702, Dec. 1. The tenants of burgage-houses, by lease, for years absolute, have a right to vote.

1715, June 1. Is in every tenant of any burgage-tenement in fee, for lives, of ninety-nine years, determinable on lives, or by copy of court-roll, paying a burgage-rent of four-pence or two-pence yearly, being resident within the said borough, and not receiving alms.

NUMBER OF VOTERS—Twenty-four.

RETURNING OFFICER—The mayor.

PROPRIETOR—Earl of Abingdon.

CALNE.

CALNE.

Political character—This borough has had the honour of giving seats in parliament to John Dunning, Esq. the late lord Ashburton, and to colonel Barré. The right of election is in twenty-four ancient burgesses, who annually elect, out of their own body, two guild stewards to be the returning officers at elections of their members of parliament.

The influence, which formerly prevailed here, was that of Richard Bull, Esq. and Mr. Ducket; but the marquis of Lansdown, from his popularity, and occasional residence at Bow Wood Park, in this neighbourhood, has had, for more than twenty years, the sole command and absolute controul over it.

Corporation—Consists of twenty-four capital burgesses; out of which two constables are annually chosen.

Right of election—1710, Dec. 22. Is in the inhabitants of the borough, having a right of common, and being sworn at Ogbourn-court.

1723, Feb. 25. Is in the ancient burgesses of the said borough only.

That the right of returning burgesses is in the guild stewards.

DEVIZES.

NUMBER OF VOTERS—Twenty-four.
RETURNING OFFICERS—The guild stewards.
PATRON—Marquis of Lansdown.

DEVIZES.

POLITICAL CHARACTER—The right of election in this borough is exclusively in the corporation, consisting of a mayor, aldermen, and common council. The influence which prevails here is that of James Sutton, Esq. of New Park, in this county, brother-in-law to the speaker of the house of commons, who was once member for this borough.

This town, which is of a very considerable magnitude, labours under the same disadvantage with Salisbury and Marlborough, respecting the right of voting being limited to the body corporate, and not extending to the people at large.

The same exclusion existing likewise in the cities of Bath and Winchester, the town and county of Poole, and in the large towns of Portsmouth, Plymouth, Andover, Tiverton, Banbury, Wycombe, Dartmouth, Scarborough, Thetford, St. Edmund's Bury, Newport in the Isle of Wight, Bewdley, and Harwich, our observations on those respective places will apply to the chartered monopoly of this borough.

CORPORATION

CORPORATION—By charter of King Charles I. it confifts of a mayor, recorder, ten magiftrates, and twenty-four common-councilmen, who have liberty of making what burgeffes they pleafe, all of whom have votes in election of members to parliament.

RIGHT OF ELECTION—1688, Mar. 21. Is in the mayor and felect number of burgeffes only.

NUMBER OF VOTERS—Thirty.

RETURNING OFFICER—The mayor.

PATRON—James Sutton, Efq.

CHIPPENHAM.

POLITICAL CHARACTER—The corporation of this borough confifts of a bailiff and eleven burgeffes, who in the year 1624, on the 9th of April, contended, that the exclufive privilege of voting for members of parliament was vefted in them; but the houfe of commons then *Refolved*, " That " the burgeffes and freemen, more than twelve, " have voices in the election."

In the year 1741, on the 28th of January, they fet up a fimilar claim, when the following propofition was put to the houfe; That the words " burgeffes and freemen," mean only fuch burgeffes and freemen as are inhabitant houfeholders of the ancient houfes, called free or burgagehoufes, houses, within the said borough; which passed in the negative. This right is, therefore, still unconfirmed, though exercised by these burgesses and freemen who inhabit ancient houses.

The number of these houses is one hundred and twenty-five, from amongst whom the twelve burgesses are chosen, who elect a bailiff.

Corruption was first introduced into this borough in the administration of Walpole, when the court made a violent opposition to Sir Edward Baynton and Sir Edmund Thomas, who were of the Leicester House faction, and which was afterwards a subject of serious investigation in the house of commons. Ten pounds was then the price of a vote in this borough, but so little has the progress of venality been checked since that period, that ten, and twenty times that sum is given at the present day.

The patronage is equally divided between Sir Edward Baynton, Bart. Sir Samuel Fludyer, Bart. and Henry Dawkins, Esq. An union of interests between two of these gentlemen, renders void, and effectually excludes, the influence of the third. A coalition at present exists between Sir Samuel Fludyer and Mr. Dawkins.

CORPORATION—By charter of Queen Mary it is governed by a bailiff and twelve burgesses.

RIGHT

RIGHT OF ELECTION—1624, April 9. The burgeſſes and freemen, more than twelve, have voices in the election.

1741, Jan. 28. " That the words " burgeſſes and freemen" mean only ſuch burgeſſes and freemen as are inhabitants, houſeholders of the ancient houſes called free or burgage houſes within the ſaid borough."

It paſſed in the negative.

NUMBER OF VOTERS—One hundred and twenty-five.

RETURNING OFFICER—The bailiff.

PATRONS—Sir Samuel Fludyer, Bart. and Henry Dawkins, Eſq.

MALMESBURY.

POLITICAL CHARACTER—The right of election in this borough, is, by the reſolution of the 13th of December, 1702, veſted in *thirteen* individuals, an alderman, and twelve burgeſſes, who are all the dependants of Dr. Wilkins, a phyſician of this town. This gentleman holds the lucrative place of receiver-general for the county; from which circumſtance it may be inferred, that the repreſentatives for this place are ſeldom inimical to adminiſtration. Mr. Paul Benfield, one of the gentlemen returned at the laſt general election,

becoming

becoming a profelyte to oppofition, fhortly after his acceffion to that fituation, did not fail to receive a hint from the grateful doctor, that the vacation of his feat became an indifpenfible etiquette; in confequence of which the Chiltern Hundreds were given, and Sir James Sanderfon fucceeded to the reprefentation of this immaculate body of conftituents.

CORPORATION—By charter of King William III. it is governed by an alderman and twelve capital burgeffes.

RIGHT OF ELECTION—1702, Dec. 13. Agreed to be in the alderman and twelve capital burgeffes.

NUMBER OF VOTERS—Thirteen.

RETURNING OFFICER—The alderman.

PATRON—Dr. Wilkins.

CRICKLADE.

POLITICAL CHARACTER—This borough has rendered itfelf remarkable by its venality, and the number of its petitions on undue elections. The firft of thefe was in confequence of a double return of John Dewar, Efq. and Samuel Peach, Efq. in 1774, which election was declared void in February 1775. The fecond fucceeded in confequence of the election of Mr. Peach to fupply

ply this vacancy; which, in the month of February 1776, was determined againſt the ſitting member, and in favour of John Dewar, Eſq. The third was the petition of Samuel Petrie, Eſq. againſt the return of Paul Benfield, Eſq. and John Macpherſon, Eſq. at the general election in 1780; which complained, that at the late election of members to ſerve in parliament for the borough of Cricklade, in the county of Witto, Paul Benfield, Eſq. John Macpherſon, Eſq. and the petitioner, were candidates; and that, previous to, and during and after the poll, the ſaid Paul Benfield and John Macpherſon, by themſelves and their agents, were guilty of many groſs and notorious acts of bribery and corruption, whereby many of the voters were influenced to give their votes for the ſaid Paul Benfield and John Macpherſon; and did, by themſelves or their agents, entertain and allow to the ſaid electors, who had a right to vote in the ſaid election, money, meat, drink, entertainment or proviſion; and by ſuch unlawful means, and by threats and promiſes, and divers other corrupt and unwarrantable practices and proceedings, of the ſaid Paul Benfield and John Macpherſon, their agents and abettors, they have procured themſelves to be unduly returned to ſerve in parliament for the ſaid borough,

to

to the manifest injury of the petitioner, and in violation of the rights and privileges of the said borough, and of the commons of England; and that the returning officer, during the course of the said election, admitted many persons to poll for the said Paul Benfield and John Macpherson, who were not duly qualified, and rejected the legal votes of other persons who tendered them in favour of the petitioner; and that the petitioner conceives he had a great majority of the legal and uncorrupted votes at the said election, and was duly elected, and ought to have been returned; and therefore, praying the house to take the premises into consideration, and to grant unto the petitioner such relief as to the house shall seem meet.

A committee was appointed on the 4th of January 1782, to try the merits of this petition, when a scene of bribery and corruption presented itself, equal to what we have reported, either of Shoreham, Shaftesbury, Hindon, or Arundel; but to enter into a detail of the evidence, would exceed the limits of all the rest put together.

The committee reported to the house, on the 1st of February following, by Sir Harbord Harbord, their chairman,

That Paul Benfield, Esq. is duly elected.

That John Macpherson, Esq. is not duly elected.

That Samuel Petrie, Esq. is not duly elected a burgess to serve in parliament for the borough of Cricklade.

Sir Harbord Harbord also reported, " That it " appears to this committee, that there was the " most notorious bribery and corruption at the " last election of burgesses to serve in parliament " for the borough of Cricklade, in the county of " Wilts."

" That it is the opinion of this committee, that " the said bribery and corruption require the most " serious consideration of parliament."

It was ordered, that the said report be taken into consideration upon the 18th of February instant; and,

That the minutes of the proceedings taken before the said select committee be laid before the house.

It was at the same time ordered, that no new writ for electing a burgess for the borough of Cricklade should issue, until the house shall have proceeded to take the said report into consideration.

On the 18th of February the house resolved to agree with the committee in the above resolutions, and ordered a bill to be brought in, to prevent

vent bribery and corruption in the elections of members to serve in parliament for the said borough of Cricklade.

Three petitions were presented against the said bill, by certain electors of Cricklade, on the 5th of March following; which were ordered to lie on the table, and the petitioners allowed to be heard by counsel against the bill upon the second reading.

On the 7th the petitioners were heard by counsel, and the bill was ordered to be committed.

After going through the several stages, the bill passed, and received the royal assent on the 17th of May following. In the preamble it recites, that, " There was the most notorious bribery and " corruption at the last election of burgesses to " serve in parliament for the borough of Crick- " lade, in the county of Wilts; and that such " bribery and corruption is likely to continue and " be practised in the said borough in future, unless " some means are taken to prevent the same. In " order therefore to prevent such unlawful prac- " tices for the future, and that the said borough " may from henceforth be duly represented in " parliament; be it enacted by the king's most " excellent majesty, by and with the advice and

" con-

"consent of the lords spiritual and temporal, and
"commons, in this present parliament assembled,
"and by the authority of the same, that from
"henceforth it shall and may be lawful to and for
"every freeholder, being over the age of twenty-
"one years, who shall have, within the hundreds
"or divisions of Highworth, Cricklade, Staple,
"Kingsbridge, and Malmsbury, or one or more
"of them, in the county of Wilts, a freehold of
"the clear yearly value of forty shillings, to give
"his vote at every election of a burgess or bur-
"gesses to serve in parliament for the said bo-
"rough of Cricklade.

"II. And it is further enacted by the autho-
"rity aforesaid, That the right of election of a
"member or members to serve in parliament for
"the said borough of Cricklade, shall be, and is
"hereby declared to be, in such freeholders as
"aforesaid, and in the persons who, by the cus-
"tom and usage of the said borough, have, or
"shall hereafter have, a right to vote at such
"election; and the proper officer for the time
"being, to whom the return of every writ or pro-
"cess does belong, is hereby required to return
"the person or persons to serve in parliament
"for the said borough who shall have the major
"number of votes of such freeholders and other
"persons

" persons having a right to vote at such election;
" any law or usage to the contrary notwithstand-
" ing.

" III. It likewise provides, That such free-
" holders only shall be entitled to vote as shall be
" duly qualified to vote at elections for knights
" of the shire for the said county of Wilts, ac-
" cording to the laws now in being for regulat-
" ing county elections."

Mr. Petrie would clearly have established his right to a seat in parliament, upon the merits of the above petition, but for the admissibility of evidence which was afterwards proved to have been perjured. His country is certainly considerably indebted to him for exposing such a system of venality; and the electors of Cricklade owe him their gratitude for restoring them to the situation of freemen.

A number of actions were afterwards brought, upon the act of 2 Geo. II. chap. 24, against the principals and agents, concerned in bribing and corrupting the electors in order to recover the penalties of five hundred pounds for each offence; when Mr. Petrie was fortunate enough to recover upon most of them.

The election next after passing this act, happened in June 1782, when the Hon. George Richard

Richard St John, and Samuel Petrie, Efq. were candidates, to fupply the place of Mr. Macpherfon. The conteft at the poll was only between Mr. St. John and Mr. Petrie, the other candidates having previoufly declined. The election was decided, by a great majority, in Mr. St. John's favour: but Mr. Petrie petitioned againft him. This petition, which was not tried during the feffion in which it was prefented, was renewed in the feffion following, but foon after withdrawn.

At the general election, in 1784, Charles Weftley Coxe, Efq. and Robert Adamfon, Efq. were candidates in the Oppofition, or, what was then called, the Coalition intereft, and were oppofed by John Walter Heneage, Efq. and Robert Nicholas, Efq. who were on the fide of Adminiftration. The poll, according to the return of the bailiff, was as follows:

Mr. Coxe	442
Mr. Adamfon	435
Mr. Heneage	373
Mr. Nicholas	358

A petition was prefented by Mr. Heneage and Mr. Nicholas, againft this return; which came to be heard before a committee on the 14th of February, 1785; when it appeared, that a number of fictitious voters had been made under the

right

right of the borough of Cricklade, where the inhabitants poffeffing houfes, who are freeholders, copyholders, or leafeholders, for any term not lefs than three years, or for any fuch term, or greater term, determinabe on life or lives, *fuch freeholder, copyholder, or leafeholder, having been in the occupation of the houfe, for which he may claim to vote, forty days preceding the election.*

One hundred and thirty-fix of thefe votes were objected to, for having *fraudulent leafes,* or none at all; fome, as not having been refident *forty days;* and others, as inmates, or having fplit tenements. Forty votes were objected to as parifh poor; befides twenty of the hundred voters who were alfo objected to for different reafons. It appeared in evidence, that moft of thefe votes had been *faggoted,* and that the returning-officer had been guilty of grofs partiality in favour of the fitting members. On the 4th of April the committee reported to the houfe, " That the pe-
" titioners were duly elected, and ought to have
" been returned."

The chairman at the fame time reported, " That
" the conduct of the returning-officer, in taking
" the poll, and making the return, at the laft
" election of members to ferve in parliament for
" the borough of Cricklade, was partial and ille-
" gal,

"gal; whereby a colourable majority was ob-
"tained on the poll for Mr. Coxe and Mr.
"Adamfon."

This report, which was taken into confideration by the houfe, after long and tedious debates, and repeated adjournments, the whole feffion was fpent without coming to any conclufion upon the fubject.

In 1790 Mr. Nicholas was made a commiffioner of excife, and Thomas Eaftcourt, Efq. was chofen in his room.

At the laft general election Mr. Petrie again offered himfelf a candidate, in oppofition to the old members; when the numbers were, for

  Mr. Eaftcourt — — 246
  Mr. Heneage — — 194
  Mr. Petrie — — — 111

The two former gentlemen being returned, in confequence of their majority, Mr. Petrie again became a petitioner; which was decided in favour of the fitting members.

RIGHT OF ELECTION—1684, April 1. Is in the freeholders and copyholders of the boroughhoufes, and leafeholders, for any term not under three years only.

1685, June 10. Agreed, by the counfel on both
            fides,

sides, to be in the freeholders, copyholders, and leaseholders for three years.

1689, April 1. Agreed, by the counsel on both sides, that the right of election is in the freeholders and copyholders of borough-houses, and leaseholders for any term not under three years.

1776, Feb. 8. Is in the inhabitants possessing houses within the said borough, who are freeholders, copyholders, or leaseholders, for any term not less than three years, or for any such term, or greater term, determinable on life or lives; such freeholder, copyholder, or leaseholder, having been in the occupation of the house for which he may claim to vote, four days preceding any election.

That the houses which were in the occupation of Thomas Bound, Thomas Kilmaster, sen. Richard Liddel, William Mabson, John Pounds, and Robert Strange, at the last election, are within the boundary of the said borough.

1782. By act of parliament it is further vested in the freeholders of the five hundreds or divisions of Highworth, Cricklade, Staple, Kingsbridge, and Malmsbury.

NUMBER OF VOTERS—Twelve hundred.

RETURNING OFFICER—The bailiff.

GREAT BEDWIN.

POLITICAL CHARACTER—The right of election here is in the freeholders and inhabitants of ancient burgage messuages, in number about eighty, and returned by the portreve, called mayor, who is chosen at the lord's court, and appoints a bailiff to act under him.

The earl of Aylesbury is the lord of the manor; in consequence of which he has the appointment of the returning-officer. His lordship also possesses the major part of the property; so that his nomination of the representatives can neither be opposed nor contradicted, with any prospect of success.

RIGHT OF ELECTION—1729, March 29. In the freeholders and inhabitants of ancient burgage-messuages.

NUMBER OF VOTERS—About eighty,

RETURNING OFFICER—The portreve, who is called a mayor, and is chosen at the lord's court, and appoints a bailiff under him.

PROPRIETOR—Earl of Aylesbury.

LUGGERSHALL.

POLITICAL CHARACTER—This place, which in its dimensions is only a small village, has a right,

of

of a very complicated kind, to send members to parliament, " being in such persons who have any " estate of inheritance, or freehold or leasehold, " determinable upon life or lives, within the " borough, not confined to entire ancient houses, " or the sites of ancient houses within the said " borough."

The majority of these estates were formerly the property of George Augustus Selwyn, Esq. of facetious memory; at whose demise they descended to the present lord viscount Sydney: the minority of them are the property of Mr. Everett, a banker in London.—This division of local suffrage has been the cause of litigation between the parties, and produced a petition to the house of commons, against the return of the two members in the interest of lord Sydney; which being heard in 1791, was determined in their favour.

Mr. Selwyn, one of the sitting members, dying in the interim, a new writ was accordingly issued; when, at the ensuing election, another contest arose, Samuel Smith, Esq. being proposed a candidate in the interest of lord Sydney, and Mr. Alderman Newnham in that of Mr. Everett; when Mr. Smith was returned, and a petition, of a similar tendency with the last, was presented to the house of commons; which was, on a compromise

of

of the parties, afterwards withdrawn. The matter in question, between the contending parties, depends upon the legality of splitting those estates to which the right of voting is annexed: the number of votes, in Browne Willis's time, were seventy; but they are now divided into one hundred and forty-nine, and are held by the tenants and friends of the two proprietors, who reside in different parts of Wiltshire and Hampshire, but who are kind enough to come here, at the time of election, to perform the ceremonial part of delegating a representative for this borough to the legislative assembly of the British nation.

RIGHT OF ELECTION—1689, Feb. 11. Is in such persons as have an estate of inheritance, or freehold or leasehold, determinable upon life, within the said borough.

1705, Jan. 17. Is in the freeholders or leaseholders of the said borough, determinable upon life or lives.

NUMBER OF VOTERS—About seventy.

RETURNING OFFICER—The lord's bailiff.

PROPRIETOR—Lord viscount Sydney.

OLD SARUM.

POLITICAL CHARACTER—This borough was quite decayed, and reduced to only one house, in the time of Browne Willis, occafioned by the tranflation of the old city to the new one, which is about a mile lower on the river, of which there is now only a fmall veftige remaining. The members are chofen by a bailiff and fix burgeffes, who are appointed by lord Camelford, the lord of the borough, and entrufted by him with burgage fcites.

This borough, with the *affiftance* of Midhurft, fends four members to parliament, although there is not a fingle houfe ftanding, nor a perfon living, within the limits of either, to be reprefented. The boroughs of Gatton and Caftle Rifing have each *two houfes only*, and they have each *two reprefentatives*.

Thus is the legiflative part of our conftitution made, of fome members who reprefent neither houfes nor perfons, of others, who are the reprefentatives only of fingle individuals, and of many whofe conftituents do not exceed ten in number.

RIGHT OF ELECTION—1688, Nov. 14. Is in the freeholders, being burgage-holders of the faid borough.

NUMBER OF VOTERS—Nominally SEVEN, but actually only ONE.

RETURNING OFFICER—The bailiff.

PROPRIETOR—Lord Camelford.

WOOTON BASSET.

POLITICAL CHARACTER—This fmall borough was ftrongly contefted in the year 1784, between the interefts of the earl of Clarendon, and lord vifcount Bolingbroke.

George Tierney, Efq. was a candidate in the intereft of the former; and the prefent lord North, and the Hon. H. S. Conway, in that of the latter. Thefe two laft gentlemen had a majority on the poll, and were accordingly returned; but a petition was prefented by George Tierney, Efq. which was heard in the month of April, 1785, when the committee decided in favour of the fitting members.

Since the above conteft, thefe noblemen have agreed, to avoid future litigation and expence, to permit each other to return one member.

CORPORATION—It is governed by a mayor, two aldermen, and twelve capital burgeffes.

RIGHT OF ELECTION—Is in the inhabitants paying fcot and lot.

NUMBER OF VOTERS—About one hundred.

RETURNING OFFICER—The mayor.

PATRONS—Earl of Clarendon and lord vifcount Bolingbroke.

MARLBOROUGH.

MARLBOROUGH.

POLITICAL CHARACTER—In this town, which, from the number of its inhabitants, and the trade it carries on, may hold a rank equal to some of the first in the county, the right of voting for members of parliament is in the corporation only, consisting of a mayor and two bailiffs, chosen out of twenty capital burgesses. Here, like as at Gatton, two men, who are a majority of the electors, returning two representatives: now, according to the principles of the constitution of this country, and the common acceptation of the word *representative*, these persons, who are thus elected, are bound, not only to listen to the instructions of their constituents, but also to obey them; suppose, therefore, this possible case; that a subject should be debated in parliament, in which the interests of this country were deeply concerned, but where, at the same time, the good of the whole might be injurious to, and militate against, that of those two individuals; would not the members be, upon every account, bound to give their voices in the senate agreeably to the will of those who sent them thither, without consulting the benefit of those with whose welfare they are not so immediately concerned? yet what must be the state of

that

that country, where this principle, which is the foundation of representative government, is forced to be denied by the representatives themselves, in order to avoid the absurdity of acting under the instructions of such a fictitious body of constituents?

CORPORATION—It consists of a mayor and two bailiffs, chosen out of twenty capital burgesses.

RIGHT OF ELECTION—1717, 13 May. Is in the mayor and burgesses of the said borough only.

NUMBER OF VOTERS—THREE.

RETURNING OFFICER—The mayor.

PATRON—Earl of Aylesbury.

WORCESTERSHIRE.

POLITICAL CHARACTER.

THIS county is not under the immediate influence of either aristocracy or administration. The earl of Coventry, lord Foley, and lord Somers, have residences and considerable estates here; but an union of their interests could not, in opposition to the inclinations of the independent freeholders, procure a return of the members to represent it in parliament. If the above noblemen should make such an attempt, we doubt not

not but that their expectations would be fruſtrated, and their deſigns rendered abortive, by the vigorous exertions of the people.

The political hiſtory of this county has been rendered remarkable for the unconſtitutional interference of the biſhop of this dioceſe, at the general election in 1702, in the firſt year of the reign of Queen Anne.

A complaint was made to the houſe, on the 2d of November following, that the lord biſhop of Worceſter, and Lloyd his ſon, had been guilty of a breach of privilege at the laſt election for that county. The ſame was ordered to be taken into conſideration on the 18th of the ſame month; when the houſe, according to the order of the day, proceeded to take into conſideration the complaint of Sir John Pakington, the 2d inſt. againſt the lord biſhop of Worceſter, and Mr. Lloyd, his ſon, relating to the rights and privileges of the houſe of commons: and Sir John Pakington, in his place, acquainted the houſe, that he had reduced the matter of the ſaid complaint into ſeveral heads; which he read in his place, and is as follows: viz.

"1ſt. That, ſoon after the parliament roſe, the biſhop of Worceſter took upon him to ſend to me to deſiſt from ſtanding to be elected knight for that county, and to threaten me, that if I did not defift, he fhould think himfelf obliged to fpeak againft me to his clergy.

" 2dly, He fent fome letters himfelf, and his fecretary fent others, to feveral of his clergy, with directions to make what intereft they could againft me in their feveral parifhes; and where they could not prevail with fuch who voted fingly for me in the laft election, to give a vote for one or both the other candidates, they fhould defire them to ftay at home; and, in order to this, his lordfhip fent them copies of the poll of their refpective parifhes.

" 3dly, He afperfed me to his clergy, branding me and my anceftors with feveral vices; and, at his confirmation and vifitations, folicited his clergy to vote againft me, reprefenting me as very unfit to ferve in parliament, and threatening them with his difpleafure, if they did not vote againft me.

" 4thly, He afperfed me and my anceftors to feveral of the laity, who were his tenants, and threatened them, that, if they would not vote againft me, they fhould never renew any eftate under him; and that he would fet fuch marks upon them, that his fucceffors fhould not fuffer them nor their children to renew any more.

" 5thly,

" 5thly, Mr. Lloyd, the bishop's son, aspersed
me, and gave scandalous characters of me to several
freeholders, whom he solicited to vote against me,
and told them I voted for bringing in a *French* government.

" 6thly, The bishop's secretary aspersed me to
several freeholders in the like manner; represent-
ing me as unfit to sit in the house, threatening
them with the bishop's displeasure, and said they
might as well vote for the Prince of Wales, as for
me."

After which, the witnesses to the respective
heads were called in, and examined at the bar
thereunto; and then they severally withdrew.

Resolved, nemine contradicente, " That Sir John
 " Pakington has, by evidence, fully made
 " out the charge which he exhibited against
 " the lord bishop of Worcester."

Resolved, nemine contradicente, " That Sir John
 " Pakington hath fully made out the charge
 " against Mr. Lloyd, the said lord bishop's
 " son."

Resolved, " That it appears to this house, that
 " the proceedings of William lord bishop
 " of Worcester, his son, and his agents, in
 " order to the hindering the election of a
 " member for the county of Worcester, have

       " been

"been malicious, unchriftian, and arbitrary,
"in high violation of the liberties and pri-
"vileges of the commons of England."

Refolved, "That an humble addrefs be pre-
"fented to her majefty, that fhe will be gra-
"cioufly pleafed to remove William lord
"bifhop of Worcefter from being almoner
"to her majefty."

Refolved, "That the faid refolution and addrefs
"be prefented to her majefty by fuch mem-
"bers of this houfe as are of her majefty's
"moft honourable privy-council."

Ordered, "That the further confideration of the
"matter relating to the lord bifhop of
"Worcefter, be adjourned till this day
"fe'nnight."

Ordered, "That Mr. Attorney-General do pro-
"fecute Mr. Lloyd, the lord bifhop of Wor-
"cefter's fon, for his faid offences, after his
"privilege, as a member of the lower houfe
"of convocation, is out."

The lords took the alarm at thefe proceedings of the commons againft a member of their houfe, and endeavoured to fcreen him from their refentment. An addrefs from the lords to the queen was agreed to, in which they ftated, "That it was
"the undoubted right of every lord of parliament,
"and

" and of every subject of England, to have an op-
" portunity of making his defence before he suf-
" fers any sort of punishment, and therefore
" humbly desired her majesty that she would be
" pleased not to remove the lord bishop of Wor-
" cester from the place of lord almoner, nor to
" shew any mark of her displeasure towards him,
" till he be found guilty of some crime by due
" course of law." This address being presented
to the queen, she returned for answer, " That she
" agreed that every peer and lord of parliament,
" and indeed every other person, ought to have
" an opportunity of being heard to any matters
" objected against him before he be punished;
" that she had not yet received any complaint
" against the bishop of Worcester; but she looked
" upon it as her undoubted right to continue or
" displace any servant attending upon her own
" person, when she should think proper." The
lords upon this answer, resolved the same day, unanimously, " That no lord of their house ought to
" suffer any sort of punishment by any proceed-
" ings of the house of commons, otherwise than
" according to the known and ancient rules and
" methods of parliament."

Mr. Comptroller reported to the house of commons that their resolutions, and address to her

majesty, for the removing *William* lord bishop of *Worcester* from being lord almoner to her majesty, had been presented to her majesty, and that her majesty had been pleased to give this most gracious answer:

" I am very sorry that there is occasion for
" this address against the bishop of *Worcester*. I
" shall order and direct, that he shall no longer
" continue to supply the place of almoner; but
" I will put another in his room, to perform that
" office."

Resolved, " That the most humble thanks of
" this house be returned to her majesty, for
" her majesty's most gracious answer to their
" address relating to *William* lord bishop of
" *Worcester*."

Ordered, " That Mr. Comptroller of her ma-
" jesty's household do return the said most
" humble thanks of this house to her ma-
" jesty."

March 25, *Ordered*, " That the evidence given
" in at the bar of this house, upon the charge
" of Sir John Pakington against *William*
" lord bishop of Worcester, and Mr. Lloyd,
" his son, be printed, together with the pro-
" ceedings of the house thereupon."

Ordered, " That the week's books, in relation
" to

" to the said evidence, be examined, and that
" Mr. Speaker do take care of the printing
" the said evidence and proceedings."

Ordered, " That the further confideration of
" the matter relating to the lord bifhop
" of Worcefter be adjourned till this day
" fe'nnight."

On the 23d, 1703, the folicitor-general reported to the houfe the proceedings which had been made againſt Mr. Lloyd, the lord biſhop of Worcefter's fon.

This county is divided into feven hundreds, containing the city of Worcefter and ten market-towns, viz. Bewdley, Bromfgrove, Droitwich, Dudley, Evefham, Kidderminfter, Parfhore, Shipton-upon-Stour, Stourbridge, Tenbury, and Upton. It is in the province of Canterbury, and diocefe of Worcefter; contains one hundred and fifty-two parifhes, and fends nine members to parliament; two knights of the fhire, two members for the city of Worcefter, two for the borough of Droitwich, two for Evefham, and one for Bewdley.

WORCESTER.

POLITICAL CHARACTER—We enter with reluctance upon the painful tafk of introducing the political character of a populous and opulent city, under the stigma of venality and corruption. To the honour of the majority of its electors, however, and to that persevering spirit which they manifested through three expensive contests, and the trial of as many petitions, it affords us the satisfaction of demonstrating, that practices subversive of national liberty cannot be used in popular elections without detection, nor escape under the ordeal of justice without punishment.

Upon the death of Henry Crabb Boulton, Esq. in 1773, who was one of the representatives for this city, Sir Watkin Lewes was invited, by a committee of the independent electors, deputed by them for that purpose, to become a candidate to supply the vacancy. Thomas Bates Rous, Esq. was opposed to him by the interest of the ministry, the corporation, and the earl of Coventry, who is recorder of this city, and has a seat in the neighbourhood. Mr. Rous was returned by the sheriff, after a poll of several days; and on the 20th of January, 1774, a petition was presented to the house of commons by Sir Watkin Lewes, setting forth, " That, at the late election of a member to represent the city of Worcester in parliament, in the room of the late Henry Crabb Boulton,

Boulton, Efq. deceafed, the petitioner, and Thomas
Bates, Rous, Efq. were candidates; and that the
faid Thomas Bates Rous, by himfelf and agents,
after the faid vacancy happened, and previous to
and during the poll, was guilty of bribing and
corrupting, and attempting to bribe and corrupt,
thofe who had a right to vote in the faid election,
in order to procure himfelf to be elected to ferve
in parliament for the faid city; and that many
of the aldermen of the faid city acted as agents
for the faid Thomas Bates Rous, and alfo did
bribe, and attempt to bribe, with money and
otherwife, a great many freemen of the faid city,
to induce them to give their votes for the faid
Thomas Bates Rous, at the faid election; and
that William Mathews, Efq. fheriff and returning
officer of the faid city, acted partially and unfairly,
before and during the poll, in rejecting good votes
for the petitioner, and admitting perfons not
qualified to vote for the faid Thomas Bates Rous,
and in many other refpects was guilty of partiality
in the execution of his office; and that, by thefe
and other illegal means, the faid Thomas Bates
Rous procured a majority of votes upon the poll,
and was returned to ferve in parliament for the
faid city, in prejudice to the petitioner, and in
open defiance of the law, and the freedom of
elections."

On the 2d of February following, a committee was appointed to try the merits of this petition, who, on the 8th of the same month, reported to the house,

"That Thomas Bates Rous, Esq. the sitting member, is not duly elected." And also,

"That Sir Watkin Lewes, Knt. is not duly elected to serve in this present parliament for the city of Worcester."

A new writ was therefore ordered to be issued for a new election.

At this second election colonel Lechmere was set up by the ministerial party, in opposition to Sir Watkin Lewes, and was returned by a small majority; but as the parliament at that time was nearly expiring, and the dissolution almost daily expected, the citizens of Worcester deferred contesting their cause any further, till the general election.

When the dissolution took place, in September following, Mr. Rous was again a candidate, on the old interest, in conjunction with Mr. Walsh, the late member; and Sir Watkin Lewes, and Edward Bearcroft, the counsel, were opposed to them by the independent interest of the city of Worcester. At the close of the poll the numbers were,

For

For Mr. Rous, — — — 981
Mr. Walſh, — — 893
Sir Watkin Lewes, — 736
Mr. Bearcroft, — — 312

Upon which the two former were returned.

On the 31ſt of October following, Sir Watkin Lewes preſented a ſecond petition to the houſe, ſetting forth, "That, at the late election of members to repreſent the city of Worceſter in parliament, John Walſh, and Thomas Bates Rous, Eſqrs. and the petitioner, were candidates; and that, previous to and during the late election, the ſaid Mr. Walſh and Mr. Rous did, by themſelves and their agents, bribe and corrupt, and attempt to bribe and corrupt, thoſe who had a right to vote at the ſaid election, in order to procure themſelves to be elected to ſerve in parliament for the ſaid city; and that previous to and at the ſaid election, William Mathews, Eſq. mayor of the ſaid city, and ſeveral aldermen and juſtices of the ſaid city, with many of the common-council, acted as agents for the ſaid John Walſh and Thomas Bates Rous, and threatened, and publicly canvaſſed and ſolicited great numbers of the freemen of the ſaid city to vote for Mr. Walſh and Mr. Rous; and promiſed that they ſhould be ſet down as conſtables, and have a certain reward for their

their votes; and alſo did bribe, and attempt to bribe, with money, and otherwiſe corrupt, a great many freemen of the ſaid city, to induce them to vote for the ſaid John Walſh and Thomas Bates Rous, or one of them, at the ſaid election; and were guilty of divers other corrupt and illegal practices, in order to procure a majority for the ſaid Mr. Walſh and Mr. Rous; and that, by means thereof, and other undue influence, the ſaid mayor, aldermen, and common-council, as agents for the ſaid Mr. Walſh and Mr. Rous, procured many freemen to vote in their intereſt for the ſaid Mr. Walſh and Mr. Rous, who would otherwiſe have voted for the petitioner; and that the ſaid mayor, ſeveral of the aldermen and juſtices of the ſaid city, and their town-clerk, for ſeveral days before and during the election, met together, nominated, appointed, and ſwore in, many freemen, and, as the petitioner believes, to the number of three hundred and upwards, to be conſtables, under a promiſe from ſuch perſons that they would vote for Mr. Walſh and Mr. Rous; for which they ſhould have certain rewards in money; which was afterwards paid to them out of the money and funds of the corporation of the ſaid city, or by the ſaid Mr. Walſh and Mr. Rous; by which means the ſaid mayor

and

and aldermen did corruptly obtain a majority of votes for Mr. Rous and Mr. Walsh upon the poll; and that a peer of this realm, and a lord of parliament, did, by himself and his agents, interfere in the said election, by canvassing and soliciting votes on behalf of the said John Walsh, and using threats to intimidate the freemen from giving their votes to the petitioner, in violation of the privileges of the house, the freedom of election, and a high infringement of the rights of the Commons of Great Britain; and that John Williams, gentleman, sheriff and returning-officer of the said city, acted partially and unfairly, before and during the election, in rejecting good votes for the petitioner, and admitting persons, not qualified, to vote for the said John Walsh and Thomas Bates Rous, and in many other respects was guilty of partiality in the execution of his office; and that, by these and other illegal means, the said John Walsh and Thomas Bates Rous, procured a majority upon the poll, and were returned to serve in parliament for the said city, in prejudice of the petitioner, who had a majority of legal votes, and ought to have been returned; and therefore praying the house to take the premises into consideration, and to grant him such relief therein as shall, upon examination, appear to be just."

The objects of the petitioner were,

1st, To prove that bribery had been committed by the sitting members, or their agents; and thereby to make the election void, as to them.

2dly, To disqualify such a number of the voters for the sitting members, and to add such a number to the poll of the petitioner, as to leave a majority in his favour, and entitle him to be declared duly elected.

3dly, To induce the committee to make a special report to the house of the various matters particularly alledged in the petition against the sitting members, the corporation, the returning-officer, the peer whose influence was complained of, and the corrupted voters.

On the first head, witnesses were produced, who swore to positive acts of bribery, and promises, by Mr. Walsh himself, and by his agents. There was no attempt to charge Mr. Rous directly; but it was contended, that Mr. Walsh, and his agents, were to be considered as agents for Mr. Rous, who, therefore, must be affected by what they had done.

On the second head there were the following objections to different classes of voters for the sitting members.

1st, To a great number, that their votes had been procured by money or promises. This was the

the main point of the cafe; being fufficient, if proved to the full extent, to have given the petitioner a majority over both the fitting members.

By a charter of James I. the city of Worcefter, which was, before that time, and continues to be, a county of itfelf, is incorporated by the name of the mayor, aldermen, and citizens of the city of Worcefter. There is a common-council, compofed of two bodies, one of twenty-four, the other of forty-eight, making together seventy-two common-councilmen. The number of citizens is indefinite; the mayor and fix aldermen are chofen annually out of the twenty-four by the feventy-two. Thefe fix aldermen, and the mayor, are, by their offices, juftices of the peace for the city.

The day before the election began, the common-council, the greateft part of whom were in the intereft of the fitting members, made the following refolution and order:

11th Oct. 1774, *Refolved*, "That it be recom-
"mended to the mayor and juftices to ap-
"point fuch a number of conftables as they
"fhall think proper, to preferve the peace
"during the election of members to repre-
"fent this city in parliament."

Ordered,

Ordered, "That the expences attending such
"appointment be defrayed by this corpora-
"tion."

Accordingly, about three hundred were sworn in; and they received one shilling and sixpence a day from the chamberlain, out of the money of the corporation, for a week: all the constables, except about ten or twelve, were freemen, and voted for the sitting members. At former elections it had been usual to appoint a certain number of special constables to keep the peace; but they were not so numerous as at this election; and they were paid, in equal proportions, by the candidates, and not by the corporation. There were several of the persons appointed, on this present occasion, lame, or so infirm as to be incapable of doing the duty of the office; insomuch that, a riot having happened during the course of the poll, it was thought necessary to swear in about ten or twelve able-bodied watermen. These watermen were the only constables who were not freemen.

From the circumstances just stated, it was contended, that the appointment of so many freemen to be constables was only colourable; that being all voters, and having voted for the sitting members, the money paid to them must be considered as bribes given them by the corporation, who were agents of Walſh and Rous; that all the votes of the conſtables therefore ought to be ſtruck off the poll.

Beſides this, there were witneſſes who ſaid, that two agents of Walſh, in their preſence, had offered, on the 30th of September, to a company of about twenty-five freemen, to make them conſtables if they would vote for Walſh and Rous; and ſaid they ſhould have a guinea from each candidate; and that many of them accepted on that condition. One of the witneſſes ſaid, he aſked whether he might not be half a conſtable, if he polled for Walſh; and that he was told he could not be a conſtable, unleſs he would vote for Walſh; ſeveral perſons ſwore to declarations of voters who were made conſtables; that they had received money from or on the behalf of Walſh; and that they were promiſed more.

There was a conſiderable number of out-voters, reſident in London, Birmingham, Kidderminſter, and other places, whoſe expences were defrayed by the ſitting members. It was alſo ſworn, that they were promiſed money for their trouble by the agents. Many declared that they had voted, in expectation of a reward; ſome that they had received the money after they had polled.

On Thursday the 18th of April, the committee, by their chairman, informed the house, that they had determined,

That the two sitting members were duly elected.

No vacancy for this city happened afterward till the general election of 1780, when Mr. Rous was again a candidate, on the interest of the corporation, in conjunction with the Hon. William Ward, now lord viscount Dudley, and again opposed by Sir Watkin Lewes, on the independent interest. Mr. Rous and Mr. Ward were successful; and on the 20th of November following, a third petition was presented to the house, from the freemen of Worcester, complaining, " That, at the last election of members to serve in parliament for the city of Worcester, the Right Hon. Sir Watkin Lewes, Knt. now lord-mayor of the city of London, the Hon. William Ward, and Thomas Bates Rous, Esq. were candidates; and that several of the aldermen, justices, and others, of the said city, hawked about, and offered the representation of the said city for sale, at the last general election, for a sum of 4000l. or other

large

large fum of money; and did treat with feveral perfons for that purpofe; and that, in confequence of bribery and corruption, and by undue and oppreffive influence, committed and practifed by the faid William Ward, or feveral of the aldermen, juftices, and others, of the faid city, as agents for the faid William Ward, a majority of votes was procured upon the poll, contrary to the general fenfe and wifhes of the freemen, who would otherwife have elected the faid Sir Watkin Lewes, if it had not been for illegal means made ufe of in favour of the faid Mr. Ward, as aforefaid."

This petition was tried by a committee appointed the 6th of February, 1781, who, on the 15th of the faid month, reported to the houfe,

" That the Hon. William Ward was duly
" elected.

The limits of our work will not fuffer us to go at large into the evidence on thefe feveral petitions; nor would it prove more than what appears almoft through every cafe which comes before the houfe of commons;—that corruption prevails;— and that the influence of magiftrates and corporations is generally exerted to deftroy the freedom of elections;—that freemen and burgeffes are admitted, or refufed their admiffion, by corporations,

tions, with little or no regard to claims legally and juftly founded, but merely to fuit the purpofes of whatever party the leading men in each city or borough may find it their intereft to efpoufe; and even the poor-rates in fcot and lot boroughs are corrupted into engines of defpotifm. The taxing a number of perfons who have no right, and omitting another defcription, who poffefs or occupy rateable houfes, has been the means of giving a colourable majority in many elections.

As a teftimony of the public approbation, the city of London unanimoufly voted their thanks to Sir Watkin Lewes, by their corporation, for the manly defence he had made in fupport of the freedom of election; and the ladies of Worcefter prefented lady Lewes with a complete fet of Worcefter-manufactured porcelain, emblazoned with the arms of Sir Watkin Lewes and thofe of the city of Worcefter; with a filver table, engraved with appofite devices, and finifhed with exquifite tafte and magnificence.

At the general election, in 1784, the Hon. William Ward, and Samuel Smith, Efq. of Aldermanbury, were chofen without oppofition. Upon Mr. Ward's fucceeding to the peerage, Mr. Wigley was elected in his room. A conteft arofe at the

laft

last general election, the two late members being oppofed to Mr. Lechmere, the barrister; when the numbers at the final close of the poll were, for

  Edmund Wigley, Efq. — 959
  Edmund Lechmere, Efq. — 892
  Samuel Smith, Efq. — — 692

This city, which is a county of itfelf, was anciently governed by two bailiffs, two aldermen, and a common-council, and fent members to parliament *ab origine.*

CORPORATION—By charter of James I. it confifts of a mayor, recorder, fheriffs, fix aldermen, twenty-four common-councilmen, and forty-eight affiftants.

RIGHT OF ELECTION—1693, Feb. 7. Is in the freemen not receiving alms.

1747, Feb. 11. Is in the citizens of the faid city not receiving alms, *and admitted to their freedom by birth, or by fervitude, or by redemption,* in order to trade within the faid city.

NUMBER OF VOTERS—Seventeen hundred.

RETURNING OFFICER—The fheriff.

DROITWICH.

POLITICAL CHARACTER—The right of election in this borough is in two bailiffs, a recorder, and eleven burgesses, who are stiled the corporation of the salt-springs of Droitwich.

This place is under the influence of lord Foley and Sir Edward Winnington, Bart. the latter of whom derives it from the family of Salway, of Stanford, in this county, and is now one of its members; the other is the Hon. Andrew Foley, second brother to the late lord Foley.

Sir Herbert Pakington has also an interest in this borough, but not sufficiently strong to oppose the present members.

CORPORATION—This place, which was originally incorporated by King John, and afterwards by charter of *inspeximus* of James I. consists of two bailiffs, a recorder, and eleven burgesses.

RIGHT OF ELECTION—1690, Nov. 11. Is in the burgesses of the corporation of the salt-springs of Droitwich.

NUMBER OF VOTERS—Fourteen.

RETURNING OFFICER—The bailiffs.

PROPRIETORS—Lord Foley and Sir Edward Winnington.

EVESHAM.

POLITICAL CHARACTER—This borough, which was incorporated by a charter granted by King James I. is only under partial influence. The corporation

corporation have been always much attached to the family of the Rushouts, of Northwick, in this neighbourhood, whose interest has been confidered as the prevailing one, and sufficient to procure a seat in parliament for one of that family. The other seat is open.

At the last election, in 1790, there were three candidates; viz. Sir John Rushout, in his own interest; Thomas Thompson, Esq, in that of Opposition; Mr. Sullivan, in that of Administration; when the numbers, on the close of the poll, were,

For Sir John Rushout, Bart. — 418
    Thomas Thompson, Esq. — 407
    Mr. Sullivan — — 374

CORPORATION—Consists of a mayor, recorder, seven aldermen, and twelve capital burgesses.

The mayor and four of the aldermen are justices of the peace, and of oyer, terminer, and gaol delivery, for all offences committed within the jurisdiction of the borough, high treason excepted.

RIGHT OF ELECTION—1669, Sept. 22. Is in the common burgesses.

NUMBER OF VOTERS—About eight hundred.

RETURNING OFFICER—The mayor.

PATRON—Sir John Rushout, partially.

BEWDLEY.

POLITICAL CHARACTER—The right of election in this borough is confined to the corporation only; confifting of a bailiff, recorder, and twelve burgeffes; which right, if it may be fo diftinguifhed, it received by a charter from King James I. It returns to parliament, in common with Abingdon, Monmouth, Higham Ferrers, and Banbury, but one member. The influence which prevails here, is that of Lord Weftcote, whofe fon, the Hon. George Fulke Lyttleton, is the prefent reprefentative.

CORPORATION—By charter of James I. it confifts of a bailiff, recorder, and twelve capital burgeffes. The bailiff is a juftice of the peace, and of the quorum for the year he officiates, as alfo for the fucceeding year.

RIGHT OF ELECTION—1662, April 28. In the bailiffs and burgeffes appointed by the charter of 3 Jac. I. exclufive of all others.

1679, May 27. All the inhabitants of the borough of Bewdley have not a right to vote.

1710, Dec. 19. The charter of 1708 is void.

1691, Jan. 24. The five perfons elected burgeffes had no right to vote.

NUMBER OF VOTERS—Fourteen.
RETURNING OFFICER—The bailiff.
PATRON—Lord Westcote.

YORKSHIRE.

POLITICAL CHARACTER.

THIS county is the first in the kingdom, in territory, population, and opulence; the number of freeholders being upwards of sixteen thousand; and its share in the representation, agreeable to the ratio of its taxes, would be forty-six out of five hundred and fifty-eight, which at present constitute the representative body of the nation: yet the boroughs of Midhurst and Old Sarum, neither of which have a house remaining in it, and those of Gatton and Castle Rising, where there are no more constituents than members, singly possess an equal share in the democratic branch of the legislature, with this extensive and populous county.

If this will not convince the most prejudiced minds of the necessity of a reform, neither argument

ment nor eloquence can be used to any purpose.

This county has the honour to give a seat in parliament to William Wilberforce, Esq. whose extensive abilities, so laudably exercised in the cause of humanity, have rendered his name sacred in the present times, and will transmit it to posterity, to be preserved by it as a pledge of a peculiar excellence. The abolition of the slave-trade was an object in which his benevolent mind was continually employed; nor did he forget that the negroes were men, although of a colour different from himself, and therefore entitled to the natural freedom and privileges of man. His labours will now be amply rewarded by the blessings which they have procured to this unfortunate and hitherto ill-fated people.

This county, which consists of three ridings, subdivided into twenty-six wapentakes, is situated in the province and diocese of York, Richmond excepted, which belongs to the diocese of Chester, and contains one city, fifty-four market-towns, and five hundred and sixty-three parishes. It sends thirty members to parliament, two knights of the shire for the county, two citizens for York, and two burgesses for each of the following

ing places; viz. Aldborough, Beverley, Boroughbridge, Heydon, Kingston upon Hull, Knaresborough, Malton, Northallerton, Pontefract, Richmond, Rippon, Scarborough and Thirske.

YORK CITY.

POLITICAL CHARACTER—This city is independent in the exercise of its constitutional rights. Were there the same number of electors in every other city, and in the respective boroughs, we should not have the baneful effects of influence and corruption to complain of. An equalization of the country into districts, would supply at least five thousand housekeepers to elect the representatives of each place; and why a mode so simple and practicable cannot be instantly adopted, we must confess we have not sagacity to divine?

CORPORATION—This was made a mayor-town by Richard I. but Richard II. changed the title into a lord-mayor, and appointed two sheriffs; besides which, there are a recorder, twelve aldermen, twenty-four assistants, and seventy-two common-councilmen.

RIGHT OF ELECTION—In the corporation, together with the freemen of the city; which freedom

dom is acquired by patrimony, servitude, purchase, or gift of the corporation.

Number of Voters—In the contested election in 1758, which was a very expensive and smartly-disputed one, and probably, therefore, very thoroughly canvassed, the number of voters was 2233. In the election of 1774, there appeared to be for Mr. Turner, 828; for Lord John Cavendish, 807; and for Mr. Hawke, 647. Most of the last being single votes, it may be fairly concluded, that upwards of 1450 voters appeared at that election. But as Mr. Hawke gave up the poll long before it would have been concluded, great numbers of persons who were entitled to vote were not called upon; besides which, it was not thought necessary to bring in all the voters who lived at a distance: from which it may be presumed, that the number of voters are not less now than in 1758; but, by those most competent to the knowledge of the fact, they are supposed to be at least a thousand more.

Returning Officers—The sheriffs.

HULL.

Political Character—About nine hundred of the electors are resident, fifty of whom were
disqualified

disqualified by Mr. Crewe's bill. The town contains nearly three thousand houses. For upwards of thirty years the candidates have paid the poorer order of voters two guineas for each vote. The number who took money was commonly two-thirds of the voters. So established is this species of corruption, that the voters regard it as a sort of birth-right. Very few of the voters are independent of the higher ranks of people in the town. The candidates have each their friends amongst the higher ranks, who canvas the town, and apply with great emphasis to their respective dependents; so that several tradesmen are at a loss how to conduct themselves with safety: they are between Scylla and Charybdis; and some have been known to put the number of their employers on the side of the two candidates, and hand about the list as their justification. Other tradesmen, having more than one voter in their families, split their votes, for the sake of peace, and the preservation of their friends in trade.

Besides the above two guineas being paid for each vote, the out-voters have been paid one guinea for expences, if resident twenty miles or under from Hull, and two guineas for above twenty miles, and under fifty: above fifty, as
could

could be agreed. This is to be underſtood, if the voter gave a ſingle vote for one candidate: if one vote for each candidate, then half a guinea; and one guinea from each. So ſoon as the candidates declare their intentions of offering themſelves, and the canvas is begun, the needy voters offer themſelves as aſſiſtants, or runners, as they are called; and if one candidate refuſes to accept their generous ſervices (for which they are paid five ſhillings per day), they threaten to go to his antagoniſt; ſo that three hundred and upwards of theſe Swiſs troops have been known to be engaged *to do nothing*, at five ſhillings per day each, ſeveral days before the poll was taken. Meſſengers ſent to canvas the non-reſident or out-voters, promiſe of places, coach-hire, horſe-hire, chaiſe-hire, treats, &c. add to the enormity of the crimes above ſtated. Another matter worthy of notice is, that Hull, being a town and county of itſelf, the freeholders and inhabitants in it, and in its diſtrict (which comprehends a quadrant of about five or ſix miles radius), have had no opportunity of voting at any election for the county of York, or for the corporation itſelf, unleſs privileged as burgeſſes.

The fifty revenue-officers are burgeſſes of Hull;

Hull; and the government candidates have ufually had about one hundred and twenty votes, by the connexions of the cuftoms and excife, and from expectants.

Many of the voters are not houfeholders, and many of the mariners have no fixed refidence in Hull, or elfewhere. It appears, that every election exceeds the preceding one in corruption.

CORPORATION—By charter of Henry VI. it confifts of a mayor, fheriff, recorder, and twelve aldermen.

RIGHT OF ELECTION—In the burgeffes, which is derived, either from being born the fon of a burgefs, from having ferved feven years apprenticefhip to a burgefs, from purchafe, or from donation for public fervices.

NUMBER OF VOTERS—From the copy of the laft poll, taken in September 1780, eleven hundred and eighty burgeffes voted, of which forty-two were cuftom-houfe, and three were excife-officers, who are now disfranchifed.

As the former parliament had been fuddenly diffolved, and writs for the new parliament immediately iffued, and as the election came on in the autumn, when many feamen in the merchants fervice were not returned from their voyages, and in time of war too, when many

were

were abroad in the service of government, it may be computed that there are fourteen hundred burgesses of this town.

Returning Officer—The sheriff.

KNARESBOROUGH.

Political Character—This borough has returned members to parliament ever since the first year of Queen Mary's reign. The right of election was then vested in eighty-four or eighty-eight burgage-houses, the owners of which were entitled to vote. The elections continued free till about the year 1719, when two gentlemen, striving against each other in canvassing, first began the practice of purchasing the burgage-houses: by these means a majority of the votes was always in the possession of some particular family. The duke of Devonshire is now, and the family has for a long time been, in possession of all the burgage-houses, except four. When an election comes on, a number of men are sent from a distant part of the country, and a certain burgage-house conveyed to each of them, for the day: they are then told who they are to vote for, and the " *cry goes* " *round.*" Some man is chaired as proxy for the absent member. The steward of the house is the returning-officer. There are no refident electors: the men who are fent to vote are the Duke's tenants: they come, if there is occafion, from his eftates in the Eaft Riding: but generally they are thofe about Bottonbridge, near Skipton, twenty miles from Knarefborough, on the other fide of the wild mountainous foreft. The number of houfes in Knarefborough is about five hundred. If the burgage-tenures were taken away, it is fuppofed there would be found three hundred or four hundred men, who pay all manner of affeffments; and thefe are chiefly manufacturers, farmers, and fhopkeepers. No diminution of votes has taken place in confequence of the act refpecting revenue officers. The principal land owners are Sir Thomas Slingfby, Mr. Roundhill, the heirs of the late Mr. Rhodes of Rippon, and Sir John Coghill, befides a great many tradefmen, who have fmall eftates in the borough. The circumftance of the members never appearing at the elections, but having fome old pauper chaired by way of proxy, which is faid to be the conftant practice, is really infulting. It cannot be faid, however, that there is bribery and corruption, as the elections are managed almoft without any vifible expence whatever.

VOL. II.   T   RIGHT

RIGHT OF ELECTION—1690, 1691, May 17. In the burgage-holders.

NUMBER OF VOTERS—About one hundred; two thirds of which are in the poffeffion of the duke of Devonfhire, and the remainder in Sir Thomas Turner Slingfby.

RETURNING OFFICER—The lord's bailiff.

PATRON—Duke of Devonfhire.

SCARBOROUGH.

POLITICAL CHARACTER—The right of election, in this town, is in forty-four individuals; a corporation confifting of two bailiffs, who are the returning-officers, and forty-two burgeffes. The patron of one feat was the late duke of Rutland, whofe influence is managed, during the minority of the prefent duke, by his uncle the duke of Beaufort, who likewife holds the recorderfhip of the corporation, until his nephew comes of age; and lord Mulgrave commands the other.

By Mr. Crewe's bill, ten of the common-councilmen are incapacitated to vote for reprefentatives; but as thofe incapacitated to vote may happen to be feniors of the body, they may, confequently, have a voice in the election of new common-councilmen, and therefore be inftrumental to corruption, by bringing fuch into their body

body as may be dependent upon them. It has, therefore, not struck at the evil, in this or any other corporation, which it was meant to remedy.

Scarborough, which is a large country-town, may be ranked with Andover, Banbury, Tiverton, and Dartmouth, whose rights are likewise monopolized by chartered corporations.

RIGHT OF ELECTION—1736, April 21. Is in the common house, or common-council of the said borough, consisting of two bailiffs, two coroners, four chamberlains, and thirty-six burgesses only.

Agreed to by the house.

NUMBER OF VOTERS—Forty-four.

RETURNING OFFICERS—The bailiffs.

PATRONS—The duke of Rutland and lord Mulgrave.

RIPPON.

POLITICAL CHARACTER—The right of election for this borough is vested in burgage-tenures; the greatest part of which belong to the Aiflabie family. The present representative of whom is William Laurence, Esq. of Kerby Fletcham, in this county.

CORPORATION—By charter granted in 1604, it is governed by a mayor, recorder, twelve aldermen, and twenty-four affiftants.

RIGHT OF ELECTION—In the burgage-holders.

NUMBER OF VOTERS—One hundred and forty-fix; of which a great majority are in the family of the Aiflabie's.

RETURNING OFFICER—The mayor.

PROPRIETOR—Mr. Aiflabie.

RICHMOND.

POLITICAL CHARACTER—The influence which prevails here is that of Sir Thomas Dundas, and Mr. York; but the former of thefe gentlemen holds a complete majority of votes, the latter poffeffing only thirty borough-houfes. Some of the aldermen, and independent freeholders, alfo have votes which they may give according to their inclinations; but thefe are an inconfiderable number.

CORPORATION—Confifts of a mayor, recorder, twelve aldermen, and twenty-four common-councilmen.

RIGHT OF ELECTION—1727, March 9. Is in fuch perfons as are owners of ancient burgages in the faid borough, having a right of pafture in a common field, called Whitecliffe Pafture.

NUMBER OF VOTERS—Two hundred and seventy, of which Sir Thomas Dundas possesses a complete majority.

RETURNING OFFICER—The mayor.

PROPRIETOR—Sir Thomas Dundas.

HEYDON.

POLITICAL CHARACTER—In this borough every burgess, with the exception of a few indeed, thinks it incumbent on him to lay the candidates under as severe a contribution as possible. Ribband-bills will amount to 100l. The candidates' agents will lend the burgesses money, which is never returned. The families of several burgesses have almost lived by their exactions, and yet their idleness has ruined them. Voters have been known to ask 100l. and 80l. has been bid for a single vote. The nominal price of a vote is 20l. that is, 20l. is expected by each voter, in case there is no opposition. Where such enormities prevail, inferior vices will necessarily flourish.

CORPORATION—Consists of a mayor, recorder, two bailiffs, and nine aldermen.

RIGHT OF ELECTION—Is in the burgesses of the said borough, whose privileges are gained either by descent, by serving seven years to a freeman refiding only in the borough, or by an honorary gift, at the difcretion of the chief officers for the time being; which latter power is feldom exercifed, on account of the jealoufy and oppofition of the common burgeffes.

NUMBER OF VOTERS—Was, in 1775, about one hundred and feventy-five; deducting from which about thirty revenue officers, who are now disfranchifed, the number will hardly exceed one hundred and forty.

RETURNING OFFICER—The mayor.

PATRON—The higheft bidder.

ALDBOROUGH.

POLITICAL CHARACTER—This parifh, which does not contain one hundred and forty houfes, fends *four members* to parliament, under the names of the boroughs of Aldborough and Boroughbridge. They do not, like Steyning and Bramber, in Suffex, confift of one paltry ftreet, or, like Weymouth and Melcombe, in Dorfetfhire, unite in choofing four members, but are feparate and diftinct boroughs, without arms or corporations, and almoft deftitute of every thing elfe but reprefentatives. A bailiff, appointed at the court-leet of the lord of the manor, is the returning-officer, and the right of election is in fixty-four houfe-

keepers

keepers, paying scot and lot; these houses are all the property of the duke of Newcastle, and Andrew Wilkinson, Esq. but as the latter has only a minority, the election interest is wholly in the duke of Newcastle.

This village never sent members to parliament till the last year of Philip and Mary, 1558.

RIGHT OF ELECTION—1679, 15 May. In all the inhabitants paying scot and lot only.

1690, 17 May. Is not only in the select number of burgesses, holding by burgage-tenure in the said borough, but in all the inhabitants paying scot and lot.

NUMBER OF VOTERS—Nominally sixty-four.
RETURNING OFFICER—The lord's bailiff.
PROPRIETOR—The duke of Newcastle.

BOROUGHBRIDGE.

POLITICAL CHARACTER—The right of election here is not, like that of the other part of the parish, in the inhabitants paying scot and lot, but in burgage-holds. These tenures, like the houses in Aldborough, are the property of the duke of Newcastle, and Andrew Wilkinson, Esq. but the former possessing the majority of them, has consequently the disposal of its representation.

The returning-officer here, as at Aldborough,

is a titular bailiff, appointed at the court-leet of the lord of the manor.

This borough never sent to parliament till 1553, being the first year of Queen Mary's reign.

RIGHT OF ELECTION—In the burgage-holders.

NUMBER OF VOTERS—Nominally seventy-four.

RETURNING OFFICER—The lord's bailiff.

PROPRIETOR—The duke of Newcastle.

MALTON.

POLITICAL CHARACTER—This town has no corporation. The returning-officer is a titular bailiff, appointed at the court-leet of earl Fitzwilliam, lord of the manor. There is no resolution respecting the right of election, but it is exercised by the burgage-holders, in number about a hundred; these are mostly the property of earl Fitzwilliam, who has the sole disposal of its political favours.

RIGHT OF ELECTION—In the burgage-holders.

NUMBER OF VOTERS—About forty.

RETURNING OFFICER—The lord's bailiff.

PROPRIETOR—Earl Fitzwilliam.

THIRSK.

POLITICAL CHARACTER—This town is divided into two parts, the old and new town. The new town has a market, is well built, full of inhabitants, and improving. The burgage-tenure, in which the right of election is vested, is in old Thirsk, now much depopulated: the owners of fifty of the burgage houses have, however, the privilege of electing two members, forty-nine of which really belong to Sir Thomas Frankland, though they are occasionally conveyed to several of his friends and dependants for the purpose of voting only, as he receives the rents and profits.

RIGHT OF ELECTION—In the burgage-holders of the village of Old Thirsk.

NUMBER OF VOTERS—Fifty.

RETURNING OFFICER—The lord's bailiff.

PROPRIETOR—Sir Thomas Frankland.

BEVERLEY.

POLITICAL CHARACTER—About two hundred of these voters are under what is called the bar-interest, and generally abide by the interest of Mr. Anderson Pelham. The ill effects of canvassing are growing conspicuous. It has been said, that
some

some of the burgesses take half a guinea or a guinea of the candidates. In the year 1774 and 1780, three or four hundred of the burgesses were exceedingly eager for an opposition, without attending to the political opinions of the candidates, which seems to indicate something very vague and unsubstantial in their ideas of freedom. They were afraid, it seems, that if the bar-interest, or Mr. Pelham's, was not opposed, the loaves and fishes, if not the liqour they swam in, might escape from their possession.

CORPORATION—Consists of a mayor, recorder, twelve governors, or superior burgesses, and thirteen inferior ones.

RIGHT OF ELECTION—Is in the freemen of the town, who acquire this right by birth, servitude, or purchase. First a freeman's son, if born within the liberties of the town of Beverley, but not otherwise, is intitled to his freedom, when of the age of twenty-one years. 2dly, An apprentice, for seven years, to a freeman residing within the liberties of the town of Beverley, but not otherwise, upon the expiration of that term, is admitted to his freedom, on paying a fine of forty-eight shillings. 3dly, Several persons are admitted to their freedom by purchase; and there is a standing order, that a day-labourer shall not be made free for a less sum than thirty guineas; and that every other person shall pay proportionally, according to his circumstances, trade, or occupation, at the discretion of the body corporate; and a candidate to represent the borough, if not already free, may purchase his freedom for fifty pounds, or guineas.

The body corporate have refused to admit to his freedom a capital tradesman in that town, although he offered them fifty pounds for the purchase of it; neither would they fix any other sum.

NUMBER OF VOTERS—About one thousand.
RETURNING OFFICER—The mayor.
PATRON—C. A Pelham Esq. partially

NORTHALLERTON.

POLITICAL CHARACTER—The right of voting is annexed to the scite of the greater part of the houses adjoining to, and fronting the street; few or none of the back tenements are considered as part of the burgage-tenures, or consequently entitled to votes. Some of those tenures now subsist in the form of stables, or cow-houses, in which the appearance of one or more chimneys is usually preserved, as a memorial of their right; others are

are let out to poor perfons, at a fmall annual rent, on the condition of their keeping them in repair; and many are totally ruinous and uninhabited. The vote is in fome inftances feparated from the houfe, by the practice of granting a leafe of the latter for the term of nine hundred and ninety-nine years, fubject to an annual pepper-corn rent; in either cafe, of the vote being referved or fold with the houfe, it is confidered as one hundred pounds in the purchafe. We are informed, that the right of voting in the borough has been invariably annexed to the ancient and eftablifhed burgage-tenures, and never, as in fome others, enlarged to the houfeholders in general. A majority of thefe houfes are known to be the property of Henry Pierfe, Efq. brother-in-law to lord Monfon, and Edward Lafcelles, Efq. firft coufin to lord Harewood, the prefent members, or their families. The number advertifed to be fold fome time ago, as the property of one gentleman, was thought to be fifteen. The remainder is divided fingly, or in fmall fhares, among various proprietors. Previous to an election, in cafe an oppofition is expected, the affignments, we are informed, of the feveral tenures, are prepared for fuch perfons as the refpective

spective proprietors can confide in; but they are
not executed unless called for, nor even then
usually entrusted to the custody of the voters.

Sir Charles Turner has ten or twelve burgage-
houses; Mr. Metcalf and family, five; Mr.
Meek, three or four; and the Rev. Mr. Peacock,
about the same number.

It is an ancient borough, without a corporation, governed by a bailiff, deputed and authorised by the bishop of Durham, for the time being, by patent for life.

The bishop is lord of the manor; and his bailiff, or deputy, presides at the election of members of parliament.

This borough, having sent 26 Edw. I. intermitted, and made no other return till called upon,
as Malton was, to send members, by order of the
house of commons, anno 1640.

RIGHT OF ELECTION—In the burgage-holders.

NUMBER OF VOTERS—About two hundred.

RETURNING OFFICER—The bishop of Durham's bailiff.

PROPRIETORS—Henry Pierse, Esq. and Edward
Lascelles, Esq.

POMFRET.

POLITICAL CHARACTER—The right of election
in this borough has been contested upon every

vacancy that has happened since the passing of the Grenville act. The question has been, whether that right was in the inhabitants householders, resiants here, or in burgage-tenures, the number of which is about three hundred and twenty; one hundred and ninety belonging to lord viscount Galway; to Sir Rowland Wynn, Bart. ninety; to Mr. Walsh, forty-two; and about one hundred to individuals.

The first investigation of these claims, was on the petition of the Right Hon. Charles James Fox, and James Hare, Esq. who were candidates on the suffrages of the inhabitants, in the general election of 1774, against Sir John Goodricke, Bart. and Charles Mellish, Esq. who were returned on the votes of the burgage-holders. The committee, which was appointed on the 28th of February, 1775, determined, on the 3d of March following, that the right was in the burgage-holders; and that the sitting members were duly elected.

The second contest was in 1782, when John Smyth, Esq. petitioned, on the votes of the inhabitants, against Nathaniel Smith, Esq. who had been returned by the burgage-holders. This committee determined, on the 11th of April, 1783, contrary to the former one, that the right was in the inhabitants.

The

The fame point was again contefted at the general election, in 1784, when the Hon. William Cockayne, and John Walfh, Efq. were petitioners, on the right of the burgage-holders, and John Smyth, Efq. and William Southeron, Efq. were fitting members, on the election of the inhabitants; when it was determined, on the 11th of June following, to be in the inhabitants, and that the fitting members were duly elected.

At the laft general election, in 1790, this point was again contefted; when John Anftruther, Efq. and Charles Mellifh, Efq. were petitioners, on the claim of the burgage-holders; and John Smyth, Efq. and William Southeron, Efq. were fitting members, on the oppofite intereft; when the committee determined, for the third time, that the right was in the inhabitants. An appeal from this decifion has been made to the houfe of commons, where it now remains for a final decifion.

In cafe the next committee fhould determine, with the three laft, that the right is in the inhabitants, this borough will be independent of controul, unlefs an honourable attachment to John Smyth, Efq. and Mr. Southeron, who have vindicated the right of the people through fo many expenfive litigations, can come under that denomination.

CORPORATION—Confifts of a mayor, recorder, and twelve aldermen, who are all in the commiffion of the peace.

RIGHT OF ELECTION—1624, May 28. There being no charter prefcription for choice, the election is to be made by the inhabitants (houfeholders) refiants there.

 1700, Jan. 17. *Agreed*, " That the right of
 " election is in fuch perfons as have an inhe-
 " ritance, or freehold of burgage-tenure,
 " within the faid borough."
 1715, March 22. *Agreed*, " That Pontefract
 " was a borough by prefcription; and that
 " the right of election is in perfons having
 " a freehold of burgage-tenure, paying a
 " burgage-rent."
 1770, Feb. 6. Is in perfons having, within the faid borough, a freehold of burgage-tenure, paying a burgage-rent.

NUMBER OF VOTERS—About three hundred and thirty.

RETURNING OFFICER—The mayor.

HISTORY

OF THE

CINQUE PORTS.

INTRODUCTION.

THE name of Cinque Ports is derived from Quinque Portuus, five havens oppofite to France, thus called by way of eminence, on account of their fuperior importance. Our kings have thought them worthy a peculiar regard; and in order to fecure them againft invafions, have granted them a particular form of government. They are under a keeper, who has the title of Lord Warden of the Cinque Ports (an officer firft appointed by William the Conqueror), who has the authority of an admiral among them, and iffues out writs in his own name.

The privileges anciently annexed to thefe ports and their dependants, were,

I. An exemption from all taxes and tolls.

II. A power to oblige all that lived in their jurifdiction to plead in their courts, and to punifh offenders in their own bounds; as alfo murderers, and fugitives from juftice.

III. A power to punifh foreigners, as well as natives, for theft; to have a pillory, and tumbrel or cucking-ftool*,

IV. A power to raife mounds or banks in any man's land againft breaches of the fea.

V. To appropriate to their own ufe all loft goods, and wandering cattle, if not claimed within a year and a day.

VI. To have commons, and to be at liberty to cut down the trees growing upon them.

VII. To convert to their own ufe fuch goods as they found floating on the fea; thofe thrown out of fhips in a ftorm; and thofe driven afhore when no wreck or fhip was to be feen.

VIII. To be a guild or fraternity, and to be allowed the franchifes of court-leet and court-baron.

---

* A machine formerly ufed for the punifhment of fcolds and brawling women; as alfo for brewers and bakers, who tranfgreffed the laws, and were, in fuch chair or ftool, to be immerged in fome muddy or ftinking pond. What pity fuch a machine fhould be out of ufe in thefe days, when fo many worthy wights daily afpire to the honour!

IX. A power to assemble and keep a portmote, or parliament for the Cinque-Ports; to punish all infringers of their privileges; make bye-laws, and hear all appeals from the inferior courts.

X. Their barons to have the privilege of supporting the canopy over the king's head at his coronation.

In return for these privileges, the Cinque-Ports were required to fit out fifty-seven ships, each manned with twenty-one men and a boy, with which they were to attend the king's service, for fifteen days, at their own expence; but if the state of affairs required their assistance any longer, they were to be paid by the crown.

It is certain that the Cinque-Ports were, at a very remote period, endowed, by royal grant, with divers very valuable privileges and immunities, as a compensation and remuneration for the shipping which they engaged to supply the sovereign with, whenever he should require it of them, and for other public services, which they were bound to the performance of.

As the exact time at which they were enfranchised has never been, with any certainty, discovered, they are held to enjoy all their earliest liberties and privileges, *as time out of mind*, *by prescription.* These were confirmed to the inhabitants of the Cinque Ports, and their members, by Magna Charta, wherein they are ſtyled the barons of the Cinque Ports; and again, by a general charter of Edward I. which, by *inſpeximus*, received confirmation, and ſometimes additions, from moſt of the kings and queens of this realm, till the time of Charles II. whoſe general charter is the laſt.

As the term baron occurs continually throughout all the charters of the Ports, it may not be improper to inform our readers, that it is of the ſame import as burgeſs or freeman. From the mode in which it is uſed, there is great reaſon to think, that every inhabitant of the Ports, contributing to the common expences, and other ſervices, was a baron, that is, a freeman. In ſome of the oldeſt boroughs in the kingdom, wherein the lands were holden in ancient demeſne, every inhabitant, who paid a rent to the crown, was intitled to the electtive franchiſe; by analogy it ſhould ſeem probable, that the ſame rights formerly prevailed in the Ports, as to thoſe inhabitants who were aſſeſſed to the exigencies of the public. There are many other circumſtances which give great ſtrength to this ſuppoſition,

supposition, which will be hereafter touched upon.

The representatives of the Ports in parliament are, to this day, styled barons, because they were formerly, as they still ought to be, chosen from amongst the inhabitants at large.

HASTINGS.

HASTINGS.

BEFORE the passing of Mr. Crewe's bill, the appointment of the representative in parliament for this town was wholly in the Treasury; the number of voters was usually about twenty, the whole of whom had places under, or were otherwise provided for, by government. The management and conduct of this faithful, and well-disciplined corps of treasury auxiliaries, was, for a long series of years, vested in Mr. Collier, who, in this situation, acquired a very princely fortune, whereby he was enabled to provide for five co-heiresses, his daughters, in a very handsome manner. Upon his death, Mr. Edward Milward, (who had married a Miss Collier) succeeded to this post of agent to the treasury, and, by way of compensation for the proper discharge of his election duties, was appointed to the very lucrative office of *surveyor general of the riding officers*; from which post, about seven years ago, he was removed by the board of customs, notwithstanding the whole interest and influence of the treasury was exerted to prevent his being displaced.

That this opposition between two such great powers may not appear strange to our readers, we think it neceffary to inform them, that at this time the board of cuftoms (owing to a change in adminiftration) were in oppofition to the lords of the treafury; moft of the commiffioners, having been appointed under former adminiftrations, felt no very great affection for the prefent. Mr. Henry Pelham, and Mr. Papillon, however, having fince been *prevailed* on to retire, the treafury have now regained the favourable opinion of that office.

This lofs was, however, made up to Milward, by the appointment of his fon to the office of deputy comptroller of excife, who, on coming of age, was made a jurat; but it was judged expedient to unite alfo, in his perfon, in addition, the more lucrative office of town clerk; accordingly, Mr. Thatcher, the old town clerk, was turned out of his place, to make room for this young gentleman. A trial in the court of King's Bench, between thefe two competitors for office, was the confequence; when it was determined[*], that a jurat of the corporation of Haftings might be elected town clerk; but that the two offices are incompatible, and that the acceptance of the latter, though an inferior office, will vacate the former.

[*] Firft Term Reports, Durnford and Eaft.

—He has since resigned the office of town clerk, on getting his more valuable place in the excise, and is now again a jurat; these two places, it is presumed, not being incompatible.

It would be very difficult to pronounce whether, at this time, the treasury, or Mr. Milward's interest in this borough, be the superior; indeed, this point is not likely to be brought to a very speedy determination, as this gentleman invariably sides with the minister for the time being, whose appointees he returns to parliament upon very moderate terms and conditions, without making any inquiry as to their capacity, or fitness for that situation. In fact, the only indispensible requisite is, an ability and disposition to say yea and nay, according to the mandate of the minister.

At present, the whole patronage of government, in this place, is in the hands of Mr. Milward, who disposes of the various places as he imagines will be most conducive to the common interest of himself and the treasury. Since Mr. Crewe's bill, it has been necessary to keep up a certain number of freemen (just enough to go through the farce, and to perform the various ceremonies, of an election) who do not ostensibly hold any place or post under government. These,

These, however, do not go unprovided for; they are, as of course, quartered on such of their brother freemen as are in possession of the more lucrative situations; others, rather than lose their franchises by the operation of that bill, have given up their places to their sons, and other near relations; by which measure the freeman preserves his vote, and the treasury its influence.

Whatever personal interest Mr. Milward may have at this place, apart from and independent of the treasury, is obtained and preserved by lending small sums of money, on bond, to the more indigent freemen; which obligations are never meant to be enforced, so long as they are, as electors, in a state of passive obedience and non-resistance; but if, at any time, they should venture to give the smallest indication of an inclination to an independence of opinion and sentiment, a payment of their debts is required, and a prison the certain consequence of the smallest delay.

In a contested election, between colonel Beaumont and Mr. Grey, in 1689, the number of voters polled, was 67; in 1698, between Mr. Austen and Mr. Gott, 70. In 1690, a petition of Robert Munns, Esq. was delivered to the house of commons, shewing, that the petitioner was duly elected

elected one of the barons of this port, and ought to have been returned; but John Beaumont, Esq. governor of Dover Castle, who pretended to have a power over the several Cinque Ports, wrote several mandatory letters to the mayors, and returning-officers of the Cinque Ports, requiring them not to engage their votes for any particular person, for that his majesty would recommend to them such persons as he should think convenient for them to choose; and, by several menaces and threats, procured a majority of the electors to vote for him to serve in parliament for the Port of Hastings, and prevailed on the mayor to return him, though not legally elected, to the prejudice of the petitioner; which petition was referred to a committee to report upon, &c.

We make no comment on the above, but leave the reader to form his judgment of the purity of this borough from a naked statement of facts; and we will venture to assert, since the time of this petition, that it is no way amended—but this by way of sample. From the evidence, on the trial of the mandamus brought by H. Moore, against the mayor and jurats of this town, it appears, that the right of the elective franchise in this place, according to its true constitution, and

according

according to the cuftumal then produced, is as follows:

In 1736, a writ of mandamus was brought by Henry Moore, to require the mayor, jurats, and commonalty of the town and Port of Haftings, to admit him into the place and office of one of the freemen of that town; and the writ fets forth, that he is the eldeft fon of a freeman, born within the town; after the admiffion and fwearing of his father into the place and office of one of the freemen of the faid town and Port; and that he has a right, in refpect thereof, and alfo upon paying a reafonable fine, to be admitted into the place and office of one of the freemen of the faid town and Port.

The above was the matter at iffue for the jury.

Lord Hardwicke, who was then the lord chief juftice of the court of king's bench, in fumming up the evidence, faid to the jury:

" The point infifted on by the plaintiff's counfel, and the firft thing produced to be confidered by you is a book, in which is an ancient entry of the cuftumal of the Five Ports and their members; the time whereof the memory of man is not to the contrary.

" The evidence relied on for the plaintiff is this,

this, " concerning the making of freemen, &c.
" as stated."

" After reading these entries, the counsel for the defendants objected, that this was not a particular custumal of Hastings, and therefore not so conclusive. But Hastings, in the mandamus, is said to be one of the Five Ports. " They " have given evidence of three different species " of persons admitted under this right."

" The first is, where persons were admitted as eldest sons of freemen, born within the borough, and after the swearing and admission of the father.

" The next is, where admission has been of eldest sons, born within the borough; but it does not appear, whether before or after the admission of the father. And,

" The third species of persons, who were admitted as the sons of freemen in general; but they have not shewn that they were born in the town, or after the father's freedom.

" For the defendants, the gentlemen on the other side insist, there is no right at all to freedoms in this borough; but that all admissions depend upon the will and pleasure of the mayor and jurats; that they may admit or refuse, a stranger or a son, just as they please. And they
insist,

infift, that if there be fuch a right, that it is reſtrained by thefe two qualifications, of being born in the town, and after the fwearing and admiffion of the father.

" And another qualification infifted on by the defendants is, that he fhould be refiant within the borough.

" Gentlemen, the matter of law which will arife, if you are of opinion that there is fuch a cuftom, will be whether the fine be a reafonable fine, as the plaintiff has laid it, or whether this is a certain fine of 6s. 8d.?

" The firſt evidence that has been produced for the defendants, is an old book, in which there are entries of an old cuftumal, and a byelaw, dated the 12th of April, 15 Elizabeth, by which it is decreed, " That if any freeman, now, " or at any time hereafter, an inhabitant of this " town, fhall depart or dwell out of the town, " by the fpace of a year and a day, he or they, fo " dwelling out of the town, fhall lofe his or their " freedom for ever." I own I do not know fo extraordinary a cuftom any where, for a man to have a right to be admitted a freeman who was not refident, and yet the corporation could diffranchife a man for non-refidence.

" But

"But this bye-law will not be of much weight one way or the other. It only ſhews the act of the corporation, to disfranchiſe any perſon that goes out of the borough.

"They have alſo produced, for the defendants, another book, in which, they ſay, is contained the uſage of Haſtings, time out of mind, and they have read out of it an entry, in old French; the purport of which is, "That if a "foreigner reſides in Haſtings a year and a day, "he may come before the bailiff and jurats, "and be admitted to the freedom, upon taking "an oath." The witneſs who read this, ſwore, that there was no other evidence in the book, relating to the making of freemen.

"They read this to ſhew, that there is no right of freedom at all in this borough, if a ſtranger, who has lived in the town a year and a day, may come before the bailiff and jurats, and they may admit him, upon taking an oath.

"The next evidence the defendants have produced, is from entries of admiſſion of the ſons of freemen, without mentioning that they were either eldeſt or youngeſt ſons; and they only ſhew, that the fact is, that other ſons, as well as eldeſt ſons, have been admitted for a fine of 6s. 8d.

"It

" It will be proper, therefore, for you, gentlemen, to confider,

" Firſt, If you believe, on the evidence, that there is no right in the fon of any freeman to demand his freedom of the mayor and jurats, but that all depends on their pleaſure; but, if you believe, that there is a right in the fon of a freeman, and that the mayor and jurats cannot deny him his freedom, then you will confider, whether the two qualifications, of being born in the borough, after the freedom of the father, are neceſſary or no?

" If you believe they are not neceſſary, but that, whether he be born in or out of the borough, or before or after he was made free, makes no difference; in that caſe you muſt find for the defendants.

" But if you believe a right in the fons of freemen, and that being born in the borough, and after the father's freedom, are eſſential, then you will confider the matter of refiance.

" And, if you believe refiance not neceſſary, then you muſt find a verdict for the plaintiff.

" But, on the other hand, if you believe being born in the borough, and after the father's freedom, are not neceſſary; or, if neceſſary, that it is equally neceſſary that the perſons
ſhould

should be resiant, then you must find a verdict for the defendants."

Verdict for the plaintiff.

Foreman. "We find that the eldest son of a freeman, born within the borough after his father's freedom, has a right."

Lord Hardwicke. "What do you find as to the commorancy?"

Foreman. "My lord, we find residence not necessary; and that the eldest son, born within the borough after his father's freedom, has a right, upon paying a customary fine?"

Lord Hardwicke. "What do you find the fine?"

Foreman. "We find the fine to be 6s. 8d. and that is reasonable."

Lord Hardwicke. "That point of the reasonable fine must be saved for the opinion of the court, and let the *postea* stay."

We should here observe, that Moore was completely successful upon this occasion. It is true, that he claimed his freedom merely as an eldest son; but the same evidence by which he availed himself, went the full length of establishing the right of every other son of a freeman to his freedom.

The verdict, given by the jury upon this occasion

casion, came under the review of the court of king's-bench, as appears from Strange's Reports, 1070, which, after solemn argument, was confirmed by the unanimous determination and sanction of the judges.

We wish, in a very particular manner, to draw the attention of the reader to this very important trial, as it not only clearly and satisfactorily demonstrates what was originally, and what ought still to be, the constitution of Hastings, but throws great light upon the true constitution of the rest of the Cinque Ports, notwithstanding the usurpations and corruptions which, in these latter days, prevail more or less, in all of them.

In the course of the Seaford contests, it became important for some of the parties to inspect this custumal; and a rule was accordingly obtained from the court of king's-bench for that purpose; but lo! it was missing, and not to be found! Through fear that some future claimant of a freedom should attempt to accomplish and perfect what Moore left undone, it was thought expedient to commit this highly important and venerable record to the flames. But, notwithstanding this destruction of it by fire, we congratulate

congratulate the public, that the moſt material and confequental part of it has been preſerved in the State Trials, by reaſon of the mandamus brought by Moore. Of which cuſtumal Jeake makes mention, page 35 and 123.

By the laſt determination of the houſe of commons, which took place in the year 1698, it appears, that the right of election of members of parliament for the Port of Haſtings, is in the mayor, jurats, and freemen, reſident, and not receiving alms. But here ariſes a very important queſtion, which is, who are entitled to be freemen? Mr. Milward contends, that only the firſt born ſon of a freemen, and ſuch as are annually nominated by the mayor; we have very little ſcruple to ſay, that if this queſtion ſhould ever be fairly brought before an impartial committee of the houſe of commons, we have no doubt but that the determination would be, that the right of freedom is according to the cuſtumal above ſet out.

Government have at this place a cuſtom-houſe; a cuſtom-houſe boat, under pretence of watching the ſmugglers, the crew of which are all landmen, but taken from amongſt the freemen; an Ordnance fort, of no utility whatever;

and

and an establishment of twelve riding officers; besides the usual retainers of the excise and of the post office.

A complaint was exhibited to the commissioners of the customs against the patrons of this borough, by the town-clerk, in 1787, for quartering freemen, at five, ten, and twenty pounds a year each, upon the revenue officers of this port; in which complaint were specifically mentioned the names of Bevins, Hide, Meadow, Bourne, and others, who had paid such sums. A copy of this memorial is now in our hands, which we will take good care of, as it may hereafter, in common with similar proofs in our possession, be a subject of more serious enquiry.

We must not omit to add, that it was in consequence of this complaint, that the elder Mr. Milward was deprived of his place of surveyor-general of the riding officers by the board of customs.

A List of the Whole Body of Electors of Hastings, taken the twenty-fifth day of April, 1792; many of whom have small places in the Customs, Excise, and Ordnance, which it is unnecessary to specify.

MAYOR.
Mr. Edward Milward.

DEPUTY MAYOR.
Mr. Edward Milward, Junior, Controller of Excise, £.1425 per annum, resides in London.

JURATS.
‡ Rev. William Hicks Coppard.
Thomas Evitt, collector of the customs.
John Stevens, officer of ditto.
John Thatcher, a superannuated officer.
John Crouch, ditto.
Thomas Crouch.
Lovell Crouch.
John Goldsworthy Shorter.
Walter Crouch.
William Polhill.

FREEMEN.
‡ John Sargent

Honourable

Honourable General James Murray, Milward's brother-in-law and friend.

Robert Meadow, fen. a fuperannuated boat-officer.

William Lintott.

‡ Henry Sargent.

Thomas Morfee, relation of Milward.

John Thatcher.

‡ Rev. William Coppard.

William Scrivens, tenant of Milward.

Alexander Godfrey, a prifoner in the king's bench, at the fuit of Milward.

John Weatherman.

Robert Thatcher, a riding-officer of the cuftoms.

Jofeph Edwards.

Robert Meadow, Jun.

Edward Evitt, purfer of the Leopard man of war.

John Williams.

John Hide.

Spencer Kent.

Jofeph Diplock.

Richard Ball.

Thomas Mannington.

Nathaniel Crouch, a bomb-bailiff.

Richard Edwards, fen.

Thomas Hide.
Thomas Godley.
Robert Ball.
‡ Stephen Penight.
Charles Stevens Crouch.
Benjamin Boffom.
Richard Edwards, jun.
John Williams, jun.

Those with this mark ‡, are in oppofition to Milward; but the numerous family of the Crouch's are all his immediate dependants.

CORPORATION—By charter of queen Elizabeth, it confifts of a mayor, recorder, and twelve jurats. The corporation is exempted from toll, and has the power of holding courts of judicature in capital cafes.

RIGHT OF ELECTION—1698, 30th January. Is in the mayor, jurats, and freemen, refident and not receiving alms only.

NUMBER OF VOTERS—Twelve.
RETURNING OFFICER—The mayor.
PATRON—The Treafury.

DOVER.

DOVER.

POLITICAL CHARACTER—This town is properly called the capital of the Cinque Ports, and stands in nearly the same situation, with respect to the others, as the chief town of a county does with those of less note; the lord warden's court being held here, and the castle being used as the prison of all the Ports.

The right of freedom is the same here as described in the custumal of Hastings, with the addition of its extending to the husbands of freemen's daughters, as well as to the sons of freemen; freeholders are also entitled to the elective franchise in this place; which privilege is at this day retained here only; at the other ports it has long since, by corrupt contrivances and practices, been stifled. The number of voters being upwards of twelve hundred, they cannot all be provided for out of sinecure places, and revenue officers, as in most of the other Ports; nevertheless, government obtains such a degree of influence from the custom-house, packet-boats, military and naval appointments, &c. as always to nominate one of the members; the other is usually a gentleman in opposition.

Mr. Trevanion, who was firſt introduced to the electors of this town by the celebrated Charles Churchill, in the days of Mr. Wilkes's popularity, has continued in his ſituation as member for this port, in oppoſition to all the influence of ſucceeding adminiſtrations (with only one exception, which was in the year 1784), till the preſent time.

This town was formerly of infinitely more importance than at preſent, the caſtle having been conſidered as the key to the kingdom. In its proſperity it had twenty-one wards, each of which furniſhed a ſhip for the ſervice of the nation, and maintained it forty days, at the expence of the inhabitants. It had likewiſe ſeven churches, though there are now only two remaining. It is ſtill, however, a large town, and not like the decayed villages of Winchelſea and Seaford, a burleſque upon the exerciſe of legiſlative and judicial powers.

CORPORATION—It is governed by a mayor, twelve jurats, and thirty-ſix common councilmen.

RIGHT OF ELECTION—1623, 24 March. Is in the freemen, and free burgeſſes, inhabitants of Dover. Every ſon of a freeman, and every perſon marrying a freeman's daughter, is entitled to

his

his freedom, as is every freeholder within the jurifdiction of the corporation; befides all thofe who are made free by redemption, gift, or purchafe. We muft here obferve, that this is the only one of the Ports that has preferved any traces of its true conftitution. We are, however, of opinion, that by a fpirited exertion, the rights of the inhabitants might ftill be recovered in many of the Ports.

1770, 12 March. That the *non*-inhabitant freemen, as well as the inhabitant freemen, and free burgeffes of the town and port of Dover, have a voice in the election.

NUMBER OF VOTERS—According to the poll at the laft general election, appears to be about twelve hundred.

RETURNING OFFICER—The mayor.

PATRON—The admiralty, of one feat; independent as to the other. Mr. Peter Fector has the beft intereft of any individual in this place, always fiding with government.

SANDWICH.

POLITICAL CHARACTER—This is the only Cinque Port, except Dover, which has the leaft claim to independence, and that arifes from the extenfive number

number of its electors. Sandwich, which has for many years been ranked as an admiralty borough, from the influence of innumerable places, and the douceurs which the voters hold under the patronage of that board, has been generally reprefented by two members of their nomination; but, at the laft election, Sir Horace Mann, who refides in the neighbourhood, having the largeft Kentifh eftate of any man in the county, and is fo much refpected for his hofpitality and convivial talents, that no other perfon would have ftood the fmalleft chance of fuccefs in oppofition to government, became a candidate on his own intereft, in oppofition to lord Parker, comptroller of the houfehold, (who was fupported by government, in conjunction with Mr. Stephens, fecretary to the admiralty) was fuccefsful, as will appear by the clofe of the poll; the numbers being, for

   Philip Stephens, Efq. — 474
   Sir Horace Mann   — 311
   Lord Parker   — — 290

Thus the independent intereft fucceeded, for the firft time, in the election of one of their members. The other is ftill confidered as being at the difpofal of the admiralty.

The mayor and jurats of this port, like the

corporations of most cities and boroughs, have not neglected to use their utmost endeavours to obtain a monopoly of the right of election, to the exclusion of the freemen*.

At the election in 1620, the third parliament of James I. lord Cobham, warden of the Cinque Ports, *made an order*, which he got confirmed by the *lords of the privy council*, that the *mayor and jurats only*, should make the elections of members of parliament. The freemen, or commons, were therefore debarred from giving their voices, with threats of imprisonment. Sir Robert Hatton was returned by the mayor and jurats. The commons, who intended to choose Mr. Borrowes, were intimidated by the magistrates. The house of commons, however, held the election void, and ordered a new writ, for the freemen at large to make the election.

It likewise appears, that the corporation of this port have not been exempt from the charge of corruption, any more than their neighbours; as on the 25th of November, 1695, a petition of John Thurban, serjeant at law, was presented to the house, setting forth, that he was duly elected a baron to serve in parliament for this port; but

* In Glanville's Reports, case 7th, there is much curious information as to this.

that

that Edward Brent, and John Taylor, Esqrs. had prevailed with the mayor to return them, though they were not duly chosen.

Upon the examination of evidence, the following matter came out before a committee:

Ralph Goodchild said, a great while before the writ came down, and he believes a month before the election, at the desire of some of Mr. Taylor's friends, he went to Mr. Taylor's house, with an account of what men they thought would engage for him; and that Mr. Taylor said to him, and, as he believes, Mr. Paramour, Mr. Mandy, and Mr. Gregg, were by, that he had heard some people got places of profit by being parliament-men; and that, if the town chose him, and he got any, *he would give half to the corporation*, and 20l. a year to the poor, and give the corporation a treat on the day he was chosen, yearly; that Mr. Taylor bid him speak of it, and he did, accordingly, make use of it, to persuade several to vote for Mr. Taylor; that he voted so, and designed to do so before the said promise; and said, he believed he saw bills of charges of 300l. on Mr. Taylor's account, and that Mr. Cricket was Mr. Taylor's agent.

Twisden said, that Mr. Taylor, the day before the election, declared, Mandy being present, *if he got a place of* 100ol. *or* 50ol. *a year, as he hoped he should, or whatever it was, he would give one half to the town;* and Mr. Cricket said, he would give his bond, that Mr. Taylor should expend 40l. or 50l. yearly, upon the town, and give 20l. yearly to the poor; and Turner, sitting by, said, he would drink the petitioner's health, but durst not vote for him, for if he did, they would never employ him again.

John Chapman said, Cricket declared, that Mr. Taylor had promised, and he (Cricket) would give his bond as before testified; and that, on account of his voting for Mr. Brent, Cricket had received forty shillings of Rickfey, which he paid in part of 7l. owing from him to the serjeant, but owned Cricket was bound with him for it; but it did not appear Mr. Brent had employed Cricket.

Cricket and Moor said, the mayor went to several to vote for Mr. Brent; and Moor owned, that he himself had spoke to several to vote for the serjeant.

Clark, Jenkinson, and Stone, said, that a letter was read, as from Sir Cloudesly Shovel, by which they pretended, that all the seamen who would not vote for Mr. Brent should be pressed. Rickfey and

and others were prefent, and fome feamen were feared out of the town by it.

Rickfey produced a letter which, being read, he faid was only a recommendation of Mr. Brent, without any threatening or promifes.

John Vatchelor faid, Broderly, who voted, and made intereft for Mr. Brent, offered him two half crowns to vote for Mr. Brent, and Rickfey and Fifher were by, and was threatened to be ruined, becaufe he would not vote againft the ferjeant.

N. Vatchelor, his brother, faid, he had heard his brother John declare, that Broderly had offered him no money.

Hutton faid, he had a debt of 3l. odd money owing to him from Curfer; but he dying, it became dubious; and that he was offered to have it paid if he would vote for Mr. Taylor.

There is at this place a harbour with a large revenue, a mere job; a cuftom-houfe; cuftom-houfe cutter; two cuftom-houfe boats; a fort; two caftle, in the neighbourhood, officered by freemen; and ten riding officers. Any owner of a veffel or hoy, being a freeman, may have his fhip taken into the fervice of the admiralty, upon application; at this time feven veffels are fo engaged.

Cor-

CORPORATION—By a charter, dated in the year 1685, it confifts of a mayor, recorder, twelve jurats, and twenty-four common-councilmen.

RIGHT OF ELECTION—1690, 31ft Oct.—The freemen of the port of Sandwich, inhabiting within the faid port, although they receive alms, have a right to vote.

Not agreed to by the houfe.

NUMBER OF VOTERS—About four hundred and eighty.

RETURNING OFFICER—The mayor.

PATRON—Admiralty.

Mr. Stephens, the fecretary to the admiralty, has been returned for this port ever fince he has been in place, now upwards of thirty years. The inhabitants are bound to this gentleman by every tie of gratitude, as there is fcarcely a fingle family, fome part of which has not been provided for by him, in the admiralty, navy, or marines. Since the laft election, the people of this town have feverely felt the inconvenience of having prefumed to reject Mr. Stephens's friend, lord Parker. Some have been alfo difplaced, and no new places have been granted, but upon a promife of implicit obedience.

HYTHE.

HYTHE.

POLITICAL CHARACTER—The bailiff of this port was appointed by the archbishop of Canterbury, till the 31st year of Henry VIII. when the archbishop exchanged the manor of Saltwood, together with the bailiwick of Hythe, with the king, for estates elsewhere. After which a bailiff was appointed annually by the crown, till the reign of Elizabeth, who in the 17th year of her reign, granted it a particular charter of incorporation, by the name of mayor, jurats, and commonalty, under which they still continue to be governed.

The corporation, out of whom are chosen two chamberlains and a town-clerk, with the assistance of ninety freemen, making in the whole one hundred and twenty-six, elect the two members; out of which number, only *twenty-two* are residents; the remaining hundred and four being dispersed over different parts of the country.

The charters of this corporation, as well as those of the other Cinque Ports, were, in 1685, by the arbitrary command of Charles II. surrendered up to colonel Strode, then governor of Dover castle, and were never afterwards returned; but they are supposed to be in possession of government at this moment.

The influence of this place is not so easily managed as the insignificant corporations of Rye, Winchelsea, Hastings, Seaford, or Romney. One hundred and twenty-six electors, five-sixths of whom are not immediately under the controul or persecution of a treasury agent, cannot be trained to the word of command so easy as a dozen custom-house officers, or pensioners, upon the emoluments of the sinecures. By one artifice or other, however, government always contrive to have both members constantly in its interest.

The corporation of Hythe are under the absolute direction of Mr. Robert Tournay*, an attorney, who is every other year chosen mayor; and, in spite of legal incapacity, unites with the office of chief magistrate, that of town clerk; thereby consolidating the master and servant in the same personal agency; but, as pluralities of livings, as well as places, are sanctioned by the example of church and state, we must not suppose, that the emoluments arising from the ministerial duties of one office, can influence the judicial deportment of the other.

The interest amongst the electors, is nearly equally divided between government and Mr.

---

* The joint agent of the treasury and Mr. Evelyn.

Evelyn, one of the prefent members. Mr. Alderman Sawbridge has indeed attempted the eftablifhment of an independent intereft; but, while the reprefentation remains in its prefent debilitated form, fuch exertions, though they might fucceed on a fingle occafion, can neither give permanency nor fecurity to the freedom of election.

CORPORATION—By charter of incorporation, granted by Queen Elizabeth, it confifts of a mayor, twelve jurats, and twenty-four common-councilmen.

RIGHT OF ELECTION—1710, 27th Jan.—Is in the mayor, jurats, common-councilmen, and freemen.

Agreed to by the houfe.

NUMBER OF VOTERS—One hundred and twenty-fix, about half of whom are non-refidents.

RETURNING OFFICER—The mayor.

PATRON—The treafury partially.

Mr. William Deedes and Sir Charles Farnaby Radcliffe, who have both confiderable intereft here, are entirely at the devotion of the minifter.

NEW ROMNEY.

POLITICAL CHARACTER—This place enjoys the same exclusive privileges with the other ports; in addition to which, it had a charter of incorporation from Edward III. by the style of the barons of the Port of New Romney; afterwards by that of jurats and commonalty; and lastly, by Queen Elizabeth, in the fifth year of her reign, by the style of the mayor, jurats, and commonalty; at which time, by letters patent, she ratified all the privileges they had enjoyed in the reign of Edward the Confessor, or at any other time. By the *forms* of this charter, the corporation is governed at this time; but the charter was seized, by order of King Charles II. in 1685, by colonel Strode, and has never been returned since.

The corporation should consist, according to *that* charter, of a mayor, twelve jurats, twenty-six common-councilmen, and an indefinite number of freemen; but, as the patron of this, as well as those of the other Cinque Ports and boroughs, finds a convenience in not supplying the vacancies as corporators fall off, nineteen are deemed sufficient to exercise the same constitutional powers in this borough, which is deposited with three only at Winchelsea, and with six individuals at Rye.

Sir Edward Deering has, by a very simple method, possessed himself of an influence in this port, not easily to be rendered insecure. His property in the neighbourhood is tenanted out, *without lease*, at *very easy* rents, to the electors; who, feeling that gratitude, which never fails to inspire those immediately interested in the present possession of a good thing, could not be so ungenerous as to oppose the inclination of a passive landlord, in so *trifling* a concern as that of the election of a member of parliament.

The two great meetings of all the Cinque Ports are still held here; the members belonging to which are, Old Romney, Bromehill, Orlaston, and Dungeness.

CORPORATION—By charter of Queen Elizabeth, before mentioned, it ought to be governed by a mayor, twelve jurats, and twenty-six common-councilmen*.

RIGHT OF ELECTION—Is in the mayor, jurats, and commonalty.

NUMBER OF VOTERS—Nineteen.

* See the Appendix to 10th vol. State Trials, in which are two trials containing much light on this corporation.

RETURNING OFFICER—The mayor; who is alternately Mr. Coates, Mr. Walter, or Mr. Cobb, Sir Edward's agents.

PATRON—Sir Edward Deering.

Sir Edward Deering having been engaged in the fashionable pursuits of the present day, has found it expedient to accommodate Sir Elijah Impey, and Mr. Sullivan, both gentlemen of Indian celebrity, with their present seats.

The number of places in the possession of Sir Edward's friends, *and their relations*, renders the return of treasury candidates an indispensible duty.

The following is a correct list of the freemen of New Romney:

Benjamin Cobb, mayor; he holds no land of Sir Edward Deering, at present; but is a capital grazier, and will have the first farm that is vacant.

W. Witwick; he holds about 300 acres, at a low rent.

Rev. T. Cobb, of Hardness, aged 90; non-resident.

Bartholomew Tookey, of Savington; he has 100 acres at an inconsiderable rent: non-resident.

Odiarne

Odiarne Coates, William Coates, his fon; jointly hold a large quantity of land, at about 200l. a year fhort of its real value.

Jacob Walter; 200 acres, low rent.

Edward Tookey; maintained by Sir Edward, but holds no land.

The above are jurats and freemen—the following are freemen only:

John Walker; he holds 150 acres of Sir Edward.

Abraham Walter; a riding officer, through the intereft of Sir Edward.

Thomas Knight, Efq. of Godmorfham; non-refident.

Robert Wightwich; maintained by Sir Edward, in low circumftances.

Edward Deering, Efq. Cholmondely Deering, Efq. fons of Sir Edward; non-refident.

Rev. W. W. Fowle; he has the livings of Burmarfh and Snargate, and the free fchool, a finecure falary 60l. a year; all given him by Sir Edward.

Charles Rolfe; ufes 50 acres of Sir Edward's land; his fon is a riding officer by the intereft of Sir Edward.

John Buckhurft, John Walter, furgeon; 50 acres each.

Edward

Edward Ruffel; 200 acres of Sir Edward.

William Fowle, jun. town-clerk, and clerk to Romney and Walland Marsh; so made by Sir Edward.

RYE.

POLITICAL CHARACTER—This is one of those places, usually, though somewhat improperly, called a Cinque Port. It was with the neighbouring town of Winchelsea, annexed as a member of the Cinque Ports generally, (but not of Hastings in particular, as is commonly but erroneously supposed) before the time of Henry III; in a charter of which king, these two places are denominated *nobiliora membra Quinque Portuum.*—They have enjoyed, from all antiquity, the peculiar appellation of the two ancient towns, and are possessed, in every respect, of equal franchises, immunities, and privileges, with the original Cinque Ports.

Rye was burnt by the French in the time of Richard II. and again in the 26th of Henry VI. in one of which fires it is supposed, that the old records and charters of this town perished, as none older than the 27th of this king, except some fragments, are at this day to be found,

Before Mr. Crewe's bill, this place was, in the strictest sense of the appellation, a treasury borough, all the freemen, with scarcely an exception, being possessed of places in some revenue department. Since this bill has passed, it has become absolutely necessary to make a small addition to the usual number of freemen, in order that there may be *some* people duly qualified to go through the formal part of the *farce* of an election to return members to parliament: all which new-made freemen, who are not ostensibly holders of a place, are quartered upon, and, in a certain degree, divide the profits with, those who are in possession of the more lucrative posts.

At this place there is a custom-house, with a very large establishment; a custom-house boat, as it is called, whose crew consists wholly of landsmen, and who are of course all freemen; and seven riding officers in the service of the customs; a cutter is likewise stationed here, under pretence of cruising against the smugglers, but in truth, by way of giving additional influence to the treasury; and here we must not omit to remark, that this vessel is actually employed and paid by the treasury, and is immediately under its controul, though it is usually called a custom-

house

house cutter; there is but one other vessel in the kingdom thus peculiarly circumstanced.

This cutter, which is named the Stag, is commanded by captain William Haddock, who alone has freemen quartered on him to the amount of 350l. a year. However, it is clear that this place will bear this incumbrance, as he is rapidly making a very large fortune. This gentleman, being very active and diligent in his professional pursuits, as a revenue officer, the emolument accruing to this vessel, by means of its captures from the smugglers, and of its pay from the treasury, being very large, serves as an inexhaustible fund for the quartering those freemen upon, who either have no places, and who do not think the ordinary profits of them sufficiently ample.

This town, being situated at a considerable distance from the sea, could not have any particular occasion for fortifications; however, it has been thought expedient, of late years, to erect a couple of forts, which have, of course, their proper officers, gunners, and assistants; here arises another opportunity for government influence. In addition to the above, Rye has the usual excise and post office establishments, which take place in other towns.

We must not here omit to make mention of
the

the new harbour of Rye; for the making of which, an act was paffed about fifty years fince. The only real object of which ftatute, was the giving additional force to treafury patronage and influence. After much labour and expence, the new harbour was wholly abandoned in the year 1788; notwithftanding which circumftance, the enormous tax of two-pence per ton, on all veffels of this kingdom, as often as they pafs the ftreights of Dover, is ftill continued. The mode in which the produce of this vaft burthen on the commerce of the nation is now applied, is well worth the inveftigation of parliament: certain it is, that all the officers, artifans, and workmen (moft of whom are freemen), ftill continue to enjoy their penfions and falaries, though their places are now become, in the ftricteft fenfe of the word, finecures.

The conduct and management of this enormous mafs of influence, is vefted in Mr. Thomas Lamb, who has been, for a long time paft, agent, and firft officer of the treafury in this borough; to which poft he fucceeded about forty years ago, on the death of his father; and, as he has conftantly fided with the firft lord of the treafury for the time being, he has been continued in quiet and undifturbed poffeffion of it ever fince. Indeed,

deed, upon the firſt paſſing of Mr. Crewe's bill, he, for a ſhort time, made an attempt at ſetting up a private intereſt of his own, independent of the treaſury; in conſequence of which he actually returned——Dickenſon, Eſq. to parliament (a gentleman in the intereſt of lord North) with the government candidate. However, he was quickly given to underſtand, that the treaſury were determined to have *both* the members of its own nomination, and that loſs of places, &c. would be the immediate and certain conſequence of diſobedience. In a very ſhort time after, he returned to his duty and allegiance, having previouſly ſtipulated, that in future he would return treaſury nominees only; but, that they ſhould make him ſome ſmall douceur or compliment; far ſhort, however, of the market price of a ſeat, the bulk of which is appropriated to the commander in chief*; the portion ſet apart for the ſubalterns and under-ſtrappers of the corporation being but trifling and inconſiderable.

* This was never done till Mr. Crewe's bill had ſomewhat leſſened the treaſury intereſt; that the candidates before merely paid the expences of the election, which were about 150l. The preſent members are, Mr. Long, ſecretary of the treaſury, and Mr. Jenkinſon, ſon of a former ſecretary of the treaſury.

ANCIENT

ANCIENT REPRESENTATION—In confequence of the flaughter which took place at the battle of Evefham, in the time of Henry III. this place, for that time, returned four members to parliament, as did the reft of the Cinque Ports. It is probable that the Cinque Ports were reprefented in the national council before that period. Ever fince 42 Edward III. this place has conftantly returned two members to parliament without any intermiffion.

CORPORATION—Ought to confift of a mayor and twelve jurats; at prefent there are only a mayor and four jurats. The office of mayor is conftantly filled up by the Lambs, father and fon.

RIGHT OF ELECTION—1702, 9 Dec. Is only in the mayor, jurats, and freemen, inhabiting in the port of Rye, and paying fcot and lot.

1710, 17 Feb. Thomas Hills, W. W. T. B. and J. Y. having been propofed to be made free, and rejected at a court of affembly, and afterwards made free in the fame mayoralty, are not legal freemen of the port of Rye.

It is not neceffary that the freemen of the Port of Rye fhould qualify themfelves according to the corporation act before they be allowed to vote in the affembly court of the faid port.

It

It appears from the old cuſtumal of Rye, ſtill in exiſtence, that the right of voting formerly belonged, ιof courſe, to every perſon poſſeſſed of a freehold within the corporation, and to every ſon of a freeman; there was, beſides, a third way of obtaining the freedom of this town, viz. by redemption. But, by the contrivance and manœuvres of the agents of the treaſury, this conſtitution has of late years been wholly changed. By a determination of the houſe of commons, in 1702, (which is the laſt we find upon the ſubject), it appears, that the right of election for barons to ſerve in parliament for this port, is in the mayor, jurats, and freemen, inhabiting in the ſaid port, and paying ſcot and lot. But here a great and important queſtion ſuggeſts itſelf: Who are the people that are entitled to their freedom? As to this point there has been no determination.—If this ſhould ever be put fairly in iſſue, the probable reſult would be, that the right is, at this day, as ſet forth in the old cuſtumal, notwithſtanding the uſurpation and innovations of modern days. At this time, the practice is, to admit freemen upon the following grounds only; viz. eldeſt ſons of freemen, at the age of twenty-one, are allowed to have a right; the mayor has a right to

name

name one on coming into office; the others are to be propofed by him, in the affembly, and approved by the majority of freemen prefent. From the account given by Carew, of fome contefted election at this place, it appears, that the number of freemen was, till very lately, about 50; but at prefent it is found expedient to keep the number much lower, in order that the claimants to a portion of the good things produced by an election, may be as few as decency will admit. Should the eldeft fon of a freeman have the prefumption to demand his birth-right of the corporation, if he be a poor man, it is refufed him; if he chance to be in a fuperior fituation, he is perfuaded, if poffible, to be made the mayor's freeman the year enfuing; the object of which manœuvre is, to erafe, if poffible, all traces of a right to freedom by birth. If the fon of a freeman, chance at any time, either before or after his father's admiffion, to have a brother born before him, and by whofe death he becomes the eldeft, his right is (ridiculoufly enough) utterly denied; becaufe, forfooth, he is not the *firft born* fon, which the wifeacres of this corporation infift is the meaning of the eldeft fon.

It is very unufual to make more than the

mayor's

mayor's annual freeman in the courfe of a year, who is, invariably, a perfon advanced in years, an old batchelor, or a man not likely to have progeny; by which means, the future claims of an eldeft fon, who perchance might not be fo well difpofed to fubmit to the doctrines of paffive obedience as the father, are effectually guarded againft.

Poverty is another effential qualification to the office of baron of this port. A perfon in an independent fituation of life, might, by poffibility, object to fome things which are expected at the hands of a freeman; but the danger of being turned out of place, or of being called upon to pay the money due from him on bond, compel an indigent man to the moft implicit obedience.

It is a very common cuftom in this, as well as the other ports, to lend fmall fums upon bond, which are never put in force, unlefs fymptoms of difobedience appear in the obligor; in which cafe, the penalty of the obligation is rigoroufly demanded; when, if the debt be not immediately difcharged, imprifonment is the certain confequence.

NUMBER OF VOTERS—SIX; all made free

since Mr. Crewe's bill; the rest of the jurats and freemen are all disqualified by that bill.

The present state of the electors of Rye, is as follows: viz.

JURATS.

Mr. Thomas Lamb, a tally-cutter in the exchequer, a place of 400l. a year, and cursitor of Hampshire.

Mr. Thomas Phillipps Lamb, his son, cursitor of Kent, and late a king's waiter of the customs at this place, which he has given to his son, Thomas Davis Lamb, a minor.

Mr. James Lamb, collector of the customs.

Mr. Nathaniel Procter, brother of the above, farms the estate of the corporation, at a very low rent.

Mr. William Proffer, a superannuated riding officer.

FREEMEN.

John Swaine,
John Pilcher,
Thomas Cook,   } Riding Officers.
James Small,
John Christmas,

Richard Butler, comptroller of customs.
Samuel Millar, post-master, &c.

Thomas Allen, mate of the custom-house cutter.

Wm. Millar, jun.
J. Allene,
T. Proffiter, jun.
James Barrey,
Thomas Bourne,
Richard Thiman,
} Officers and crew of custom-house boat, but all landmen.

John Hogben, surveyor of customs, and guager.

John Haddock, captain of the Stag Custom-house sloop.

Mr. C. Lambe, a superannuated captain of a custom-house cutter.

Richard Pollard, chamberlain, &c. to the corporation.

Lewis Maryn, a place in the stamp office.

John Giles,
James Elliot,
John Kennett,
John Buckhurst,
Richard Jarrott,
} Lately made freemen; as yet they have no ostensible places, but are all quartered on some of the aforementioned placemen.

RETURNING OFFICER—The mayor.

PATRON—The treasury.

We think it proper here to observe, that what we have said concerning the ministerial agent in this borough, relates solely to his conduct in that capacity; being convinced, from good authority, that in private life, this gentleman's department has been at all times truly respectable and honourable, and wholly different from that which usually results from being hackneyed in the ways and tricks of corruption. As a magistrate, both of the town, and of the two counties of Kent and Sussex, his conduct has always been clear, even of the suspicion of impropriety. Both the freemen and the inhabitants (which is not a little remarkable) are contented and satisfied with the mild sway of their borough monarch.

WINCHELSEA.*

POLITICAL CHARACTER—Were we to set forth at length, all the instances of corruption, venality, and profligacy, that have come to our knowledge in having traced the election history of this borough, it would much exceed the space we can allot to the account of any indivi-

---

* If the reader wishes to enter more particularly into the particular rottenness of this borough, we refer him to Glanville's Election Reports, Carew and Burrow's Reports, vol. II. and Term Reports, vol. I.

dual

dual place, in this work. Some of the moſt remarkable, however, we ſhall point out, and recite as much at length as our room will admit of. In the year 1623, Paul Wymond, the mayor, having been convicted of threatening and terrifying ſome of the voters, and of unlawfully excluding others from giving their votes, and of other corrupt and indiſcreet practices, was placed on his knees at the bar of the houſe of commons, as a delinquent, and was there ſeverely reprimanded, and ſentenced to be committed to priſon under the cuſtody of the ſerjeant at arms, for a certain time, and afterwards, to make ſubmiſſion on his knees, at the bar of the houſe of commons, and again at Winchelſea, in court, before the jurats and freemen.

In the year 1702, Mr. Edwards, the mayor, for the ſame improper conduct as his predeceſſor, Paul Wymond, was taken into cuſtody; was reprimanded by the ſpeaker in the ſame diſgraceful manner; and, in conſequence of a reſolution of the houſe of commons, was turned out of all his places in the cuſtoms, notwithſtanding every effort was made by the treaſury bench, whoſe tool and creature he was, to protect him from the vengeance of the legiſlature.

In the year 1702, two petitions were preſented

ed against undue returns, on the ground of bribery. In 1711, it appeared in evidence, to a committee of the house of commons, that Sir Francis Dashwood had paid 30l. to each of those who voted for him, besides giving a douceur to all the wives and daughters of freemen.

Winchelsea may be considered as having been wholly a treasury borough, till the year 1754, when the late Arnold Nesbitt, Esq. an Irish gentleman, and till then entirely unknown in this place, was returned by the then minister, the duke of Newcastle. Mr. Nesbitt began immediately to make purchases to a considerable amount of estates within the town, and in the neighbourhood, with a view of securing to himself thereby a controul over the borough in future. In this project he succeeded so far, as to establish fully the command over *one* of the seats, and, occasionally, when he chanced to be well with the treasury, over *both*.

About the year 1762, Mr. Nesbitt, being at that time in opposition, a violent attack was made by government on this borough, under the auspices of the late earl of Egremont, who had a large estate in the neighbourhood, in order to bring it back to its former allegiance to the treasury.— This contest gave birth to the famous Winchelsea

causes,

caufes, fet forth at length in the fecond volume of Burrow's Reports. The Nefbitt intereft was, upon the whole, fuccefsful upon this occafion. The treafury have fince made fome other rude attacks on the Nefbitt intereft, in which they have at times fo far fucceeded, as to return one member.

In the courfe of thefe conflicts, which were of long continuance, and of courfe very expenfive, the death of the earl of Egremont took place, and, in confequence, a temporary deficiency of cafh; Mr. Wardroper, the treafury agent, who was then in the office of town-clerk, having occafion for larger fums of money to carry on the battle, than it was convenient for government to fupply him with, actually pawned the charters, cuftumal, and all the records of the corporation, with a Mr. Wilfon, an underftrapper to the minifter; at a convenient feafon, the pledge was redeemed by the treafury, where it was, till very lately, in fafe keeping.

Since the late transfer of the borough, it is probable that the purchafers, who are entirely at the devotion of the miniftry, may have poffeffed themfelves of the inftrument and documents above-mentioned, as they, eventually, may be of great confequence; though, upon the whole, if

this

this be the cafe, it is highly probable, that the fate of the cuftumal of Haftings, (annihilation by fire) will await the charters and records of Winchelfea. We pledge ourfelves for the authenticity of this anecdote.

The late Arnold Nefbitt having died indebted to the crown, to nearly the amount of 100,000l. and otherwife much embarraffed in his circum-ftances (to which his expences, at this place, not a little contributed, as he had the character of being a liberal pay-mafter to his *virtuous* confti-tuents,) a decree for the fale of all his property was made by the court of chancery, for the bene-fit of his creditors. Mr. J. Nefbitt, the prefent member for Gatton, (confcious that his confe-quence in this place wholly depended on the eftate, which the world had hitherto fuppofed to have defcended to him from his uncle, free from any incumbrance whatever) a very fhort time before the promulgation of this fatal decree in chancery, entered into a treaty with the earl of Darlington, and with Mr. Barwell, the nabob, and owner of Tregony, for the fale of this borough. At firft, a much larger price was required of them than they were willing to give. After many difficul-ties about the mode of payment and transfer, as with Mr. Nefbitt time was preffing, a bargain was
ftruck,

struck, and the price agreed for 15,000l. which, considering the present market price, may, upon the whole, be considered as a cheap purchase, especially as immediate possession was given. Taking 5,000l. to be the market price at the last general election, the fee of the future good-will of the borough stands the purchasers in but 2,500l. a-piece.

Where the right of voting in a borough depends upon property, as in a scot and lot, or burgage-hold borough, it is easy to conceive that the seats in parliament may be merchantable commodities; but, as the elective franchise in this place is not connected with property, but depends upon freedom, it is probable, that in the sale above alluded to, the voters themselves, like so many beasts in a pen at Smithfield, were bartered in the transfer.

But what is not a little curious; it is certain that the bargain was made, and terms fully settled and agreed upon between the parties, without the consent, knowledge, or privity of any one of the voters. They, however, concluded, that their customary fee of 100l. per man, would be paid to the electors, by either their present or former owners; in truth, this point had not been properly adjusted between them, and the freemen of

Winchelsea were referred from one party to the other, for upwards of two years, without being satisfied in their demands; at length they began to shew some serious signs of discontent, and even of revolt; insomuch, that their present owners thought it prudent to comply with their requests, and let them have the long delayed douceur, which they received at Easter 1792.

At the time of the sale of the borough of Winchelsea, the state of the corporation was as follows:

JURATS.

Mr. Thomas Marton, commander in chief.

Richard Lamb, his nephew; a riding officer.

Mr. Stace, a riding officer, and has a farm of late Nesbitt's, now Barwell's.

FREEMEN.

Benjamin Tree, mace-bearer and chamberlain to the corporation.

Charles Stephens, surveyor of customs.

Thomas Marton, jun. son to the commander.

Richard Butler, comptroller of customs; he, having been in opposition to Mr. Nesbitt, did not constitute a part of the sale.

Since the sale, the following additions have been made to the corporation:

JURATS.

JURATS.

Captain Coffin, brother-in-law to Barwell.

———— Scholey.

Lord Bernard (son of lord Darlington) and Mr. Barwell, the members.

Mr. Douce, partner with Mr. Lloyd, the attorney, who managed the sale.

———— Paddy, an American refugee, living at Windsor.

Perry Coffin, brother to Mrs. Barwell.

A short time previous to the sale, Mr. Nesbitt made a lease of all his property in this town, consisting of about 50 houses and tenements, to the present members; which, as it was without the consent of the mortgagees, and other claimants on the estate, cannot be of any validity. As it is necessary that every voter should be rated, to get possession of these houses, either by lease or purchase, was of great consequence. At the sale before the master in chancery, this town lot was knocked down to Mr. Coffin, as agent to Barwell, for 1200l. a Mr. Hull opened the biddings for the benefit of creditors, who was the best bidder at 3,000l. Mr. Barwell finding that the fate of his borough, very much more than he imagined, depended on securing this lot, made

application

application to the chancellor for a third fale, which requeft (ftrange to relate) was complied with; but had not this nabob been in the treafury intereft, it is more than probable it would have been refufed.

The third fale has fince taken place, when the agent of lord Darlington and Mr. Barwell was the beft bidder, at the price of 5,200l. We fhould obferve that this borough has been in a conftant ftate of fermentation for upwards of thirty years. —At this time, from the want of confidence, and the diftruft which exifts between the patrons and the old agents under Mr. Nefbitt, we will venture to predict, that great revolutions are at hand. Mr. Marton and his friends have difcovered, that though they are ftill nominally the agents, there is an interior cabinet of non-freemen, who have the direction and management of all tranfactions of fuperior importance.

CORPORATION—When complete, confifts of a mayor and twelve jurats; this body feldom, in fact, exceed four or five.

RIGHT OF ELECTION—1711, 11 Feb. The freemen of the port of Winchelfea are not obliged to qualify themfelves, by receiving the facrament, according to the corporation act.

According to the old cuftumal, and the true conftitution

constitution of the place, every son of a freeman, and every freeholder, were entitled to their freedom; but, according to the modern constitution, the relations and nominees of Mr. Barwell. As lord Darlington, at Easter 1792, suffered Barwell to appoint his own dependants, it is supposed, that he has disposed of his share in the borough to the nabob.

NUMBER OF VOTERS—THREE.

Mr. Marton is allowed two hundred pounds a year for the management of the borough, and for keeping the voters in good order, who receive one hundred pounds a man at each election.

It is supposed, that the only good voters in this place are the elder Marton and Tree; as young Marton lives in London, and the rest are placemen.

The newly-made junto are only fictitiously rated; do not reside, and, on account of divers informalities in their appointment to their freedoms, it is presumed they might be disfranchised with great ease.

RETURNING OFFICER—The mayor.

The fee of the mayor at an election is 200l.

PATRONS—Mr. Barwell and the earl of Darlington; both in the interest of the treasury;

wherefore

wherefore the patronage of government is in their hands as to this borough.

SEAFORD.

POLITICAL CHARACTER—The influence of this borough, or port, has been exercised for near two centuries by the family of the late Sir William Thomas, of West Dean, near this place, whose title became extinct for want of male heirs; but his estate, together with the patronage of the borough, descended to the late Mr. Harison, of Sutton-place, and from him to the present Lancelot Harison, Esq.

This gentleman, at the age of fourteen, was put into possession of the lucrative sinecure of comptroller of cloth and petty customs in the port of London, which produces him a net salary of 200l. per annum; to this place was afterwards added that of supervisor of the riding officers, worth 150l. per annum, and captain of the custom-house boat, with an income of 120l. per annum more; all those places Mr. Harison was allow to hold as sinecures. Not having ever been at sea, an additional 60l. per annum was allowed for a deputy captain, or chief-mate of the boat; and as the only duty of the riding officers, in this district, was to support the interest of the patron at

an

an election, the fupervifing of them did not require any great vigilance.

From the year 1747 to the prefent time, the right of election has been the fubject of continual litigation. In 1670 the houfe determined it to be in the populacy, and in 1761 the word populacy was explained to mean inhabitants houfekeepers paying fcot and lot. The ufe made of this explanation, was to rate fuch of the houfe-keepers only as were revenue officers or dependants on the will of the patron; the number of ratable houfes within the borough was one hundred and thirty-two, though not more than twenty-four had ever been known to be taxed, previous to Mr. Flood's fuccefsful oppofition in 1786; out of this number *feventeen* were revenue officers, when Mr. Crewe's difqualifying bill was paffed in 1782.

The firft petition which is deferving of the attention of our readers, was occafioned by the interference of the late duke of Newcaftle, at the election in 1747, when the late Right Hon. William Pitt, afterwards earl of Chatham, and William Hay, Efq. were candidates on the minifterial intereft of that day, and the earl of Middlefex, uncle to the prefent duke of Dorfet, and the Hon. W. H. Gage, afterwards lord vifcount Gage, oppofed posed them on the opposition, or what was then termed the prince of Wales's interest. The petition set forth, that at the last election of barons to serve in this present parliament for the town and port of Seaford, in the county of Sussex, the petitioners, together with the Right Hon. William Pitt, Esq. and William Hay, Esq. were candidates. That on the day before the said election, a noble peer of this realm did invite to, and entertain at his house most of the voters of the said town and port; and in the town, where they were assembled, spake to them one by one, and did solicit and influence them, with respect to giving their votes at the said election; by means whereof several persons who had promised to vote, and would have voted for the said petitioners, were prevailed upon by the said noble peer to vote for the said Mr. Pitt and Mr. Hay. Which proceeding the petitioners conceive is an high infringement of the liberties and privileges of the commons of Great Britain. That on the day of election, in order to awe and influence the voters in favour of the sitting members, and deter them from voting for the petitioners, the said noble peer came into the court, accompanied by other peers of this realm; and being seated near to the returning officer, did continue there until the poll was closed; notwithstanding the presence of him, and the said other peers, was objected to by one of the petitioners, and the returning officer applied to by him not to take the poll while the peers remained present in the court. In all which the said petitioners thought themselves fully justified, as they apprehended their presence obstructed the freedom of the election, and from the several declared resolutions of the house of commons, was a violation of the rights and privileges of the commons of Great Britain; and that by these, and other illegal practices, the petitioners lost a great number of votes, which would otherwise have been given for the petitioners: and therefore praying the house to take the premises into consideration, and to grant the petitioners such relief as to the house shall seem meet. The house moved, That the resolution of the 16th day of this instant November, That it is an high infringement of the liberties and privileges of the commons of Great Britain, for any lord of parliament, or lord lieutenant of any county, to concern themselves in election of members to serve for the commons in parliament, might be read. And the same was read accordingly. A motion was made, and the question being put, That the matter of the said petition be heard at

the

the bar of this house: upon which a debate arose. In this debate, Mr. Pitt, one of the sitting members, treated the petition with great contempt, and turned it into a mere jest.

On this occasion, Mr. Potter (son of the archbishop) spoke as follows: "Mr. Speaker, I rise up to do myself justice: for as I look upon the matter contained in this petition to be of the utmost importance to the honour of the house, and even to the existence of parliament; and as, to my very great amazement, I see this question treated with the greatest contempt and ridicule by an honourable gentleman, whose weight may perhaps persuade a majority to be of his opinion, I think I owe it to myself to declare my sentiments on this great occasion by something more than the vote which I shall give. I hope, Sir, things are not yet come to such a pass, as to make it necessary for any man to go about to prove that the constitution is destroyed, whenever the house shall lose its independency. After all the noble struggles made in the house by great patriots, after all the laws passed by the legislature to preserve that independency, I should hope, that out of decency, as well as out of regard to truth, I may be allowed to argue upon that as upon an indubitable maxim. The
representa-

representatives of the people, when they are chosen to that office, have been said to be independent, even on their constituents; how necessary then, Sir, is it for this house to take care that there be no other improper or corrupt dependency? But, Sir, if the ministers are to be allowed to nominate to the burghs the persons who shall be their representatives, how are we to expect an independent parliament? That ministers may endeavour to subvert this independency, that they may think it even necessary, to their own security, to corrupt parliament, we have too much reason to know. But, Sir, whatever pains former ministers may have taken for this purpose, what undue methods soever they may have used to gain for themselves a corrupt majority in this house, I believe history is not able to produce an instance, equal to the present, of a wise and great statesman taking upon himself the honourable employment of being an agent at a burgh. It was not enough to signify his commands by his underlings; it was not enough to solicit votes in his own person. The voters, it seems, could not be trusted out of his presence, and therefore they were to be attended even to the poll. But, Sir, this great humility and condescension in a minister, would, in former times, have been construed a moſt notorious invaſion of the rights of the people, and of the privileges of this houſe. And, Sir, what will the people ſay to us? Or what will they think of our independency, if we are not as jealous of their rights, and as tenacious of our own privileges as any of our predeceſſors have been? What will they think, Sir, if after ſeeing one parliament diſſolved in a new unprecedented, I had almoſt ſaid an unconſtitutional manner, they ſhall be told, that the miniſters have been nominating their repreſentatives in the next, even without the ceremony of a *congé d' élire?* But, Sir, ſtill farther; What will they think, if they ſhall be told that this proceeding of the miniſter has been laid before the houſe of commons, and that the houſe of commons will not, or dare not cenſure him? There have been times, when no man was thought too great to be accountable to this houſe for his conduct; and I could give an inſtance, even in my own memory, of a great and able ſtateſman, whoſe long adminiſtration was an honour and benefit to his country, and whoſe conduct this houſe thought fit to enquire into by the moſt ſevere ſcrutiny.—When I firſt heard the petition read at your table, I could hardly believe it poſſible that the allegations it contained were founded upon truth. I expected to have heard

the

the friends of the noble perſon who is the object of it, boldly denying the charge, and calling loudly upon the accuſers to juſtify it; I was determined not to believe it, unleſs ſupported by the ſtrongeſt proof. But, Sir, how great was my amazement when I heard an honourable gentleman, [W. Pitt, Eſq.] who was privy to the whole tranſaction, not only admitting every fact alledged to be true, but openly avowing and attempting to juſtify them? In what light they may appear to him, Sir, he can beſt tell you; but to me it ſeems moſt manifeſt, that as the conduct complained of was the greateſt injury that could be done to our privileges, the attempt to juſtify it is the greateſt inſult upon our underſtanding. In what other light, Sir, can it appear to us, than as the laſt and utmoſt effort of one who was determined, at any rate, to procure a majority in this houſe of perſons attached to himſelf, his own creatures, the tools of his power? I wiſh to God, Sir, nothing may happen to-day to give the people room to ſuſpect that he has been too ſucceſsful. What more could he have done? Or what greater inſult is it poſſible for him to offer, unleſs he ſhould come, even within the walls of this houſe, to direct our determinations? After what he has done—I ſhould not wonder, Sir, if

he did come and take that chair, and tell you,
as we were told formerly, that your mace was a
bauble, and that you fhould keep it only while
you pleafe him. Your mace, Sir, is a bauble,
and fo is every other enfign of authority, unlefs
you can preferve your independency. A dependance upon the crown, Sir, would in the end
prove fatal to our liberties; but a dependance
upon the minifter, as it is infinitely more difho-
nourable, is infinitely more dangerous. One
might fuppofe, Sir, fome fecurity to a people
from the honour of a crowned head, and from
the folid compacts that are made between the
people and their fovereign. I know of no compacts that are or can be made between a minifter and the people. I can fuppofe too, Sir, that
in fome future time a minifter may arife profli-
gate enough to carry his views fo high, as to attempt to make both king and people fubfervient
to his own ambition. I can imagine fuch a one,
Sir, taking advantage of fome general calamity,
or time of general confufion, by a corrupt parliamentary influence, oppreffing even the king upon
his throne, and making the crowned head a prifoner in his clofet. I can imagine him, Sir, fo
blown up with folly and felf-conceit, as to become a competitor even with thofe who fhall be

of

of royal blood, for posts of dignity or titles of honour; and he may, Sir, (it is hardly possible indeed) but he may even prostitute the name of the crown to support his pretensions. This, Sir, I say, is a picture which I can draw in my own mind of the miserable situation of this country if ever the parliament should become dependant on a minister. But as this can never happen but in some time of general infatuation, or general corruption, the wisdom and virtue of the present age scarce secure us from seeing it otherwise than in imagination: but, Sir, whatever I see, or whatever I feel, God forbid that by an act or vote of mine, I should make the way easy for such miseries to overwhelm any future generation. The honourable gentleman was pleased to say that this was a new case, and that there was no precedent upon our journals to guide our proceedings: but let it be remembered, that this can never be the case again, since the vote of to-day will remain upon our books an eternal precedent to posterity, and a law to this house for the future. For God's sake, then, Sir, let us consider a little what sort of a law we are going to make; let us remember, that if the present transaction passes uncensured, and is declared free from guilt, we may hereafter see every peer of parliament,

parliament, every secretary and other officer of state, every chancellor of the exchequer, with his treasury bags under his arm, attending and soliciting elections; and when they shall be called upon in this house to justify their proceedings, they shall tell you, they have done nothing but what they had a right to do, and that such was the opinion of this wise, this independent, this freely elected parliament. Sir, I am not one of those persons, who will ever be for extending the privileges of this house to any ridiculous or romantic degree: if I could but persuade myself that there was the least room to doubt upon this occasion, I should think that humanity obliged me to put the mildest construction. But really, Sir, I think the insult offered to the house is of so flagrant a nature, I think the precedent must prove so dangerous to the honour and independency of parliament, I think the consequences must be so destructive to the constitution, as to deserve and demand the severest animadversion. The honourable gentleman was pleased to ask, What is the object of the petition? Sir, I will tell him what the object is; it is the security, the freedom of parliaments, and protecting the privileges of the commons of Great Britain. Surely, Sir, from this house the

commons

commons of Great Britain have a right to expect justice. Their most valuable privileges have been trampled upon and insulted, and they come now by this petition to demand justice: Justice, Sir, they will receive, and I hope now. But of one thing I am sure, that, sooner or later, they will have it.

The house determined, by a majority of 247 against a minority of 69, *not* to receive the petition.

The next contest of importance was in 1761, when Sir James Peachy, Bart. and lord viscount Gage (the latter having changed his party since the last election), were supported by the duke of Newcastle, and the ministerial interest, and George Medley, Esq. and William Evelyn, Esq. opposed them. At this election the distinction of *populacy* and *tax-payers*, which has since been the subject of so much expence and litigation, first took place.

Under the denomination of " populacy," every man who had a legal parochial settlement, and resided within the parish, claimed, as in pot-walloping boroughs, the right of voting; and having exercised it upon all former occasions, they were deemed the legal constituent body.

A majority of the " populacy" were in the interest

tereſt of Medley and Evelyn, and precluded every chance of ſucceſs from their opponents on their ſuffrages. The ſubterfuge of ſetting up a diſ‑tinct right was, therefore, reſorted to by the mi‑niſterial candidates, as the only method by which they might, with the aſſiſtance of the houſe of commons, ground any hopes of ſucceeding.

The returning officer, Mr. Chambers, father of the *immaculate* character who filled that ſtation at the laſt general election, being in the miniſterial intereſt, and the tax-payers, by a rate, fabricated for the purpoſe, devoted to the ſame party, every elector, whoſe name was not upon the rate, was rejected when he tendered his vote. A majority being obtained by theſe means for Peachy and Gage, they were returned to parliament, and Mr. Medley and Mr. Evelyn were left to ſeek their redreſs by petitioning the houſe.

Upon the hearing of this petition, the houſe of commons, who were precluded by the 2d of George II. from *altering* the right of election, contented themſelves with *explaining it away*, by reſolving, that by the word "populacy" in the laſt reſolution of the houſe of commons, was *meant* inhabitant houſe-keepers, paying ſcot and lot, and that Sir James Peachy and lord viſcount Gage *were duly elected*.

From

From this period, until the year 1786, the practice of taxing only the revenue officers, and four or five other individuals, who were sure to obey the word of command, prevailed, to the exclusion of all the other inhabitants. Petitions against this arbitrary exclusion were presented in 1774 by Messrs. Sayre and Chetwoode, and in 1780 by Mr. Molesworth, but were not attended with success. The committees of the house of commons not choosing to admit the rateability of men, who the Seaford magistrates in their justice had deemed ineligible.

In 1784, the Right Honourable Thomas Pelham, whose father, lord Pelham, owns the tythes and about half the landed property in the neighbourhood of the borough, attempted to revive the political interest of the family, which had been neglected ever since the death of the late duke of Newcastle; and the Honourable L. T. Watson became a candidate under Mr. Pelham's patronage. A Mr. Alves, who then resided in Harley-street, had succeeded in compelling the overseers of the parish to add seven of the non-rated inhabitants to the poor-rate, became a candidate upon their suffrages; and, by *good management*, brought over eight out of the remaining seventeen electors, to his interest. With this majority

majority he muſt have ſucceeded, even againſt the united intereſts of the oppoſitional and miniſterial parties; but as the talent of *managing* was not confined to Mr. Alves, and the attachment of this deſcription of electors being neither to the perſon nor principles of their candidates, the means were ſoon reſorted to of detaching one half of Mr. Alves's confederated club from his intereſt, and uniting them with the *ſtaunch friends* of government. A junction then became neceſſary between the remaining ſupporters of Mr. Alves's cauſe, and the intereſt of Mr. Pelham; but the bewitching allurements of treaſury temptation was continually aſſailing this little party, and, by the day of election, reduced them to nearly one half of their original number.

Mr. Alderman Curtis was at this time the candidate on the miniſterial intereſt, and had obtained the promiſes of a majority of theſe virtuous electors, the whole number being at this time only *twenty-four;* and, in endeavouring to prevent any prejudice which his education in the preſbyterian principles might create in the minds of his orthodox conſtituents, embraced the opportunity, which a ſaint's day preſented, of attending epiſcopal worſhip; but as Satan is never ſo alert in his miſchievous propenſities, as when an

opportunity

opportunity prefents itfelf of refifting the purpofes of the righteous, he fo managed it, as to improve this unlucky moment, of confounding all the parliamentary fchemes of the convivial alderman; for, before he had finifhed his devotions, a new candidate was introduced, under the recommendation of the celebrated John Robinfon, who had formerly reprefented this borough, when every elector in Mr. Curtis's intereft received abfolution from his firft engagement, and embraced the more powerful intereft of a greater favourite.

Several other candidates appeared at this election with minifterial recommendation; but lord Neville, and Sir Peter Parker, having the confidence of thofe in the fecret, we forbear to mention the names of gentlemen, whofe chagrin muft have been feverely irritated, at finding themfelves the dupes of minifterial intrigue and duplicity.

At the election, which came on in March, 1784, the numbers on the poll were,

For the minifterial candidates,
  Lord Neville, — 12
  Sir Peter Parker, — 12
For the oppofition candidates,
  Hon. L. T. Watfon, — 11
  Thomas Alves, Efq. — 11

One elector did not vote, who, it has since been discovered, was in the ministerial interest; but having a majority without him, he was kept back, that he might not avow his principles to the opposite party, into whose meetings he had always been admitted as a friend.

An informality was observed in this election, which being of importance to future contests, we must not omit to mention. The 7th and 8th of William III. ch. 25. enacts, that the returning officer, after the receipt of the precept from the sheriff, or the proper officer authorised to issue the same, shall proceed to the election *within eight days* after receipt of the precept, giving *four days* notice thereof*.

The bailiff of Seaford proceeded to the election on the *fourth day* after proclamation, and it being considered that the letter of the act was not complied with, only *three days* having intervened since the proclamation, a petition of two of the electors who voted for Mr. Watson was presented to the house, complaining of this irregularity; which being heard before a committee, in the month of March, 1785, It was determined that the said election *was void*.

* This act does not include county elections. The time for making proclamation, holding county courts for election, &c. is regulated by the 25th of George III. ch. 24. f. 4.

Lord

Lord Neville, who had been returned with Sir Peter Parker, had alfo been elected for the county of Monmouth. This circumftance made a vacancy for the borough of Seaford certain, before the event of the above petition was known; to fupply which, no lefs than *fix and twenty* candidates offered themfelves, between the time of the election, in March 1784, and the hearing of the petition, in March 1785. The number of electors being, at that time, only *twenty-four*, it could not fupply a fingle vote to each of thefe gentlemen, if they had perfevered in the conteft to the end of the poll.

One of thefe candidates was the late Right Honourable Henry Flood, who was introduced to the borough by the author of this work, not with a view of obtaining his feat by the fuffrages of the twenty-four exifting voters, who were to a man engaged in the intereft of Mr. Pelham, or that of adminiftration, though it appeared that a decided majority of them was to be obtained, on what they called *honourable terms*, but on the right of twice that number of inhabitant houfekeepers, whofe names had been omitted in the poor-rate for near thirty years, on purpofe to preclude them from the exercife of their franchifes.

Amongft

Amongst these persons, whom the overseers of the poor had placed in the legal description of paupers, by charitably disburthening them of their taxes, were the vicar of the parish, and fourteen county freeholders, besides others, who could afford, and actually had, at the time, lent money to some of the parish officers, and even to one of the magistrates who allowed the rates.

These non-rated inhabitants commenced their claim to redress, by appealing to the quarter-sessions of the borough, on the ground of being excluded to answer election purposes. Upon hearing this appeal, it appeared not to have been lodged at the sessions next ensuing the making of the rate, as the law directs; and the magistrates availed themselves of that pretence to dismiss it.

The overseers took care to prevent a second appeal on this complaint, *by maintaining the poor themselves*, and making *no rate*, till the election, which was suspended for a year by the petition then before the house of commons, was disposed of.

Sir Godfrey Webster had declared himself a candidate on the interest of Mr. Pelham, for the vacancy occasioned by lord Neville making his election for Monmouthshire; and lord Mountmorres,

morres, in oppofition, had been recommended by the treafury.

The petition being heard, and the election declared void, in March 1785, there became two vacancies; in confequence of which, Sir Godfrey Webfter united his intereft with Mr. Alves, as the Honourable Mr. Watfon had done at the former election; Sir Peter Parker, and lord Mountmorres, appeared under the treafury influence, and Sir Laurence Parfons, Bart. the prefent member for King's County in Ireland, became a candidate on the fuffrages of the non-rated houfe-keepers, in conjunction with Mr. Flood.

The day preceding the election, a third treafury candidate appeared, in the perfon of Sir John Henderfon, and exhibited fimilar official recommendations to thofe already produced by Sir Peter Parker and lord Mountmorres. The government voters, who had all engaged to fupport the two laft, were at firft a little ftaggered how to act under thefe contradictory orders; but receiving inftructions from a proper perfon, they difmiffed lord Mountmorres with as little ceremony as they had, upon a former occafion, done Mr. Alderman Curtis, under fimilar circumftances. His lordfhip, however, did not

acquiefce

acquiesce in this treatment with quite so much indifference and condescension; a very serious meeting had nearly taken place between him and Sir John Henderson, and which was only prevented by the intervention of friends, who suggested the propriety of an interview with a person high in office, that they might know to whom the blame was imputable.

This meeting actually took place in a few days after, which we since understood terminated so little to the satisfaction of the noble viscount, that he took the first opportunity, in a dignified place in a neighbouring kingdom, to make some strong comments in his speech, on the impropriety of a minister's not paying the most scrupulous attention to the observance of his word. We do not recollect that he pledged himself "as a man, " and as a minister;" but it appears, that his lordship considered the obligation as equally binding.

On the day of election, seven candidates appeared on the hustings, (if the miserable place in which the public business of the borough is transacted may be understood by that name) but lord Mountmorres, finding himself deserted by every voter who had promised him, and by the men who had received him with cordiality, and announced

him

him to the electors as the government candidate, in a speech of manly indignation, declined any further connection with this confistent body of electors.

At the close of the poll, the numbers were,

For the Right Hon. Henry Flood	— 28
Sir Laurence Parsons,	— 24
Sir Godfrey Webster	— 19
Thomas Alves, Esq.	— 18
Sir Peter Parker	— 16
Sir John Henderson	— 14

The returning officer however, thought proper to reject every vote for Flood and Parsons; eight of Sir Godfrey Webster's; seven of Mr. Alves's; two of Sir Peter Parker's; and then made a return of the treasury candidates.

At this election the celebrated Mr. Harben made his first appearance in this borough, in a political character, having taken a lodging-house for forty days, to qualify himself for an occasional voter. Mr. Harison, who, for the last thirty years had been considered as the government agent and patron, was still looked up to as preserving that situation.

Four petitions were presented to parliament against the return of Sir Peter Parker and Sir John Henderson; one, by Messrs. Flood and Parsons;

Parsons; a second, by certain electors in their interest; a third, by Messrs. Webster and Alves; and a fourth, by other electors who had voted for these gentlemen.

These petitions were tried by a committee of the house of commons, in February 1786, when, after a full investigation of the claims of those who voted for Flood and Parsons, the committee determined not to admit evidence to invalidate the resolution of 1761, by which the word populacy was explained to mean inhabitant housekeepers, paying scot and lot. The counsel then endeavoured to prove, that these persons were rateable housekeepers, within the meaning of the last resolution of 1761; but their appeal to the Seaford sessions not having been made within the time directed by law, the committee also resolved not to admit evidence to prove that fact.

The petition of these gentlemen being thus disposed of, the committee proceeded upon that of Sir Godfrey Webster and Mr. Alves, who objected to three of the votes for the sitting members, amongst whom was Mr. Harben, who voted for a lodging-house, upon a pretended residence of forty days. The whole three being deemed bad, the numbers for both parties became equal. Some strong evidence of bribery, was opened, which,

which, for reasons the author is unacquainted with, was not proceeded upon. The committee, therefore, upon the equality of numbers, declared this second election void.

Mr. Alves by this time had received a complete surfeit of the Seaford contest; and the voters in the interest of Mr. Flood, having had a second opportunity of appealing to the Seaford sessions against the poor-rate, a new one being made the instant the last election was concluded; the overseers, not expecting that the petitions against it would occasion a second void election, the non-rated inhabitants were now in a situation to prove their rateability before a committee of the house of commons; when nineteen of that description being in a state of opulence, much superior to the majority of the tax payers, Mr. Flood's success was placed beyond the possibility of doubt.

Mr. Alves having declined any pretensions to future support, all his little party, except one, were *prevailed on* to join the treasury junto; but a junction having been formed between Mr. Pelham's interest and that of Mr. Flood, they became a majority of just two to one against all the forces the treasury could muster.

At the third election, the numbers on the poll were,

For the Right Hon. Henry Flood, 32
  Sir Godfrey Webſter, Bart. 32
  Sir Peter Parker, Bart. 16
  Sir John Henderſon, Bart. 16

The returning officer again ſtruck off all ſuch votes as did not appear on the poor-rate, though that rate had been rejected by the committee as a corrupt one; and admitting the whole ſixteen votes for Parker and Henderſon, and only half that number for Flood and Webſter, made his return to parliament accordingly.

Theſe proceedings were too flagrant to meet the eye of a committee of the houſe of commons; for, however deſperate the imbecility and ignorance of a routed party of borough-mongers might make them, the characters of Sir Peter Parker and Sir John Henderſon were not to be ſported with, to gratify the chagrin of ſuch people. A petition of Mr. Flood and Sir Godfrey Webſter was preſented to the houſe, and, when the day of hearing arrived, the counſel for the ſitting members informed the committee, that their clients, being ſenſible *that the petitioners had a majority of legal votes, they would give them no fur-*

ther

ther trouble. The committee reported to the house the same day, March 13, 1786, " That the Right Hon. Henry Flood and Sir Godfrey Webster, Bart. were duly elected, and ought to have been returned."

Thus was the cause of independence, in this little borough, triumphant over the most unprecedented oppression, and in opposition to the influence of the treasury, to a family junto of borough magistrates, or jurats, and to the united exertion of seventeen sinecure placemen, pensioned on purpose to support the cause of tyranny.

The system of politics in this place now took an entire change; the whole of Mr. Flood's friends, together with the other inhabitants who had taken no part in the election, were put upon the poor rates, and Mr. Harison, who had for thirty years enjoyed the confidence of government, and been the acknowledged patron of the borough, from the ill success that attended his late management, or from a determination to introduce a manager of less scruple into the dashing concerns of the party, was treated with coolness by the treasury; but as he still retained the absolute command of the corporation, which consisted of a bailiff, three jurats, and seventeen freemen, matters were not yet quite ripe for openly insulting and dismissing him.

Mr. Harben, the present hero of these political myrmidons, had therefore time to inveigle himself into the confidence of Mr. Harison, and by an offer, apparently liberal, of undertaking to be at the expence of re-inflating Mr. Harison's influence, upon being permitted to share with him in the advantages attached to it, he obtained the purchase of several acres of land within the borough, from Mr. Harison's estate, on which he soon erected a stately house; and, having once got an establishment within the limits of its privileges, his next advance was upon the corporation.

This body consisted mostly of revenue officers, whose places were all sinecures, and were originally created here, as in the other Cinque Ports, for the establishment of a government interest. Each individual owed his place to the recommendation of Mr. Harison; and it was at first apprehended, that the moral tie of gratitude might make such an impression on the minds of some of them, as to create a difficulty in the attempt, of not only detaching them from the interest of their benefactor, but in inducing them, at the same time, to support that of his avowed opponent;

for,

for, whenever the experiment was made, the mask of friendship must be taken off.

Treasury mandates were however obtained, and the freemen were founded one by one. On the Michaelmas day following the late election defeat, this master-piece of political craft was to be played off.

It commenced with electing a creature of Harison's, but who was now privately in the interest of Harben, into the office of bailiff, and then the cloven foot appeared in Mr. Harben's being proposed to be elected a freeman. Mr. Harison, who was present, fired with indignation at the plot which was unfolding itself, intreated the freemen, as they valued *their own interest* *, and if they felt a spark of attachment to him for the places they held, or the patronage he had ever afforded them, not to suffer this attempt to succeed against his political existence, and their security. The freemen, however, heard this harangue with stoic apathy, and, when the question was put, to a man voted against their benefactor!!!

We have been particular in our relation of

* The only appeal to their feelings which seemed to make any impression.

these circumstances of political perfidy, in order to display the pernicious consequences, which the present system of borough representation must have upon the morals of the parties interested; not doubting but it will be an argument of much weight with the established clergy, whose zeal in the cause of virtue and good government will exert itself with redoubled vigour, to obtain that reform in the representation of the people, which is so immediately connected with the cause of religion and morality.

Mr. Harben having now erected a country seat in the borough, and obtained a political one in the corporation, felt his importance sufficiently established to commence open hostilities with Harison. The first act of his reign, for he now became the avowed and ostensible agent of government, was to procure Mr. Harison's dismission from the sinecure places of supervisor of the riding officers, and captain of the customhouse boat, worth together 270l. *per annum;* the first of which he disposed of to Thomas Chambers, the late returning officer, and the other he kept open for the most hungry of the opposite party to bite at. Mr. Harison's other sinecure, of comptroller of cloth and petty customs

toms in the port of London; being a patent place for life, was out of the reach of Mr. Harben's grasp.

Mr. Harben was not all this while negligent of his own interest, having procured the excise of the eastern part of the county to be paid into his hands, in its passage to the treasury, (an object of no little importance to a country banker), and obtained the place of receiver general of the stamp duties for Sussex, worth 600l. *per annum*, for his eldest son; his next care was to procure the office of warehouse-keeper of the stamp office in London, with a salary of 200l. *per annum*, for his second son, which he is allowed to hold as a sinecure, and to continue his residence at Lewes. Mrs. Harben has also a sinecure of 400l. *per annum* in her majesty's houshold.

From this period to the present, this insignificant little place has exhibited the most disgusting scene of profligacy, in all its shades of deformity. Mr. Harison had the merit of managing the government influence, in its political concerns, without persecution; but from this moment scarce a sessions, assize, or term passed, without indictments for assaults, informations against pretended riots, in which the prosecutors were

were always sure to have been the aggressors, indictments for perjury, robbery, and every crime which malicious ingenuity could give a colourable pretence of instigating. The expence and ruin brought on individuals by these means is inconceivable, independent of the disgrace and misery that the most innocent must suffer from the infamy of such proceedings.

In opposition to the treasury influence, and to these measures of iniquity, Mr. James Hurdis, a gentleman of independent fortune, incorruptible integrity, and possessing a mind pregnant with the most amiable qualities, at his own private expence, not only opposed the torrent of corruption, which, like a whirlwind, was swallowing every thing in its vortex, but, with a benevolence corresponding with his superior virtues, became the advocate of the oppressed, and in the language of the inimitable Gray,

" The little tyrant of his fields withstood."

To this village Hampden, the author, with grateful pride, acknowledges his obligations; to his humanity whole families owe their existence; to his liberality the impoverished victim of tyranny owes his rescue from the jaws of a prison; but in his praise the highest panegyrick would

would exhauſt itſelf in vain, for he has a ſenſibility which is its own reward.

With Mr. Hurdis, every gentleman of the borough, except the three penſioned jurats, had the honour to act, who vainly imagined that it was poſſible to preſerve ſuch a handful of voters from the influence of venality; ſcarce a week however paſſed without ſome one being detached from amongſt the inferior part of their intereſt. The mode of corrupting theſe people was, by advancing each individual a ſum of money (not leſs than fifty pounds) upon bond; of whom, while they continued obſequious to their dictator, neither principal nor intereſt was demanded; but the moment one of thoſe unfortunate men preſumed to exerciſe a will of his own, the bond was exacted with unexampled rigour. Another engine of undue influence is, the number of cuſtom-houſe and ſinecure places in the gift of the patron of this borough.

Our readers will naturally be led to imagine, from the number of tide-waiters, boatmen, &c. who reſide here, that there muſt be a harbour commodious for ſhipping; that the imports and exports muſt be great, and the revenues ariſing from them to government proportionable thereto; but ſo far is this from being the real ſituation

tion of the place, that the only bufinefs done here, throughout the whole year, is the difcharging one folitary cargo of coals. Newhaven, which is a confiderable port, where much bufinefs is done, with a third part of the number of officers, is only four miles diftant from hence; a convincing proof that thefe vermin are fuffered to feed on the earnings of the laborious part of the public, only becaufe their influence may have fome weight at the election of the treafury members. The patronage of the cuftom-houfe at Newhaven, on account of its vicinity, is added as an appendage to the treafury agent of this place.

The revenue offices of Rotten Dean, Eaft Dean, and the cuftom-houfe of Eaft Bourne, are alfo fupplied with placemen from amongft the electors of this borough.

Mr. Harben being ftill unable, with all his influence, to afcertain a ftrength that would conftitute a majority of the electors, had recourfe to a new expedient, which was not only contrary to the charter of the borough, but to its cuftom, practice, and conftitution; this was, to create *nineteen non-refident freemen*, which Mr. Harben and his advifers were weak enough to believe would inveft them with the rights of election.

election. A meeting of the corporation was accordingly convened, at an ale-houfe in the borough, when the following perfons were admitted to their freedom:

1. Hon. Charles Lenox, nephew to the duke of Richmond.
2. Robert Steele, Efq. brother to the fecretary of the treafury.
3. Walker Goldfmith, brother to one of the jurats.
4. Henry Chambers, ditto.
5. Nathaniel Pain, ditto,
6. Henry Plaifted, brother-in-law to Harben.
7. Harry Plaifted, coufin to Harben.
8. James Harben, brother to ditto.
9. Robert Rofam.
10. Rev. William Gwynne, of Lewes.
11. Rev. Arthur Iredel, a relation of ferjeant Kempe, has obtained two government livings.
12. William Green, a magiftrate at Lewes, and crier of the court of King's Bench.
13. Charles Gilbert.
14. Philip Mighill.
15. John Coggan.
16. James Brooke, brother-in-law to one of the jurats.

17. Gabriel

17. Gabriel Burrowes, father to the overseer.

18. Richard Talmage, an itinerant carpenter.

19. Richard Thatcher, brother-in-law to the town clerk.

Soon after which were added the following;

20. Right Hon. William Pitt!!!

21. Duke of Richmond!!!

22. John Young, a jack-ass driver.

23. William Chambers, brother to two of the jurats.

The jurats in the above list were non-residents, and selected from different parts of the kingdom.

The resident freemen and jurats, forming a list equally curious, it may not be amiss to add them in this place.

JURATS.

John Sargent, Esq. bailiff, clerk of the Ordnance, worth 2000l. per annum, slept one night in the borough to constitute a *legal residence.* Lives at Lavingdon Park, near Petworth.

2. John Aldridge, Esq. storekeeper of the Ordnance, worth 2000l. per annum, resides at Horsham.

3. Nathaniel

3. Nathaniel Tredcroft, Esq. deputy paymaster of the army under Mr. Steele. Resides in London.

4. Robert Steele, Esq. brother to the paymaster of the army. Resides at Chichester.

5. Thomas Chambers, supervisor of the riding officers, 150l. per annum.

6. William Chambers, brother to the former, a patent waiter in the customs of the port of London, 150l. per annum, resides at Bletchingdon, and carries on the business of a farmer.

7. Thomas Harben, who resides at Lewes, has the public taxes paid into his bank, and his two eldest sons have places worth 800l. per annum. and his wife a place of 400l. a year, in the houshold.

8. Duke of Richmond, master general of the Ordnance, &c. &c. &c. who was never within the borough but once.

9. Lancelot Harison, residing at Brighthelmstone, comptroller of cloth and petty customs in the port of London, 200l. per annum.

10. Robert Stone, a tenant of lord Pelham.

FREEMEN.

11. Sir James Peachey, master of the robes to the king.

12. Chatfield

12. Chatfield Turner, town clerk, who refides at Lewes, and is faid to be a rider, at 100l. per annum, upon a revenue officer.

13. Thomas H. Harben, fon of the jurat, and collector of ftamp-duties, 600l. per annum.

14. Jofeph Stevens, mate of the revenue boat, 60l. per annum, but a landfman.

15. Charles Wood, a fuperannuated revenue-officer, who has refigned his pay to be maintained by the parifh.

16. Henry Bean, a riding officer, 60l. per annum.

17. William Baker, ditto, and brother-in-law to Thomas Chambers.

18. Thomas Wood, a boat-man, 30l. per annum.

19. John Wood, fen. nicknamed Roper, a boat-man, 30l. per annum, and bully to the corporation.

20. John Hood, a fchoolmafter, and an honeft man.

21. Thomas Hughes, a fuperannuated boat-man.

22. Samuel Sage, fen. a broken tide-waiter, and beggar-whipper to the magiftrates.

23. Thomas Holman, an induftrious labourer.

24. Robert

24. Robert Spearman Bates, a well known East-India captain, resident at Lymington.

25. Thomas Simmons, a bricklayer, and a boatman, 30l. per annum.

26. William Simmons, father to the former.

27. John Simmons.

28. William Wood, son to John Wood, a bum-bailiff, nicknamed Tippler.

29. William Harmer, jun. cow-boy.

30. Henry Putland, a drunken disorderly fellow.

31. John Wood, jun. brother to Tippler.

32. Thomas Verral.

33. John Gorringe, the person reprimanded by the committee of the house of commons for prevarication.

34. Arthur Hughes son to Thomas Hughes.

35. Joseph Stevens, jun. son to the man, No. 14.

36. William Hide, nicknamed Turpin, assistant to Thomas Chambers, 30l. per annum.

37. Mr. Serjeant Kempe, recorder of this borough.

The interest of Mr. Harben, with the assistance of so many non-resident freemen, not being yet deemed secure, another expedient was resorted to. Twenty-six persons, most of whom were in the employment of Mr. Harben, as diggers of chalk, at eight shillings per week each, were brought into the borough on the eve of Christmas-day, 1789; when, a new poor rate being made the same evening, every one of them were taxed for such houses as were occupied by widows, custom-house officers who could not vote, or freemen whom they presumed had a right of suffrages by virtue of their freedom; and one was rated for the poor-house of the parish.

These twenty-six chalk diggers, together with the twenty-four non-resident freemen, making together fifty surreptitious votes, amounted to more than half of the whole number of legal electors in the borough; and if a returning officer could be found to admit persons of such descriptions to poll, little doubt could be now entertained of the treasury party succeeding at the ensuing election, as far at least as obtaining the return.

The dissolution of parliament happened to take place *seventeen days* before the *six months residence*, required by the statute of 26 George III. chap. 100, was completed; in consequence of which the treasury junto found themselves involved in what appeared to be an insurmountable

able dilemma. The craft and contrivance of their managers, however, hit upon a scheme for extricating them. The returning officer was not compelled, by law, to proceed to election till the eighth day after proclamation, which happening to be Saturday, an adjournment took place till Monday; which manœuvre carried them over to the tenth day, when it was agreed to dispose of the remaining seven in the following manner.

The candidates to insist on the six oaths required by statute *, being administered to each voter, which would take up half an hour in repeating by each individual.

The candidates and the counsel to object to every voter, objectionable or not, and to make a speech of half an hour each on his ineligibility; which mode would occupy one hour and a half more upon each vote separately.

Under these obstacles, it was deemed impossible to poll more than four votes each day, till the seven days were expired; at which time the six-and-twenty chalk diggers might be brought forward, and polled, as having completed their six months residence.

This plan was actually put in practice, and

---

* 1. Oath of allegiance. 2. Oath of supremacy. 3. Declaration of test. 4. Oath of abjuration. 5. Oath of residence. 6. Bribery oath.

this ridiculous and reproachful farce was abfolutely played off for the whole feven days.

The fcene exhibited, candidates fpeaking againſt time, counfel pleading againſt law, clergymen abjuring popery, and the immaculate electors of Seaford purging themfelves of bribery and corruption.

The feven days being at laſt got over by this management, the fix-and-twenty chalk diggers were brought forward on the eighth day, and every one of them admitted to poll, and were received as *good votes* by the returning officer.

Fourteen of the voters in Mr. Pelham's intereſt were rejected; *nine* houfekeepers, who had lived feveral years in the borough, but whofe political fentiments not correfponding with thofe of the pariſh officers, had not been affeffed to the poor-rate, though they had frequently appealed to the Seaford feſſions to be admitted to pay their taxes; *four* for not having their names marked in the poor-book, as having paid the laſt rate, one of whom was a gentleman poffeffing at leaſt a thoufand pounds *per annum* property, and who had been a houfekeeper fix-and-twenty years in the place; and *one* for having *moved out of an old refidence into a new one, fince the making of the poor rate.*

The poll, thus favoured on one fide, and fcrutinized

tinized on the other, appeared to contain the following numbers:

For the ministerial candidates,
  John Sargent, Esq. 92
  R. P. Joddrell, Esq. 91

For the opposition candidates,
  Sir Godfrey Webster 48
  John Tarleton, Esq. 48

A petition was presented to parliament by Sir Godfrey Webster and Mr. Tarleton, immediately on its meeting, complaining of the above return, and the partiality of the returning officer, &c. which did not come to a hearing till March 1792; when the twenty-four non-resident freemen, and the twenty-six chalk diggers, were declared bad votes, and ordered to be struck from off the poll, without subjecting the petitioners to the trouble of examining a single witness.

The poll of Sargent and Joddrell was now reduced to *forty-two* and *forty-one*; and the petitioners proceeded to add *nine* to their own poll, who were housekeepers within the borough, and though not assessed to the poor-rate, had paid the church and king's taxes, and had appealed against all the poor rates which had been made for several years, in consequence of their names having been omitted. It appeared, however, that their last appeal, either by *mistake* or *neglect*, had not been entered on the record of the sessions, the committee refused to hear evidence to prove their rateability.

The counsel for the petitioners next attempted to establish the four votes who had been rejected for not paying to the last rate preceding the election to which they had been assessed. The committee, however, contrary to general expectation, refused to allow them.

The last attempt of the petitioners was, to establish the vote of the man who had been rejected by the returning officer, for having changed his dwelling-house between the time of making the rate and the election. In this they succeeded.

The sitting members now opened their case, and objected to nineteen votes of the petitioners, upon grounds which appeared so very frivolous, that had complete evidence been brought up to establish their validity, the author is persuaded, that not one of them could have been deemed ineligible; however, upon summing up the evidence, the committee determined against seven of them, which put one of the sitting members upon an equality with one of the petitioners, and lost Sir Godfrey Webster his seat.

One

One of the electors having polled for Sargent and Tarleton, and a second for Webster only, the latter was one of the voters disallowed by the committee, which gave the majority of *one* to Sargent and Tarleton.

The committee, therefore, reported to the house, on the 19th March, 1792,

" That John Sargent, Esq. one of the sitting members, and John Tarleton, Esq. one of the petitioners, were duly elected."

The committee, at the same time, reported specially,

" That the right of election for the port and borough of Seaford, in the county of Sussex, is in the inhabitants housekeepers of the said town and port, paying scot and lot, *and in them only.*"

By this last resolution, the corporation, consisting of a bailiff, jurats, and freemen, which Mr. Harben, with so much difficulty and expence had attached to his interest, are intirely shut out from all election rights within the borough of Seaford, and the privilege is vested where the constitution originally placed it—in the inhabitants housekeepers, paying scot and lot.

The Right Hon. Thomas Pelham, who may now be considered as the patron of this borough, both

both from the influence of property, and the perfonal affections of the people, might, at any period, have fupplanted that of Mr. Harben, had he condefcended to have recourfe *to the fame means.*

The corporation, to the author's own knowledge, made an offer of their fervices to Mr. Pelham, which that gentleman never honoured with an anfwer.

Mr. Harben, fince he has fuperfeded Mr. Harifon in the confidence of the treafury, has had the recommendation to places in the gift of government, to the amount of near three thoufand pounds per annum. Amongft the perfons moft favoured are, his own fons, and Weft, Martin, and Burrowes, the overfeers, who were the framers of the poor rates, which have been the fubject of fo much litigation, expence, and oppreffion.

RIGHT OF ELECTION—Refolved, that the bailiff, jurats, and freemen, have *not only* voices in elections, but that the election is in the populacy. 10th Feb. 1670.

That by the word populacy is meant, inhabitants houfekeepers, paying fcot and lot. Dec. 15, 1761.

To refufe the admiffion of evidence, in order

to fhew, that in the above determinations of the houfe, the words " bailiff, jurats, and freemen," mean " fuch bailiff, jurats, and freemen only as are refident within the faid town and port." 10 Dec. 1761.

That the right of election is in the inhabitants houfekeepers of the faid town and port, paying fcot and lot, and in them only. 19 March, 1792.

NUMBER OF VOTERS—Eighty-three.

RETURNING OFFICER—The bailiff; who ought to be chofen by the tenants and inhabitants, refident and abiding, on Michaelmas-day in every year.

PATRON—Difputed between the Right Hon. Thomas Pelham and the duke of Richmond.

CORPORATION—Confifts of a bailiff, twelve jurats, (which are generally half or two-thirds kept vacant) and an indefinite number of freemen.

HISTORY

HISTORY

OF THE

WELCH BOROUGHS.

INTRODUCTION.

BY an act of parliament, made 27 Henry VIII. the twelve counties, and as many towns in Wales, were imprivileged to send members to parliament. The boroughs of Beaumaris, Radnor and Montgomery, can alone be said to be under absolute controul. The influence which prevails in the other towns, is not the produce of corruption, but arises from the popularity and hospitality of men of considerable property, whose residences are contiguous to them, and who are ready to serve them with that assistance and advice, which the exigencies of their situation may require. An instance of bribery is very uncommon among them, nor are their morals debauched by frequent invitations to election treats, which are the parents of drunkenness,

drunkenness, idleness and dissipation, and in their consequences more generally pernicious to society than any evil which exists in it. Unaccustomed to depend upon the precarious subsistence which they may derive from a sale of their votes, they are continually exercised by being useful to the community, by the laborious employments in which they are engaged. Unlike the inhabitants of the rotten boroughs, who enjoy at one time the extreme of luxury, and at another are reduced to the most abject poverty, they divide amongst their families the hard, but well-earned fruits of their labour and their industry.

ANGLESEA.

ANGLESEA.

Political Character.

THE reprefentation of this county was warmly contefted in 1784, between Mr. Bayley, fupported by the intereft of his brother the earl of Uxbridge, and Mr. Meyrick by that of lord vifcount Bulkeley; the former of whom was then fuccefsful. But thefe two noblemen have agreed fince that time not to oppofe each other, either in this county or Carnarvon; fo that the influence of the earl of Uxbridge returns the member for Anglefea without oppofition, and lord vifcount Bulkeley, unmolefted, procures the return of a reprefentative of his recommendation for Carnarvonfhire.

Patron—Earl of Uxbridge.

This ifland fends two members to parliament, viz. one for the county, the other for Beaumaris.

BEAUMARIS.

Political character—This town is the only place in Wales where the right of election is confined to the corporation only, which confifts of twenty-four members; thirteen perfons, which
form

form a majority of thefe twenty-four, return the member for this county-town. This body corporate is under the fole influence and direction of lord vifcount Bulkeley.

Corporation—By charter of incorporation of 4 Elizabeth, it confifts of a mayor, recorder, two bailiffs, and twenty-one burgeffes.

Right of election—1709, 18 Feb. 1729, 3 Mar. In the mayor, bailiffs, and capital burgeffes of Beaumaris only.

Number of voters—Twenty-four.

Returning officer—The mayor.

Patron—Lord vifcount Bulkeley.

BRECON COUNTY.

Political Character.

THE principal intereft in this county is in Sir Charles Morgan of Tredegar. The immenfe property of this gentleman, and the anceftors of his lady, the heirefs of the Morgan family, is diftinguifhable in the political hiftory of of Monmouthfhire, ever fince it firft fent reprefentatives to parliament; but it commenced in this county about the time of Charles I.

Patron—Sir Charles Morgan, Bart.

BRECON TOWN.

POLITICAL CHARACTER—The right of election in this town is not confined, as at Beaumaris, to a select corporation, consisting of twenty-four individuals, but extends to the burgesses at large of the town of Brecon, who are upwards of three hundred in number. The same interest which directs the political bias of the county, prevails also in this town.

CORPORATION—Consists of two bailiffs, twelve aldermen, and fifteen common-councilmen.

RIGHT OF ELECTION—In the corporation and free burgesses.

NUMBER OF VOTERS—Near three hundred.

RETURNING OFFICERS—The bailiffs.

PATRON—Sir Charles Morgan, Bart.

CARDIGAN COUNTY.

POLITICAL CHARACTER.

THE influence which prevails in this county is that of the earl of Lisburne and John Campbell, Esq. of Stackpole Court, in Pembrokeshire. The earl of Lisburne has the leading interest, and has for many years been returned without oppofition.

PATRON—Earl of Lifburne.

CARDIGAN.

POLITICAL CHARACTER—The member of parliament for this place is elected by the burgeffes at large of this town, in conjunction with thofe of the outlying boroughs of Aberyftwith, Lampeter, and Adpar, amounting in the whole to twelve hundred voters   The principal intereft in thofe feveral boroughs is that of Thomas Johnes, Efq. of Croft Caftle, in the county of Hereford, John Adams, Efq. Edward Loveden Loveden, Efq. of Bufcot, in the county of Berks, and Thomas Powel, Efq. of Nanteis.

CORPORATION—By charter of 25 Elizabeth, it confifts of a mayor, two bailiffs, and twelve aldermen.

RIGHT OF ELECTION—1730, 7 May. Is in th burgeffes at large of the boroughs of Cardigan, Aberyftwith, Lampeter, and Atpar, only.

NUMBER OF VOTERS—Upwards of twelve hundred.

RETURNING OFFICER—The mayor.

PATRONS—Thomas Johnes, Efq. &c. &c. &c.

CAERMARTHEN.

CAERMARTHEN COUNTY.

Political Character.

THIS county is principally under the interest of lord Dinevor. The interest which George Rice, Esq. acquired during his life-time, induced the freeholders of the county to elect his son, the Honourable George Talbot Rice, now lord Dinevor, at the last general election, in preference to their late member, Sir William Mansel.

Patron—Lord Dinevor.

CAERMARTHEN.

Political character—This town, which is under the influence of John George Phillips, Esq. of Cumgwilly, is remarkable for the illegal and unconstitutional interference of a right reverend bishop, in the election of its representative; but as there was no formal complaint brought against him in the house of commons, he escaped those consequences which befel the bishop of Worcester in the reign of queen Ann, for an attempt to prejudice the freeholders of that county against Sir John Packington, who was at that time a candidate to reprefent it in parliament. Mr. Phillips, the prefent member, had, by the vote which he gave in favour of the repeal of the Teft Act, fo much incenfed his lordfhip, as to induce him to write circular letters to the clergy, who had votes for the election of members of parliament, ftating the imminent danger the church would be reduced to by the repeal of this act, and requefting that they would ftrenuoufly exert themfelves in oppofing fuch candidates as were friendly to this meafure. Sir William Manfel, who was the member for the county, and voted againft the repeal, thought proper to decline a conteft at the laft general election with fo powerful an adverfary as the Honourable George Talbot Rice, of Dinevor; but he entertained hopes of fuccefs with a greater degree of probability in the borough, when affifted with the abilities and advice of his fpiritual guide and director. However, neither the threats nor intreaties of this great pillar of the church, were finally productive of any good confequences, as Sir W. Manfel declined the poll, and Mr. Phillips was chofen without oppofition.

The following is a Copy of the Letter written by the Bifhop upon that occafion.

Aberguilly, Auguft 24, 1785.

Sir William Manfel has declared himfelf a candidate to reprefent the borough of Caermarthen in the next parliament; I cannot refrain from declaring that he has my heartieft good wifhes.—Mr. Phillips, the prefent member, has received the thanks of the Diffenters, for the part he took in a late attempt to overthrow our *excellent* ecclefiaftical conftitution, by the repeal of the Corporation and Teft Acts; which, I will venture to pronounce, are as wife and falutary laws as any in our code. By this it is eafy to guefs what part he is likely to take in any future attempt for that purpofe.—I truft I fhall not have the mortification to find a fingle clergyman in my diocefe, who will be fo falfe to his own character and fame, and to his duty to the eftablifhed church, as to give his vote to a man who has ventured to difcover fuch principles.

I am, Rev. Sir,

Your affectionate brother and fervant,

SAMUEL St. DAVIDS.

CORPORATION—It is governed by a mayor, recorder, two sheriffs, and twenty common-councilmen, out of which the mayor is chosen, who is ever after reputed an alderman. By charter of James I. it also consists of a sword-bearer.

RIGHT OF ELECTION—1727, 7 March. Is in the burgesses of the said borough.

NUMBER OF VOTERS—Near five hundred.

RETURNING OFFICERS—The sheriffs.

PATRON—J. G. Phillips, Esq.

CAERNARVON COUNTY.

POLITICAL CHARACTER.

THE leading interest in this county is, like that of Anglesea, between the earl of Uxbridge and lord viscount Bulkeley; but these noblemen having agreed not to oppose each other in their respective counties, the influence of Anglesea is left to lord Uxbridge, and the controul of this county to lord Bulkeley.

PATRON—Lord Bulkeley.

CAERNARVON TOWN.

POLITICAL CHARACTER—This borough sends one member to parliament, in conjunction with the burgesses of Criccieth, Pwllely, Nevin, and Conway. The earl of Uxbridge has at present the leading interest, but it is by no means secure, like that of Beaumaris or Montgomery.

CORPORATION—Consists of a mayor, who is by patent created constable of the castle, one alderman, two bailiffs, a town-clerk, and two serjeants at mace.

RIGHT OF ELECTION—In the burgesses of Caernarvon, Criccieth, Pwllely, Nevin, and Conway.

NUMBER OF VOTERS—About seven hundred.

RETURNING OFFICERS—The mayor and bailiffs.

PATRON—Earl of Uxbridge.

DENBIGH COUNTY.

POLITICAL CHARACTER.

THE most prevailing interest in this county is that of Sir Watkin Williams Wynne, Bart. whose chief seat is at Ruabon, near Wrexham. Mr. Middleton,

Middleton, of Chirke Caftle, whofe anceftors have reprefented it, at various times, fince it firft fent members to parliament, which was in the 27th year of the reign of Henry VIII. has the fecond influence; but as the moft perfect cordiality prevails between thefe families, the firft takes the lead in the county, and the other in the town, without giving caufe for oppofition in either.

PATRON—Sir Watkin Williams Wynne.

DENBIGH TOWN.

POLITICAL CHARACTER—The member for this town is chofen by the burgeffes of Denbigh, and its two contributory boroughs, Leon and Ruthen. The influence of which is entirely in Richard Middleton, Efq. of Chirke Caftle, whofe anceftors have reprefented it, in various parliaments, from the 33d of Henry VIII. to the prefent time.

About the time of Henry III. Adam Salufbury founded and endowed an abbey of black monks, of the Benedictine order; the prefent proprietor of the ruins of which is Sir Lynch Salufbury Cotton.

CORPORATION—By charter of incorporation of 14 Charles II. it confifts of a mayor, two aldermen,

dermen, a recorder, two bailiffs, twenty-three burgesses, a town-clerk, and two serjeants at mace.

RIGHT OF ELECTION—1743, 7 Feb. Is in the burgesses, inhabitants of the boroughs of Denbigh, Ruthyn, and Holt, respectively.

NUMBER OF VOTERS—About five hundred.

RETURNING OFFICERS—The bailiffs.

PATRON—R. Middleton, Esq.

FLINT COUNTY.

POLITICAL CHARACTER.

THIS county is independent in the exercise of its political franchises. The principal individual interest here is that of Sir Roger Mostyn, Bart. its present representative; but it is by no means sufficient to dictate to the freeholders the person that shall represent them in parliament.

FLINT TOWN.

POLITICAL CHARACTER—This town, and its contributory boroughs, Caerwis, Overton, Rhyddlan, and Caergoerley, has a greater number of votes in the election of its representative than any other in the county. The chief interest which prevails here is Sir Watkin Williams Wynne's, whose relation, Major Williams, of Penbedw, is the present member.

CORPORATION—Consists of a mayor, who is, by patent, constable of the castle, and two bailiffs.

RIGHT OF ELECTION—1728, 21 May. Is in the inhabitants of the borough of Flint, Rhyddlan, Overton, Caerwis, Caergoerley, paying scot and lot.

The inhabitants of Knolton and Overton, foreign, paying scot and lot in the parish of Overton, have a right to vote for the town of Flint.

NUMBER OF VOTERS—About one thousand.

RETURNING OFFICER—The mayor.

PATRON—Sir Watkin Williams Wynne.

GLAMORGANSHIRE.

POLITICAL CHARACTER.

THIS county has recently given us an example of its being independent of, and uninfluenced by, aristocratical controul.

The duke of Beaufort, earl of Plymouth, earl of Bute, and lord Vernon, men of different parties

ties and sentiments in politics, united their several interests, and nominated the Honourable T. Windsor, brother to the earl of Plymouth, for their candidate to represent it in parliament. The independent freeholders vigorously opposed this formidable combination, which had for its object the dictation of a representative; and their exertions, previous to the election, were so effectual in favour of Thomas Wyndham, Esq. of Dunraven Castle, their own candidate, that captain Windsor, although assisted by so powerful an union, did not think it convenient to stand the poll, and left his adversary quietly to enjoy that honour, which the patriotism of his friends had so justly bestowed on him.

CARDIFF.

POLITICAL CHARACTER—This town, in conjunction with Cowbridge, Swansea, Lougher, Aberavon, Kenfigg, Neath, and Llantrissent, sends one member to parliament. The interest of the earl of Bute prevails principally in Cardiff and Cowbridge; that of the duke of Beaufort, in Swansea and Lougher; that of Thomas Mansell Talbot, Esq. of Margam, in Aberavon and Kenfigg; and that of Sir Robert Mackworth, in Neath. Lord viscount Mountstuart son to the earl

earl of Bute fucceeded to the reprefentation of thefe boroughs, upon the death of the late Sir Herbert Mackworth; which is a plain indication of the agreement of the above gentlemen, that it fhall be confined to one or other of their own families.

CORPORATION—The corporation is very ancient, and confifts of a mayor, who, as chief magiftrate, is conftable of the caftle, twelve aldermen, two bailiffs, who are annually chofen from among the aldermen, and twelve common councilmen.

RIGHT OF ELECTION—Not only in the burgeffes of this place, but in the burgeffes of Aberavon, Cowbridge, Kenfigg, Llantriffent, Lougher, Neath and Swanfea.

NUMBER OF VOTERS—About one thoufand.

PATRON—Earl of Bute.

MERIONETHSHIRE.

POLITICAL CHARACTER.

SIR Watkin Williams Wynne has the firft intereft in this county; but it is not decifive in the election of its reprefentative, as was demonftrated ſtrated at the laſt vacancy, occaſioned by the death of their old and reſpectable member, Mr. Vaughan, of Corſygedol, when a gentleman of oppoſite attachments to thoſe of the Wynne family was choſen.

There being no borough in this county adjudged proper to be made choice of to nominate a burgeſs, when the principality was firſt impriviledged to ſend members by act of parliament, which was 27 Hen. VIII. proves that ſome regard was had at that time to the equality of repreſentation, and that care was taken not to conſtitute a repreſentative body without conſtituents, as is too often the caſe in the preſent times. It was therefore enacted, that Haverfordweſt, a large town in Pembrokeſhire, ſhould elect a member to make up the deficiency.

MONTGOMERY COUNTY.

Political Character.

THE earl of Powis has been conſidered as poſſeſſing the firſt intereſt in this county. Mr. Owen, the preſent member, ſucceeded upon it on his firſt election; but Sir Watkin Williams Wynne, having now united his influence with that

that of Mr. Owen, we underſtand that gentleman can now ſecure his ſeat, in oppoſition to lord Powis.

MONTGOMERY TOWN.

Political character—This town, like all the others in Wales which were impriviļeged to ſend members to parliament, had its contributory boroughs, who participated in the invaluable right of election, until the year 1728, when one of thoſe reſolutions of the houſe, which has ſwept away the conſtituents of moſt of the Engliſh boroughs, extending the disfranchiſing arm of authority to thoſe of Llanidlos, Llanvilling, and Welchpool, which are now ſtripped of their ancient privileges, and the right declared to be in the burgeſſes of Montgomery *only*. The number of electors are now not more than eighty; conſequently the independence of its parliamentary character is at an end, and the borough, like that of Beaumaris, is entirely at the diſpoſal of a patron, the whole borough being the private property of lord Powis.

Corporation—Conſiſts of two bailiffs, and twelve burgeſſes or common-councilmen.

Right of election—1728, 16 Apr. Is in the burgeſſes of the ſaid ſhire-town only.

Formerly

Formerly the boroughs of Llanidlos, Llanvilling, and Welchpool, joined in the election; but these outlying boroughs are now excluded by the resolution of 1728.

Number of voters—Eighty.
Returning officers—The bailiffs.
Patron—The earl of Powis.

PEMBROKE COUNTY.

Political Character.

THE freeholders of this county have, upon many occasions, shewn a spirit of independence. If any influence can be said to exist here, it is that of the Owen family, of Orielton, in this county; but this partiality arises, not so much from the extent of their property, as from their invariable attachment to the cause of liberty.

In 1780, lord Milford and lord Kensington united their interest; the former of whom then became a candidate for the representation of the county. The independent party viewed this union with a jealous eye, and conceived it formed for the purpose of depriving them virtually of their rights as electors; they therefore exerted themselves with redoubled vigour, in support of their

their favourite candidate Sir Hugh Owen, who was finally fuccefsful by a great majority.

PEMBROKE TOWN.

POLITICAL CHARACTER—This town has for fome years been under the influence of the Owen family. The burgeffes of this place, in conjunction with thofe of Wifton and Tenby, elect the member. There is no fpecial refolution of the Houfe of Commons, refpecting the right of the burgeffes of Tenby, but with refpect to thofe of Wifton it has been refolved, That the mayor and burgeffes of the ancient borough of Wifton, in the county of Pembroke, have a right to vote in the election for the borough of Pembroke.

CORPORATION—It is governed by a mayor, two bailiffs, and burgeffes.

RIGHT OF ELECTION—1711, 1712, 23 Feb. That the mayor and burgeffes of the ancient borough of Wifton, in the county of Pembroke, have a right to vote in the election for the borough of Pembroke.

NUMBER OF VOTERS—Five hundred.

RETURNING OFFICER—The mayor.

PATRON—H. Barlow, Efq.

HAVERFORDWEST.

POLITICAL CHARACTER—This place, which was made a county of itfelf, firſt by charter of Edward IV. afterwards by Henry VIII. and laſtly by James I. is under the influence of lord Milford, of Piƈton Caſtle. A compromife has fome time ago taken place between this nobleman and lord Kenfington, when it was agreed between them, that the latter fhould, upon his fupporting invariably the intereſt of the former in the county of Pembroke, be quietly put into the poffeffion of a feat for this town.

CORPORATION—Confiſts of a mayor, fheriff, two bailiffs, and twenty-four common councilmen.

RIGHT OF ELECTION—1714, 4 July. The proceeding of the mayor and common-council, of the town of Haverfordweſt, in making burgeffes without the confent of the commonalty, was illegal, and contrary to the rights of the faid town; and that the burgeffes fo pretended to be made, have not thereby acquired any right of voting in any future eleƈtions.

Agreed to be in the freeholders, burgeffes, and inhabitants, paying fcot and lot, and not receiving alms.

NUMBER OF VOTERS—About five hundred.
RETURNING OFFICER—The mayor.
PATRON—Lord Milford.

RADNOR COUNTY.

POLITICAL CHARACTER.

THE interest of this county centers entirely in the earl of Oxford. No political occurrence has happened to extend our observations beyond that circumstance.

PATRON—Earl of Oxford.

RADNOR TOWN.

POLITICAL CHARACTER—This town has been subject to various contests on the right of election. The question at issue has been, whether the word *Burgesses* meant such as were resident within the boroughs of New Radnor, Ryader, Knighton, Knucklas, and Reventice, only, or whether it extended to those who did not reside within the said boroughs. Three petitions have been presented to the house since the passing of the Grenville Act, which have all originated in this dispute. The first was, that of Edward Lewes, Esq. on the 6th of December, 1774, against the election

election of John Lewes, Esq. who had been returned by the resident burgesses, which was determined on the 27th of January, 1775, in favour of the petitioner. The second was in consequence of a double return of both these gentlemen, at the ensuing general election in 1780; which, on the 31st of January 1781, was likewise determined in favour of the non-resident burgesses; and the third, arose out of a contest at the last general election in 1790, when the earl of Oxford, who is patron of this borough, thought proper to withdraw his countenance from Mr. Edward Lewes, the late member, and to support his relation, David Murray, Esq. Mr. Lewes, who had before experienced the influence of his lordship's patronage, and had twice succeeded by petition, on the claim of the non-resident burgesses, now became a candidate on that of the resident ones; when the numbers upon the poll were,

  For David Murray, Esq. - - 609
    Edward Lewes, Esq. - - 313

Mr. Murray was accordingly returned, and Mr. Lewes became a petitioner upon the same claim of right which he had formerly opposed, and against which he had twice succeeded by petition.

tion. This petition was determined in favour of the fitting member.

Corporation—Confifts of a bailiff and twenty-five burgeffes.

Right of election—1690, 12 Nov. Is in the burgeffes of Radnor, Ryader, Knighton, Knucklas, and Kevenliel only.

1769, 7 March. The feveral perfons, though they had no other claim to be burgeffes of the boroughs of Ryader and Knucklas, than by virtue only of a prefentment made in the pretended court leet, holden under the authority of certain letters patent, which appear not to have been enrolled within the time exprefsly required by the faid letters patent, in order to the validity thereof, ought not to have been admitted as legal voters at the laft election.

Number of voters—About one thoufand.

Returning officer—The bailiff.

Patron—Earl of Oxford.

HISTORY

OF THE

COUNTIES AND ROYAL BURGHS

OF

SCOTLAND.

INTRODUCTION.

THE reprefentation of the kingdom of Scotland, which according to the eftimate of Sir John Sinclair, contains one million feven hundred thoufand inhabitants, is confined to the *tenants of the crown* in the feveral counties, to a corporation of *thirty three* individuals in the city of Edinburgh, and to fixty-five delegates from the fame number of felf-elected corporations of the royal burghs of Scotland.

The whole number of electors, in fome of the fhires, does not exceed *five*, and the whole conftituent body of thirty-three counties, is no more than one thoufand three hunded and fixty-eight, a number greatly inferior to that of the freeholders

freeholders in the smallest county of England; while the number of representatives is only *one* more than is furnished from the rotten boroughs of Cornwall.

We shall forbear to make any comment, where the external evidence of defective representation is so glaring as to set at defiance all sophistry, and impress conviction on the unprejudiced part of mankind. Where the represented part of the community does not amount to a hundred in a hundred thousand, and where property, held in tenure from the crown, and corporate bodies deriving exclusive privileges from accident and intrigue, can alone exercise the rights of freemen.

To give the reader a comprehensive view of what is called the representative system of Scotland, we have extracted the report of the committee of the Friends of the People, associated for the purpose of obtaining A REFORM OF PARLIAMENT; where, to use their own words, " an unembellished detail of facts must be refuted before it can be shaken," and cannot fail to convince where interest or prejudice has not warped the mind.

Report

Report of the Committee of the Friends of the People, associated for the Purpose of obtaining a Reform of Parliament, appointed to examine into the State of the Representation of Scotland.

Before your committee proceeds to the confideration of the important objects to which they conceive you chiefly intended to direct their attention, it may not be improper to mention a fort of reprefentation which is peculiar to North Britain; which has an irrefiftible tendency to give to the crown an undue influence in the houfe of lords, and which, by a more filent but not lefs effectual operation, contributes equally to the fame end in the other houfe of parliament.

At the union of the two kingdoms, in the beginning of this century, the peers of Scotland furrendered their hereditary right to feats in parliament; and were limited to an elective reprefentation by fixteen of their number. It is not the intention of your committee to enter at large into the hiftory of their elections; it is fufficient to ftate, that, it is univerfally known, that ever fince the union, they have been confiderably influenced by the minifters of the crown; which fpecies of patronage

tronage has given them an undue preponderance in the popular branch of the legiflature, by means which will be afterwards explained.

Your committee having thus flightly touched on the ftate of the Scottifh peerage, and only as it has a reference to their immediate object; they will now endeavour to fulfil their duty, by prefenting to the fociety a true and impartial account of the reprefentation of the people of Scotland in the houfe of commons.

They will firft eftablifh, as they think incontrovertibly,

1. That the conftitution of the Scottifh parliament was originally popular and free.

2. That many laws, which have been enacted for the regulation of elections, bear evident marks of the combined efforts of the crown, and the ariftocracy, to *narrow* the rights of election.

3. That each of thefe laws deprived the people of fome right formerly enjoyed and exercifed.

4. That by various fictions of law, contrary to the fpirit of the Britifh conftitution, the right of election of members to ferve in parliament has been transferred from thofe to whom it juftly and naturally belonged, to others who had no right whatfoever.

5. That

5. That these grievances have been long and severely felt by the people; that they have been often complained of; and that various statutes for their remedy have been vainly enacted and successfully eluded.

6. That the system of representation in Scotland is now so confined and defective, that it has become a mere mockery upon the name or idea.

Although the counties, cities, and burghs, labour under the same constitutional grievance, and suffer equally from the gradual deterioration of their ancient condition, it will be necessary to consider their history separately, on account of the different modes in which their rights have been circumscribed, usurped, or destroyed.

COUNTIES.

By the constitution of Scotland, the parliament being the King's Court Baron, or *Curia Regis*, he could summon all his immediate tenants to attend him there. In these remote times, service in parliament was not considered as a profitable privilege, but as a burdensome duty; and, in the beginning of the fifteenth century, the fyſtem of repreſentation was introduced for the eaſe and benefit of the vaſſals or tenants. Yet, until near the end of the ſixteenth century, every freeholder or tenant of the crown was entitled to vote at elections, however ſmall his property might be, which ſufficiently proves the ancient popularity and freedom of the inſtitution.

In the reign of James the ſixth of Scotland, and firſt of England, (a monarch who was not diſtinguiſhed by too great an attachment to the liberty of mankind) the right of voting was firſt reſtricted to freeholders poſſeſſing lands of forty ſhillings of what was called "Old Extent;" that is, of lands which were ſo rated in the ceſs or county books about the end of the thirteenth or beginning of the fourteenth century. Your committee wiſh you to obſerve, that this was a great and fatal blow to popular election; for though forty ſhillings was made, *as in England*, the nominal ſtandard of a vote, yet, by carrying it back to a rate or valuation made three hundred years before, the value of money having confiderably fallen, the extent of the qualification required was very much raiſed.—And this circumſtance points out the efficient cauſe of the enormous difference which ſubſiſts between

England

England and Scotland with regard to the freedom and popularity of election in the counties. In England the qualification has been allowed to keep pace with the decreasing value of money, and has therefore been extended to greater numbers of electors. In Scotland, by the limitations to the rates and valuations of very remote periods, the right of voting has been confined to the possessors of very considerable estates, and the number of electors has been very much diminished.

Had the Scottish kings and nobles stopped at this point, the evil might have been endured: but they proceeded vigorously in their career of encroachment. In the reign of Charles the second it was enacted, that where the right of voting on an old forty shillings land could not be proved, which had become difficult, then, to be enabled to vote, it should be necessary to be infeft in, or seized of an estate, valued in the same reign at 400l. Scots annual rent. It is proper here to mention, that at this day, by the nearest average which can be made over the whole kingdom, the rent of those lands, which are valued at forty shillings " Old Extent," is from 70l. to 130l. sterling; and the rent of the lands valued in the reign of Charles the second

second at 400l. Scots, is now about 400l. sterling, so that this king more than tripled the qualification required of the greatest part of the kingdom, by substituting lands, worth 400l. instead of those worth 100 or 130l.

Even this infringement was not thought enough; under George the second the mode of proving the existence of those old forty shilling votes, were rendered more difficult, by details with which your committee will not trouble you; they will only state, that by these regulations many of those votes have disappeared, and that very few of them now remain.

Hitherto your committee have confined themselves to the statement of those evils which arise from the magnitude of the qualifications required in electors, and their consequent paucity: they have yet supposed that this precious right is exercised only by the real proprietors of the soil, under certain grievous and improper limitations; but they are now to describe mischiefs of another nature, which have been suffered to grow up, which have been fondly fostered in the bosom of kingly and aristocratic power; and which have totally perverted and completely overturned the real representation of the counties.

By

By the act of Charles II. 1681, the foundation
was laid for the intolerable abuses which now
exist, and which certainly were never contempla-
ted or foreseen by that parliament. It was then
enacted, that the right of voting should be in
persons publickly infeft in *property* or *superiority*
of lands of forty shillings old extent, or £.400
Scots valued rent; thus making the distinction,
and drawing the line, between *property* and *superiority*. It is necessary to explain this term of
superiority, because from an abuse of it, the principal grievances in the elections for knights of
the shire in Scotland have arisen.

The feudal law supposes the king to be the
sole proprietor of all the lands in the kingdom:
from him his vassals hold by charter; in like
manner his vassals may grant lands to be held
from them by charter: these sub-vassals may
repeat the same operation *ad infinitum;* but the
original or *immediate* vassal of the king has the
sole right of voting or being elected to serve in
parliament. From this system the following
consequences have flowed:

I. Proprietors of estates, of whatsoever value,
who hold from a subject, are not entitled to vote
or to be elected. It is computed, that in several
counties nearly one half of the lands are held in

this

this manner from subjects superior: over the whole kingdom it is believed that one fifth of the lands are so held; therefore the proprietors of one fifth of the landed property, as far as that property operates, are deprived of any voice in the choosing their representatives.

II. In this class of landholders, so excluded from this invaluable franchise, are men of estates, worth from £.500 to £.2000 per annum; but what is more to be lamented, it comprehends the best and most virtuous parts of the community, namely, the middling and smaller gentry, and the industrious yeomen and farmers who have inherited or acquired some landed property.

III. Many persons without the smallest interest in the land possess the right of voting and of being elected.

IV. It is a principle in the constitution, that no man shall have more than one vote in the same county in his own person; and it is another principle, that no peer of the realm shall have any vote at all in the election of members to serve in the house of commons.

By an ingenious device of the lawyers, these two fundamental principles have been eluded: When a person of great property wishes to multiply his votes, he surrenders his charter to the crown;

crown; he appoints a number of confidential friends, to whom the crown parcels out his estate, in lots of £. 400 Scots valued rent: then he takes charters from these friends for the real property; thus leaving them apparently the immediate tenants of the crown, and consequently all entitled to vote or to be elected. This operation is equally open to peers and great commoners, who have availed themselves of it accordingly; the peers thus acquiring an influence, from which they are excluded by the spirit and forms of the constitution; and the great commoners extending and multiplying a right in an undue and fraudulent manner—thereby depreciating or extinguishing the franchises of the smaller proprietors, with great and manifest prejudice to the general liberty of the country.

This legal fraud began in this century, and has been chiefly practised during the present reign; it therefore derives no shelter or sanction from custom, which the folly of men allows to cover a multitude of glaring abuses. Your committee will not dwell on the various modes by which it has been performed: they will briefly state, that the common methods have been by life-rent, charters, charters on wadset or mortgage, and charters in fee.

The

The legiflature has not been blind to thefe mifchievous innovations; nor has it been inactive in endeavouring to refift and prevent them. It has admitted, that thefe delufive furrenders of charters, and confequent creations of nominal and fictitious votes, are fraudulent in fact and principle; and it has been decreed, that wherever they can be detected, they fhall be illegal and void. Several laws have been paffed for the prevention of fuch proceedings, and for the detection of fuch crimes. Oaths have been enacted to be taken by freeholders claiming to poll at elections, couched in the ftrongeft terms, and providing as many guards as the zeal and wifdom of the legiflature could invent; but all thefe precautions have been conftantly defeated by the ingenuity of the learned profeffion, who have always fucceeded in finding falvos for weak confciences. Gentlemen of the faireft characters, nay clergymen, have been induced by fubtile explanations, and the niceft verbal fubterfuges, to take thefe oaths, contrary to the evident intendment of the legiflature, contrary to the received meaning and ufage of our language, and in defiance of the general fenfe of their country.

Your committee refer you to the acts, 12 Anne,

Anne, cap. 6. and 7; Geo. II. cap. 18, not only for the terms of the oaths, but for the purpose and meaning of the laws.

The court of session in Scotland have been remarkably unfortunate in their endeavours to give effect to these laws. Being composed of fifteen judges, and the sentences being decided by the majority actually present, it has necessarily happened, that from the diversity of opinions naturally incident to mankind, the decisions of the court have frequently varied, according to the absence or attendance of the several lords; and the same points at issue have often undergone very different and opposite determinations. Nor has the situation of the subject been much bettered by the appeal to the house of peers; for very contrary systems concerning these election laws have been maintained and carried into effect by the highest authorities in that final judicature. What was law one day, and under the direction of one judge, was not law another day, and under another judge: and thus, from the double uncertainty of the manner in which the majorities on the Scottish bench might decide, and of the varying opinions of the high legal characters in England, men have had no security, and have been doomed to suffer *incertum jus,*

jus, fumma injuria. It may not be wrong to state, that not lefs than fix hundred law-fuits have taken place within thefe twenty years on this fubject of county elections; which, with the the attendant legal operations, have coft above a million of pounds fterling.

The parliamentary reprefentation of the counties in Scotland has therefore, according to the expreffion of a noble lord high in the law, " completely flid from its bafis." Much undue influence has been acquired by the crown, the nobility, and the great proprietors; the laws have been eluded and perverted; the number of electors has been greatly diminifhed; and the conftitutional rights of the fubject have been invaded, ufurped, or annihilated.

By table No. I. which is annexed, it will be feen, that, in two of the counties, there are only three real voters in each; in feven, not more than ten: in all of them refpectively very few. The total number of real voters in the whole is 1,390. Total of falfe, nominal, and fictitious voters 1,201: and thirty-three counties return only thirty members, fix having only the right of fending a member to every fecond parliament.

CITIES AND BURGHS.

By the ancient and original conftitution of the cities and burghs, the magiftrates and town councils *were chofen by the* refident burgeffes and proprietors *of houfes and lands:* this, however, was a ftate of freedom too incompatible with the proud and narrow views of the kings and nobility, who conftantly in hoftility with each other, agreed in nothing but in degrading and oppreffing the people. By an act paffed in 1469, the town councils were invefted with the power of electing their fucceffors; and, in 1474, it was ordained that four perfons of the old fhould be annually chofen into the new town councils. By thefe laws, as far as they were effectual, the burgeffes and inhabitants at large were disfranchifed; they had no longer any controul over their magiftrates; and the corporations became felf-elected juntos, totally feparated in interefts from their former conftituents and fellow citizens.

Every city or burgh had certain eftates in land, houfes, fisheries, port duties, and other valuable forts of property; the revenue arifing from which was by their original charters and constitutions destined to be applied for the benefit of their communities; but as soon as the magistrates and councils acquired the power of electing themselves in perpetuity, they administered, embezzled, and dilapidated these estates at their pleasure.

This subject is now before parliament; and a great body of evidence has been compiled, which will soon be published, and which will throw very great light on the antient state of the Scottish burghs. Your Committee, however, have thought proper to mention it as one great branch of the encroachment on former rights.

It is absolutely necessary to state, that these unjust acts of 1469 and 1474 have been so detested by the people, and so much resisted in practice, that they have never been completely executed in any one place: in many of the burghs the burgesses continued for a long period to elect their own magistrates, and several charters have been granted as low down as the end of the last century, conferring the right of election on the burgesses. These acts, then, on which the present system is founded, have not the sanction derived from the submission, consent, or reverence of the people: and their repeal

repeal would not be an innovation, but a restoration of antient rights and privileges.

If the cities and burghs had suffered in their common property only, by these tyrannical laws, they would have been comparatively fortunate; but as their representatives in parliament were to be chosen by the magistrates and councils, when they lost the right of electing them, they lost all share in the choice of their legislators; and, in this unhappy situation, they find themselves at this day.

At the union, Edinburgh, being the capital, alone retained its right of sending one member to parliament: all the other towns were thrown into districts of fours and fives, each district being allowed to send one member.—This induced a regulation, which still more sensibly wounded the freedom of election. By it, every burgh now elects a delegate; these delegates meet by rotation at each of the towns to elect the representative. The place where they meet is called the presiding burgh for that election, and its delegate has a casting vote in case of an equality of voices. The burghs have no controul on their delegates; they must trust entirely to honour for the return of the person by whom they wish to be represented: and there *have* been instances where the delegates have corruptly betrayed their trust, and have acted contrary to the desire and expectation of their constituents.

Another evil, deeply felt by the great commercial towns, is their being classed with insignificant and obscure burghs: among many instances of this it will be sufficient to mention Glasgow, which is known to be one of the most opulent trading cities of Great Britain. Its number of inhabitants exceeds 60,000; its delegate is chosen by thirty-two persons, who are self-elected; and this delegate has only one voice of four in the choice of a member of parliament, in common with the delegates of three little towns, the inhabitants of which are not more than 2000.

By table No. II. it appears that of the fifteen members for the cities and burghs, one for Edinburgh is chosen by thirty-three persons; the other fourteen by 65 delegates, who are elected by 1220 persons.

The inhabitants of Scotland are supposed to be near two millions; their representatives are chosen by 2643. Scotland sends forty-five members,

members; a single county in England, namely, Cornwall, sends forty-four.

Your committee will now conclude: they have endeavoured to be as brief as possible, and to confine themselves strictly to the most material facts. Volumes might have been written on the matter which presented itself to their observation: but they hope with deference to the judgment of the society, that they have more truly executed the task which they undertook, by compressing than by expanding the subject.

TABLE,

TABLE, &c. of Number of Electors in the Counties, &c.

No I.

		1788. Real.	1788. Nom.	1790. Real and Nominal.	Valued rent of each Shire of Scotland, Scots money.		
1	Aberdeen	82	96	158	235,665	8	11
2	Argyll	23	21	43	149,595	10	0
3	Ayr	86	119	220	191,605	0	7
4	Banff	19	103	108	79,200	0	0
5	Berwick	66	87	150	178,365	7	3
6	Dumbarton	15	51	65	33,327	19	0
7	Dumfries	34	11	49	237,041	3	4
8	Edinburgh, or Mid Lothian	83	10	96	191,054	3	9
9	Fife	153	32	188	362,584	7	5
10	Forfar, or Angus	71	24	92	171,519	15	7
11	Haddington, or East Lothian	61	13	76	168,878	5	10
12	Inverness	20	83	103	73,188	9	0
13	Kinkardine	46	6	55	74,921	1	0
14	Kirkcudbright	80	72	155	114,571	19	3
15	Lanerk	55	69	148	about 160,000	0	0
16	Linlithgow, or West Lothian	29	18	64	74,931	19	2
17	Moray, or Elgin	23	53	77	65,603	0	5
18	Orkney	18	21	40	56,551	9	1
19	Peebles	32	5	37	51,937	13	10
20	Perth	128	19	145	about 330,000	0	0
21	Renfrew	32	82	128	68,076	15	2
22	Ross	46	33	72	75,040	10	3
23	Roxburgh	56	49	81	315,594	14	6
24	Selkirk	27	13	40	80,307	15	6
25	Stirling	46	30	59	108,518	8	9
26	Sutherland	8	23	35	26,193	9	9
27	Wigton	29	34	53	65,338	7	8

The following six Shires elect a Member alternately: At the last election the Shires of Caithness, Kinross, and Cromarty, returned a Member to Parliament. At the next election the Shires of Bute, Clackmannan, and Nairn, will return a Member to Parliament; that is, Caithness alternately with Bute, Clackmannan with Kinross, and Nairn with Cromarty. At the last election in 1790,

28	Caithness	10	12	22	37,256	2	10
29	Cromarty	3	6	6	12,897	2	8
30	Kinross	9	17	23	20,192	11	2
	To return next election.	1390	1201	2588	3,815,857	11	8
31	Bute	3	9	12	15,022	13	8
32	Clackmannan	5	11	16	26,482	10	10
33	Nairn	6	14	20	15,162	10	11
		1404	1235	2636	3,872,526	7	1

TABLE of the Number of Electors in the Royal Burghs.

No. II.

Number of Town-Council, who choose each one Delegate.		Number of Delegates in each district who choose the Member of Parliament.	Number of Town-Council, who choose each one Delegate.		Number of Delegates in each district who choose the Member of Parliament.
I. Edinburgh, City	33		IX. Stirling	25	
II. Dinwall	25		Inverkeithing	15	
Dornock	15		Dumfermline	26	5
Wick	12	5	Culross	19	
Kirkwall	23		Queensferry	23	
Tain	17		X. Rutherglen	19	
III. Fortrose	15		Glasgow	32	
Invernefs	21		Renfrew	21	4
Nairn	19	4	Dumbarton	15	
Forres	17		XI. Jedburgh	25	
IV. Elgin	17		Dunbar	20	
Banff	17		North Berwick	12	5
Cullen	26	5	Lauder	17	
Kintore	9		Haddington	25	
Inverarie	9		XII. Peebles	17	
V. Aberdeen	19		Linlithgow	27	
Montrose	21		Selkirk	33	4
Brechin	13	5	Lanerk	17	
Aberbrothock	19		XIII. Dumfries	25	
Inverbervie	15		Kirkcudbright	17	
VI. Perth	26		Annan	21	5
Dundee	29		Lochmaben	15	
St. Andrews	29	5	Sanquehar	17	
Cupar	31		XIV. Whithorn	19	
Forfar	19		New Galloway	20	
VII. Crail	21		Stranraer	18	4
Kilrenny	13		Wigton	18	
Anstruther, W.	15	5	XV. Irwine	17	
Anstruther, E.	19		Rothsay	19	
Pittenweem	24		Inverary	13	5
VIII. Kinghorn	22		Cambelltown	17	
Dysart	24	4	Ayr	17	
Kirkaldy	21				
Burntisland	22			1220	65

In Edinburgh 33 persons elect one Member of Parliament. In each of the other 14 districts, the respective Town Councils nominate one Delegate each, and by the majority of those Delegates in each district, the Member of Parliament is elected.

Thus in Edinburgh - - - 33 persons elect - 1 Member.
In the other Districts, 1220 choose - 65 persons who elect 14 Members.

So that ultimately in the Burghs 98 persons elect - 15 Members.

STATE

OF THE SEVERAL

COUNTIES OF SCOTLAND,

INCLUDING

REAL AND NOMINAL VOTES,

AT THE LAST GENERAL ELECTION, IN 1790.

ABERDEENSHIRE.

ON the roll being made up, at a meeting which was held at Aberdeen the 21st of July, 1790, for the election of a member to serve this county in parliament, the number of freeholders, in whom the right of election is vested, appeared to be one hundred and fifty-eight; when James Fergufon, Efq. of Pitfour, was unanimoufly elected.

PATRON—Duke of Gordon.

ARGYLESHIRE.

AT the meeting held at Inverary the 19th of July, 1790, for the purpofe of electing a member to reprefent this county in parliament, the number of voters, as appeared by the roll, was forty-three;

three; when lord Frederick Campbell was unanimously elected.

Patron—Duke of Argyle.

AYRSHIRE.

At a meeting of freeholders, held at Ayr the 19th of July, 1790, for the election of a member to serve this county in parliament, the number of electors appeared to be two hundred and twenty; when Sir Adam Ferguſſon, of Kilkerron, Bart. was unanimously elected.

Patron—Earl of Eglintoun.

BAMFFSHIRE.

At a meeting of freeholders, which was held at Bamff the 2d of July, 1790, for the election of a member to repreſent this county in parliament, the number of voters on the roll then made up was one hundred and eight; when Sir James Grant, of Grant, Bart. was unanimously elected.

Patrons—Duke of Gordon and earl of Fife.

BERWICKSHIRE.

On making up the roll at a meeting of freeholders, held at Greenlaw the 1st of July, 1790, for the purpose of electing a member to represent this county in parliament, the number of voters appeared to be one hundred and fifty; when Patrick Home, Esq. of Wedderburn, was unanimously elected.

Patron—Duke of Buccleugh.

SHIRE OF CAITHNESS.

On the roll being made up, at the meeting of freeholders, held at Wick the 1st of July, 1790, for the purpose of electing a member to represent this shire in parliament, the number of voters found in the whole county was but twenty-two; when Sir John Sinclair, Bart. was unanimously elected.

Patron—Sir John Sinclair.

SHIRE OF CROMARTY.

In this county, according to the meeting of freeholders, held at Cromarty the 8th of July, 1790, there are but six voters.

As this numerous body of voters have the exclusive privilege of electing the representatives for the county, their names may not be unacceptable to our readers.

William Pulteney, Esq. of Solway Bank.

Duncan

Duncan Davidson, Esq. of Tullock.

Alexander Ross Grey, Esq. of Cromarty.

David Urquhart, Esq. of Braelangwall.

Robert Bruce Æneas Macleod, Esq. of Cadboll.

Alexander Brodie, Esq. of Brodie.

At the last general election two out of these six electors were candidates for its representation; viz. Alexander Brodie, Esq. of Brodie, and Duncan Davidson, Esq. of Tullock.

The following freeholders voted for Mr. Davidson.

William Pulteney, Preses.

Duncan Davidson, for himself.

Alexander Ross Grey.

The following voted for Mr. Brodie.

David Urquhart.

Robert Bruce Æneas Macleod.

Alexander Brodie, for himself.

The numbers being thus rendered equal, the Preses, William Pulteney, Esq. (according to the laws of election in Scotland) gave the casting vote to Mr. Davidson, who was of course declared duly elected.

PATRON—Mr. Pulteney.

DUMBARTON-

DUMBARTONSHIRE.

ON the roll being made up, at the meeting of freeholders, held at Dumbarton the 21st of July, 1790, for the election of a member to serve this shire in parliament, the number appeared to be sixty-five; when Sir Archibald Edmonstone, of Duntreath, Bart. was unanimously elected.

PATRONS—Hon. Keith Elphinston, and lord Frederick Campbell.

DUMFRIESSHIRE.

ON making up the roll, at a meeting of freeholders held at Dumfries the 24th of July, 1790, the number was forty-nine. A contest then took place for the representation of this county in parliament, between Sir Robert Lawrie, and John Johnstone, Esq. of Alva; when the numbers were, for Sir Robert Lawrie, twenty-two, John Johnstone, Esq. thirteen; whereupon Sir Robert Lawrie was returned as duly elected.

PATRON—Duke of Queensberry.

SHIRE OF EDINBURGH.

ON making up the roll, at a meeting of the freeholders, held at Edinburgh, 25th June, 1790, the

the number of electors appeared to be ninety-six; when Robert Dundas, Esq. of Arniston, was unanimously elected their representative in parliament.

PATRON—Right Hon. Henry Dundas.

FIFESHIRE.

ON the roll being made up, at the meeting of freeholders held at Cupar the 22d of July, 1790, for the purpose of electing a member to represent this shire in parliament, the number of voters was one hundred and eighty-eight; when William Wemyss, Esq. of Wemyss, was unanimously elected.

PATRON—Earl of Fife.

FORFARSHIRE.

ON the roll made up, at the meeting of freeholders, held at Forfar the 2d of July, 1790, for the purpose of electing a member to represent this shire in parliament, the number appeared to be ninety-two; when David Scott, Esq. of Dunninauld, was unanimously elected.

PATRON—Duke of Athol.

HADDINGTONSHIRE.

ON the roll made up, at a meeting of freeholders, held at Haddington, the 28th of June, 1790, for the purpose of electing a representative to serve this county in parliament, the number was seventy-six; when John Hamilton, Esq. of Pencaitland, was unanimously elected.

PATRON—Earl of Haddington.

INVERNESSSHIRE.

AT a meeting of freeholders, held at Inverness the 27th of July, 1790, for the purpose of electing a representative in parliament for this county, the number of voters, as appeared by the roll then made up, was one hundred and three; when Lieutenant-colonel Norman Macleod, of Macleod, was unanimously elected.

PATRON—Duke of Gordon.

KINCARDINESHIRE.

AT a meeting of freeholders held at Stonehaven the 14th of July, 1790, for the purpose of electing a representative in parliament for this county, the number of voters, as appeared by the roll then made up, was fifty-five; when Robert

Robert Barclay, Esq. of Urie, was unanimously elected.

KINROSSSHIRE.

AT a meeting of freeholders, held at Kinross on the 6th of July, 1790, for the purpose of electing a representative to serve this county in parliament, the number of voters appeared to be twenty-three; when George Graham, Esq. of Kinross, was unanimously elected.

PATRONS—Earl of Leven, and Sir William Erskine.

STEWARTRY OF KIRKCUDBRIGHT.

AT the meeting of freeholders, held at Kirkcudbright the 14th of July, 1790, for the purpose of electing a representative to serve this place in parliament, the number was, as appears by the roll made up, one hundred and fifty-five; when Major-general Alexander Stewart was unanimously elected.

PATRONS—Earl of Galloway, and James Murray, Esq. of Broughton.

LANERKSHIRE.

ON the roll made up, at a meeting of freeholders, held at Lanerk the 14th of July, 1790, for

for the purpofe of electing their reprefentative in parliament, the number of voters was one hundred and forty-eight; when Sir James Steuart Denham, of Coltnefs, Bart. was unanimoufly elected.

Patron—Duke of Hamilton.

LINLITHGOWSHIRE.

At the laft general election, Sir William Auguftus Cunninghame, of Livingftone, and the Honourable John Hope, oppofed each other as candidates for the reprefentation of that county in parliament. The number of freeholders is fixty-two; of which number thirty-four voted for the Honourable John Hope, and twenty for Sir William Auguftus Cunninghame; whereupon the Honourable John Hope was returned as duly elected.

Patron—Earl of Hopeton.

SHIRE OF MORAY, alias ELGIN.

On the roll made up, at the meeting of freeholders, held at Elgin the 5th of July, 1790, for the purpofe of electing a reprefentative to ferve this county in parliament, the number of voters was feventy-feven; when Lewis Alexander Grant,

Grant, Esq. of Grant, the younger, was unanimously elected.

PATRON—Earl of Elgin.

SHIRE OF ORKNEY.

AT the last general election, a contest took place for the representation of this county, between John Balfour, Esq. Fiar of Warfater, and Colonel Thomas Dundas, of Fingask. The number of freeholders, as appears by the roll made up at the meeting held at Kirkwall, on the 28th of July, 1790, was forty; nineteen of whom voted for Mr. Balfour, and thirteen for Mr. Dundas; whereupon Mr. Balfour was returned as duly elected.

PATRON—Disputed between Sir Thomas Dundas, and the earl of Galloway.

PEEBLESSHIRE.

ON the roll made up, at the meeting of freeholders, held at Peebles the 5th of July, 1790, the number of voters was thirty-seven; when Lieutenant William Montgomery was unanimously elected.

PATRON—Earl of Eglintoune.

PERTHSHIRE.

AT the laſt general election for the repreſentative of this county, there was a conteſt between Major General James Murray, of Strowan, and John Drummond, Eſq. of Megginch; on which occaſion the number of freeholders, as appears by the roll made up at their meeting, held at Perth the 17th of July, 1790, was one hundred and forty-five; ſixty-ſeven of whom voted for General Murray, and thirty-nine for Mr. Drummond; whereupon the General was returned as duly elected.

PATRON—Duke of Athol.

RENFREWSHIRE.

AT the laſt general election for this county, there was a conteſt for its repreſentation, between John Shaw Stewart, Eſq. of Greenock, and Alexander Cunninghame, Eſq. of Craigends. The number of freeholders, as appears by the roll, made up at the meeting held at Renfrew the 24th of July, 1790, was one hundred and twenty-eight; twenty-two of whom voted for Mr. Stewart, and twenty-one for Mr. Cunninghame; whereupon Mr. Stewart was declared and returned as duly elected.

PATRON—Duke of Hamilton.

ROSSSHIRE.

On the making up of the roll, at the meeting of freeholders, held at Tain the 16th of July, 1790, for the purpose of electing a representative to serve this shire in parliament, the number of voters was seventy-two; when William Adam, Esq. the younger, of Blair, was unanimously elected.

ROXBURGHSHIRE.

At the last general election there was a contest for the representation of this county, between Sir George Douglas, of Springwood Park, and John Rutherford, Esq. of Edgarstoun. The number of freeholders, as appears by the roll made up at their meeting, which was held at Jedburgh the 24th of July, 1790, was eighty-one; thirty of whom voted for Sir George Douglas, and twenty-five for Mr. Rutherford; whereupon Sir George was declared duly elected.

PATRONS—Duke of Queensberry, and duke of Roxburgh.

SELKIRKSHIRE.

THE number of freeholders for this county, as appears by the roll which was made up at their meeting held at Selkirk the 2d of July, 1790, for the purpose of electing a member to serve them in parliament, was forty; when Mark Pringle, Esq. of Fairnilie, was unanimously elected.

STIRLINGSHIRE.

AT the last general election there was a contest for the representation of this county between Sir Alexander Campbell, of Ardkinlass, Bart. and Sir Thomas Dundas, of Kerse, Bart. The number of freeholders, as appeared by the roll then made up, at the meeting which was held at Stirling the 6th of July, 1790, was fifty-nine; twenty-eight of whom voted for Sir Thomas Dundas, and twenty-two for Sir Alexander Campbell; whereupon Sir Thomas was returned as duly elected.

PATRON—Sir Thomas Dundas.

SHIRE OF SUTHERLAND.

AT the last general election, there was a contest for the representation of this county, be-

between

tween General James Grant, of Ballindallock, Robert Bruce Æneas Macleod, Esq. of Cadboll, and Robert Home Gordon, Esq. of Embo. The number of freeholders, as appears by the roll made up at their meeting, which was held at Dornock the 14th of July, 1790, was thirty-five; nine of whom voted for General Grant, five for Mr. Macleod, and three for Mr. Gordon; whereupon the General was returned as duly elected.

Patrons—Countess of Sutherland, and earl of Wemyss.

WIGTONSHIRE.

On the roll being made up, at the meeting of freeholders, held at Wigton the 16th of July, 1790, the number appeared to be fifty-three; when Andrew M'Dowal, Esq. of Culgroat, was unanimously elected.

Patron—Earl of Galloway.

SHIRE OF BUTE.

At the making up of the roll of freeholders, at a meeting held at Rothsay the 22d of April, 1784, since which time the freeholders have had no meeting (not sending a representative to this present

present parliament) the number of electors appeared to be twelve.

Patron—Earl of Bute.

CLACKMANNANSHIRE.

At a meeting of the freeholders of this county, held at Clackmannan the 29th of November, 1788, since which time they have had no meeting (not sending a member to this present parliament) the number of voters, as appeared by the roll then made up, was sixteen.

NAIRNSHIRE.

At a meeting of the freeholders of this county, held at Nairn in Michaelmas, 1789, since which no meeting has been held, this shire not returning a member to this parliament, the number of voters, as appeared on the roll then made up, was twenty.

STATE

OF THE SEVERAL

BOROUGHS OF SCOTLAND,

INCLUDING

REAL AND NOMINAL VOTES,

AT THE LAST GENERAL ELECTION, IN 1790.

EDINBURGH.

POLITICAL CHARACTER.

THE mode of proceeding at the election of the member of parliament for this city is extremely simple, the right of election being in the whole magistrates and council, ordinary and extraordinary, united. The clerk (although perhaps he lies under no strict necessity by statute to do so) usually takes the oath against bribery, and to make a faithful return.

The whole is settled in a general, but rather inaccurate way, by an act of the 6th of Queen Ann, c. 6. 5. "The Sheriff of the shire of Edinburgh shall, on the receipt of the writ, directed to him, forthwith direct his precept to the Lord Provost of Edinburgh, to cause a burgefs to be elected for that city; and on the receipt of such precept, the city of Edinburgh shall elect their member; and their common clerk shall certify his name to the sheriff of Edinburgh, who shall annex it to his writ, and return it.

The council by whom the member is elected consists of

    A provost
    Four bailies
    Dean of guild
    Treasurer
    Old provost
    Four old bailies
    Old dean of guild
    Old treasurer
    Three merchant counsellors
    Two trades counsellors
    Six ordinary council deacons
    Eight extraordinary council deacons.

These voters are all under the influence of Mr. Dundas, their present representative. The enormous patronage which this gentleman is necessarily in possession of, from the various and lucrative places which he holds under government, insures to him the certainty of success for the representation of the city, unattended both with

with the trouble of canvassing, and the expence of an opposition to his interest.

NUMBER OF VOTERS—Thirty-three.

PATRON—Right Hon. Henry Dundas.

DISTRICT I.

This district, of which Dingwall was the presiding borough, comprises also Dornoch, Wick, Kirkwall, and Tain.

At the last general election, Sir Charles Ross, of Balnagown, Bart. was unanimously elected to represent them in parliament.

NUMBER OF VOTERS—FIVE.

PATRON—Sir Thomas Dundas.

DISTRICT II.

This district, of which Fortrose was the presiding borough, comprises also Inverness, Nairn, and Forres.

At the last general election Sir Hector Monro was unanimously elected to represent them in parliament.

NUMBER OF VOTERS—FOUR.

DISTRICT

DISTRICT III.

This diſtrict, of which Elgin was the preſiding borough, compriſes alſo Bamff, Cullen, Kintore, and Inverary.

At the laſt general election, Alexander Brodie, Eſq. was unanimouſly elected to repreſent them in parliament.

NUMBER OF VOTERS—FIVE.
PATRON—Mr. Brodie.

DISTRICT IV.

This diſtrict, of which Aberdeen was the preſiding borough, comprehends alſo Montroſe, Brechin, Aberbrothock, and Inverbervie.

At the laſt general election there was an oppoſition for the repreſentation of theſe boroughs in parliament between Alexander Callender, Eſq. of Crichton, and Sir David Carnegie, of Southeſk. The delegates of Aberdeen, Montroſe, and Inverbervie, voted for Mr. Callender, and thoſe of Brechin and Aberbrothock for Sir David; when Mr. Callender was elected, and duly returned.

NUMBER OF VOTERS—FIVE.

DISTRICT V.

This district, of which Perth was the presiding borough, comprises also Dundee, St. Andrew's, Cupar, and Forfar.

At the last general election for these boroughs, a contest took place between Captain George Murray, of Pitkeathly, and Captain Colin Campbell, of Carwhin. The commissioners for Dundee, St. Andrew's, Cupar, and Forfar, voted for Mr. Murray, and that for Perth for Captain Campbell; when Captain Murray was returned as duly elected.

NUMBER OF VOTERS—FIVE.

PATRON—Duke of Athol.

DISTRICT VI.

This district, of which Craill was the presiding borough, comprehends also Kilrunny, Anstruther Wester, Anstruther Easter, and Pittenween.

At the last general election there was a contest for the representation of these boroughs in parliament, between Sir John Anstruther and Thomas Erskine, Esq. late British Consul at Gottenburgh.

tenburgh. The delegates for Anftruther Wefter, Anftruther Eafter, and Pittenween, voted for Sir John, and thofe for Craill and Kilrunny for Mr. Erfkine; whereupon Sir John Anftruther was returned as duly elected.

Number of voters—FIVE.
Patron—Sir John Anftruther.

DISTRICT VII.

This diftrict, of which Kinghorn was the prefiding borough, comprifes alfo Dyfart, Kirkaldie, and Burntifland.

At the laft general election there was an oppofition for their reprefentation in parliament, between the Honourable Charles Hope and John Crawfurd, Efq. of Auchinames. The delegates for Kinghorn and Kirkaldie voted for Mr. Hope, and thofe for Dyfart and Burntifland for Mr. Crawfurd; when Mr. Hope was elected by the cafting vote of the delegate for Kinghorn, the returning borough.

Number of voters—FOUR.
Patron—Earl of Hopeton.

DISTRICT VIII.

This diſtrict, of which Stirling was the preſiding borough, compriſes alſo Inverkeithing, Dunferline, Culroſs, and Queensferry.

At the laſt general election, Sir Archibald Campbell was elected without oppoſition.

NUMBER OF VOTERS—FOUR.

DISTRICT IX.

This diſtrict, of which Rutherglen was the preſiding borough, comprehends alſo Glaſgow, Renfrew, and Dumbarton.

At the laſt general election, Mr. M'Dowal was unanimouſly elected.

NUMBER OF VOTERS—FOUR.

DISTRICT X.

This diſtrict, of which Jedburgh was the preſiding borough, compriſes alſo Dunbar, North Berwick, Lauder, and Haddington.

At the laſt general election there was a conteſt for their repreſentation between the Honourable Thomas Maitland and Colonel Fullarton.

The

The delegates for Jedburgh and Haddington voted for Mr. Fullarton, and thofe for Dunbar, North Berwick and Lauder for Mr. Maitland; whereupon the latter gentleman was returned.

NUMBER OF VOTERS—FIVE.

PATRON—Earl of Lauderdale.

DISTRICT XI.

This diſtrict, of which Peebles was the returning borough, compriſes alſo Linlithgow, Selkirk, and Lanerk.

At the laſt general election, William Grieve, Eſq. was unanimouſly elected.

NUMBER OF VOTERS—FOUR.

DISTRICT XII.

This diſtrict, of which Dumfries was the preſiding borough, comprehends alſo Kirkcudbright, Annan, Lochmaben, and Sanquhar.

At the laſt general election there was a conteſt for their repreſentation in parliament between Captain Millar, jun. of Dalſwinton, and Sir James Johnſtone. The delegates for Annan and Lochmaben voted for Sir James, and thoſe for Dumfries, Kirkcudbright, and Sanquhar, for

Captain

Captain Millar; whereupon Captain Millar was returned.

NUMBER OF VOTERS—FIVE.

PATRON—Duke of Queenſberry.

DISTRICT XIII.

This diſtrict, of which Whithorn was the preſiding borough, compriſes alſo New Galloway, Stranraer, and Wigton.

At the laſt general election there was an oppoſition for their repreſentation between Lord Daer and Colonel Balfour. The delegates for New Galloway and Stranraer voted for Lord Daer, and thoſe for Whithorn and Wigton for the latter; when Colonel Balfour was declared to be duly elected, Whithorn being the returning borough.

NUMBER OF VOTERS—FOUR.

PATRON—Earl of Galloway.

DISTRICT XIV.

This diſtrict, of which Irvine was the returning borough, comprehends alſo Rothſay, Inverary, Campbellton, and Ayr.

At the last general election, the Honourable Colonel Charles Stuart was unanimously elected.

NUMBER OF VOTERS—FIVE.

PATRON—Earl of Bute.

A TABLE.

A

TABLE

OF THE

COUNTIES, CITIES, AND BOROUGHS,

OF

GREAT BRITAIN;

Shewing the Period at which each City and Borough first sent Members to Parliament; the Names of those Places which have lost that invaluable Privilege; the Time that each of the existing Boroughs have been deprived of their exclusive Rights; and the different Reigns in which they have been restored.

N. B. The Names printed in *Italic* are the obsolete Boroughs.

Counties, Cities, and Boroughs.	When first summoned.	When discontinued.	When restored.
BEDFORDSHIRE.			
Dunstable - - - -	4 Edw. II.	11 Edw. III.	
Bedford - - - -	23 Edw. I.		
BERKSHIRE.			
Newbury - - - -	30 Edw. I.	11 Edw. III.	
Windsor - - - -	Ditto	14 Edw. III.	7 Edw. IV.
Reading - - - -	23 Edw. I.		
Wallingford - - -	Ditto		
Abingdon - - -	11 Edw. III.	12 Edw. III.	4 & 5 W. & M.

H h

Counties, Cities, and Boroughs.	When first summoned.	When discontinued.	When restored.
BUCKINGHAMSHIRE.			
Buckingham	11 Edw. III.	12 Edw. III.	36 H. VIII.
Wycomb	28 Edw. I.	17 Edw. IV.	33 H. VIII.
Aylesbury	1 Mary		
Agmondesham	28 Edw. I.	2 Edw. II.	21 James I.
Wendover	Ditto	Ditto	Ditto
Marlow	Ditto	Ditto	Ditto
CAMBRIDGESHIRE.			
Ely	23 Edw. I.	27 Edw. III.	
Wisbeach			
Cambridge University	1 James I.		
——— Town	23 Edw. I.	17 Edw. IV.	33 H. VIII.
CHESHIRE.	1 Edw. VI.		
Chester	Ditto		
CORNWALL.			
Polurun	11 Edw. III.	12 Edw. III.	
Launceston	23 Edw. I.		
Leskard	Ditto	17 Edw. IV.	1 Edw. VI.
Lestwithiel	Ditto	Ditto	Ditto
Truro	Ditto	Ditto	Ditto
Bodmin	Ditto	Ditto	Ditto
Helston	Ditto	Ditto	Ditto
Saltash	6 Edw. VI.		
Camelford	Ditto		
Westlooe	Ditto		
Grampound	Ditto		
Eastlooe	14 Edw. III.	14 Edw. III.	13 Eliz.
Penryn	1 Mary		
Tregoney	23 Edw. I.	35 Edw. I.	1 Eliz.
Bossiney	6 Edw. VI.		
St. Ives	4 & 5 P. & M.		
Fowey	14 Edw. III.	14 Edw. III.	13 Eliz.

Counties, Cities, and Boroughs.	When first summoned.	When discontinued.	When restored.
St. Germains	5 Eliz.		
St. Michael	6 Edw. VI.		
Newport	Ditto		
St. Maw's	5 Eliz.		
Callington	27 Eliz.		
CUMBERLAND.			
Egremont	23 Edw. I.	24 Edw. I.	
Carlisle	Ditto	17 Edw. IV.	33 H. VIII.
Cockermouth	Ditto	24 Edw. I.	16 Cha. I.
DERBYSHIRE.			
Derby	Ditto	17 Edw. IV.	33 H. VIII.
DEVONSHIRE.			
Bradnesham	6 Edw. II.	7 Edw. II.	
Crediton	35 Edw. I.	36 Edw. I.	
Exmouth	14 Edw. III.	15 Edw. III.	
Tremington	6 Edw. III.	7 Edw. III.	
Liddeford	28 Edw. I.	30 Edw. I.	
Modbury	34 Edw. I.	35 Edw. I.	
South Moulton	30 Edw. I.	31 Edw. I.	
Teignmouth	14 Edw. III.	15 Edw. III.	
Torrington	23 Edw. I.	45 Edw. III.	
Exeter	Ditto	17 Edw. IV.	1 Edw. IV.
Totnefs	Ditto	Ditto	Ditto
Plymouth	26 Edw. I.	7 Edw. II.	20 Hen. VI.
Oakhampton	28 Edw. I.	Ditto	16 Cha. I.
Barnstaple	23 Edw. I.	17 Edw. IV.	1 Edw. VI.
Plympton	Ditto	Ditto	Ditto
Honiton	28 Edw. I.	4 Edw. II.	16 Cha. I.
Tavistock	23 Edw. I.	17 Edw. IV.	1 Edw. VI.
Ashburton	26 Edw. I.	8 Hen. IV.	16 Cha. I.
Dartmouth	Ditto	17 Edw. IV.	1 Edw. VI.
Berealston	27 Eliz.		
Tiverton	18 James I.		

Counties, Cities, and Boroughs.	When first summoned.	When discontinued.	When restored.
DORSETSHIRE.			
Blandford	23 Edw. I.	22 Edw. III.	
Winborn			
Sherborn	11 Edw. III.	12 Edw. III.	
Milton			
Bere Regis			
Poole	14 Edw. III.	42 Edw. III.	31 Hen. VI.
Dorchester	23 Edw. I.	17 Edw. IV.	1 Edw. VI.
Lyme Regis	Ditto	Ditto	Ditto
Weymouth	12 Edw. II.		
Melcomb Regis	33 Edw. I.		
Bridport	21 Edw. III.		
Shaftsbury	23 Edw. I.		
Wareham	30 Edw. I.		
Corfe Castle	14 Eliz.		
DURHAM COUNTY.	31 Cha. II.		
City of Durham	Ditto		
ESSEX.			
Chelmsford	11 Edw. III.	12 Edw. III.	
Malden	2 Edw. III.		
Harwich	17 Edw. III.	18 Edw. III.	12 James I.
Colchester	23 Edw. I.		
GLOUCESTERSHIRE.			
Gloucester	Ditto		
Cirencester	13 Eliz.		
Tewkesbury	7 James I.		
HAMPSHIRE.			
Alresford	23 Edw. I.	35 Edw. I.	
Alton	Ditto	4 Edw. II.	
Basingstoke	Ditto	Ditto	

Counties, Cities, and Boroughs.	When first summoned.	When discontinued.	When restored.
Fareham	34 Edw. I.	36 Edw. I.	
Odiham	28 Edw. I.	Ditto	
Overton	23 Edw. I.	2 Edw. II.	
Winchester	Ditto		
Southampton	Ditto		
Portsmouth	Ditto		
Yarmouth	Ditto	24 Edw. I.	27 Eliz.
Newport	23 Edw. I.	24 Edw. I.	23 Eliz.
New Town	27 Eliz.		
Petersfield	35 Edw. I.	36 Edw. I.	1 Edw. VI.
Stockbridge	1 Eliz.		
Christchurch	13 Eliz.		
Lymington	27 Eliz.		
Whitchurch	Ditto		
Andover	23 Edw. I.	2 Edw. II.	27 Eliz.
HEREFORDSHIRE.			
Bromyard	33 Edw. I.	34 Edw. I.	
Ledbury	23 Edw. I.	Ditto	
Ross	33 Edw. I.	Ditto	
Hereford	23 Edw. I.		
Leominster	Ditto		
Weobly	Ditto	1 Edw. II.	15 Char. I.
HERTFORDSHIRE.			
Berkhamstead	11 Edw. III.	15 Edw. III.	
Storteford	4 Edw. II.	Ditto	
St. Albans	35 Edw. I.	6 Edw. III.	1 Edw. VI.
Hertford	23 Edw. I.	Ditto	21 James I.
HUNTINGDONSHIRE.			
Huntingdon	23 Edw. I.		

Counties, Cities, and Boroughs.	When first summoned.	When discontinued.	When restored.
KENT.			
Greenwich	4 & 5 P. & M.	6 P. & M.	
Tunbridge	23 Edw. I.	24 Edw. I.	
Canterbury	Ditto		
Rochester	Ditto		
Maidstone	Edw. VI.	Q. Mary	2 Eliz.
Queenborough	13 Eliz.		
LANCASHIRE.			
Manchester	Commonw.		
Lancaster	23 Edw. I.	5 Edw. III.	1 Edw. VI.
Newtown	1 Eliz.		
Wigan	23 Edw. I.	36 Edw. I.	Ditto
Clitheroe	1 Eliz.		
Liverpool	23 Edw. I.	35 Edw. I.	Ditto
Preston	Ditto	2 Edw. II.	Ditto
LEICESTERSHIRE.			
Melton Mowbray	11 Edw. III.	12 Edw. III.	
Leicester	23 Edw. I.		
LINCOLNSHIRE.			
Spalding	11 Edw. III.	12 Edw. III.	
Waynfleet	Ditto	Ditto	
Lincoln	49 Hen. III.		
Boston	11 Edw. III.	27 Edw. III.	1 Edw. VI.
Grimsby	23 Edw. I.		
Stamford	Ditto	11 Edw. III.	Ditto
Grantham	2 Edw. IV.		
MIDDLESEX.			
London	49 Hen. III.		
Westminster	1 Edw. VI.		

Counties, Cities, and Boroughs.	When first summoned.	When discontinued.	When restored.
MONMOUTHSHIRE.			
Monmouth	Hen. VIII.		
NORFOLK COUNTY.			
Norwich	23 Edw. I.		
Lynn Regis	Ditto		
Yarmouth	Ditto		
Thetford	1 Edw. VI.		
Castle Rising	5 P. & M.		
NORTHAMPTONSHIRE.			
Peterborough	1 Edw. VI.		
Northampton	23 Edw. I.		
Brackley	1 Edw. VI.		
Higham Ferrers	2 & 3 P. & M.		
NORTHUMBERLAND.			
Bamberg	23 Edw. I.	24 Edw. I.	
Corbrigg	Ditto	Ditto	
Newcastle			
Morpeth	1 Q. Mary		
Berwick	Hen. VIII.		
NOTTINGHAMSHIRE.			
Nottingham			
East Retford	9 Edw. II.	10 Edw. II.	13 Eliz.
Newark	29 Cha. II.		
OXFORDSHIRE.			
Burford	34 Edw. I.	35 Edw. I.	
Chipping Norton	28 Edw. I.	34 Edw. I.	
Doddington	30 Edw. I.	Ditto	
Witney	33 Edw. I.	5 Edw. III.	

Counties, Cities, and Boroughs.	When first summoned.	When discontinued.	When restored.
Oxford University	James I.		
——— City	23 Edw. I.		
Woodstock	30 Edw. I.	34 Edw. I.	1 Q. Mary
Banbury	1 Mary		
RUTLANDSHIRE.			
SALOP COUNTY.			
Shrewsbury	23 Edw. I.		
Bridgnorth	Ditto		
Ludlow	12 Edw. IV.		
Wenlock	Ditto		
Bishop's Castle	15 Eliz.		
SOMERSETSHIRE.			
Oxbridge	23 Edw. I.	17 Edw. III.	
Chard	28 Edw. I.	3 Edw. III.	
Dunster	34 Edw. III.	35 Edw. III.	
Glastonbury	12 Edw. III.	13 Edw. III.	
Langport	33 Edw. I.	36 Edw. I.	
Montacute	Ditto	34 Edw. I.	
Stoke Curcy	34 Edw. III.	35 Edw. III.	
Watchet	30 Edw. I.	31 Edw. I.	
Were	34 Edw. I.	36 Edw. I.	
Bristol	23 Edw. I.		
Bath	Ditto		
Wells	Ditto		
Taunton	Ditto		
Bridgewater	Ditto		
Minehead	1 Eliz.		
Ilchester	23 Edw. I.	12 Edw. III. 13 Edw. IV.	12 Edw. IV. 18 Jac. I.
Milborne Port	26 Edw. I.	35 Edw. I.	15 Cha. I.
STAFFORDSHIRE.			
Litchfield	33 Edw. I.	27 Edw. III.	Edw. VI.

Counties, Cities, and Boroughs.	When first summoned.	When discontinued.	When restored.
Stafford	23 Edw. I.		
Newcastle	27 Edw. III.		
Tamworth	5 Eliz.		
SUFFOLK COUNTY.			
Ipswich	23 Edw. I.		
Dunwich	Ditto		
Orford	Ditto	1 Edw. II.	Hen. VII.
Aldborough	13 Eliz.		
Sudbury	1 Eliz.		
Eye	13 Eliz.		
St. Edmondsbury	4 Jac. I.		
SURRY COUNTY.			
Farnham	4 Edw. II.	38 Hen. VI.	
Kingston upon Thames	Ditto	47 Edw. III.	
Southwark			
Bletchingley	23 Edw. I.		
Rygate	Ditto		
Guildford	Ditto		
Gatton	29 Hen. VI.		
Haslemere	27 Eliz.		
SUSSEX COUNTY.			
Chichester	23 Edw. I.		
Horsham	Ditto		
Medhurst	4 Edw. II.		
Lewes	23 Edw. I.		
New Shoreham	Ditto		
Bramber	Ditto	Edw. II.	31 Hen. VI.
Steyning	4 Edw. II.	Ditto	Ditto
East Grinstead	1 Edw. II.		
Arundel	23 Edw. I.		

Counties, Cities, and Boroughs.	When first summoned.	When discontinued.	When restored.
WARWICKSHIRE.			
Coventry	23 Edw. I.	28 Edw. I.	8 Edw. II.
		25 Edw. III.	31 Hen. VI.
Warwick	Ditto		
WESTMORELAND.			
Appleby	Ditto		
WILTSHIRE.			
Bradford	Ditto	24 Edw. I.	
Mere	Ditto	1 Edw. II.	
Highworth . . .	26 Edw. I.	27 Edw. IV.	
Salisbury	23 Edw. I.		
Wilton	Ditto		
Downton	Ditto	38 Edw. III.	1 Hen. V.
		2 Hen. V.	20 Hen. VI.
Hindon	27 Edw. VI.		
Heytesbury . . .	Ditto		
Westbury	Ditto		
Calne	23 Edw. I.	1 Edw. II.	34 Edw. II.
		36 Edw. III.	2 Rich. II.
Devizes	Ditto	20 Edw. II.	4 Edw. III.
Chippenham . . .	Ditto	2 Edw. II.	Ditto
		2 Rich. II.	12 Hen. VI.
Malmesbury . . .	Ditto		
Cricklade	Ditto	1 Edw. II.	20 Edw. II.
		21 Edw. II.	Edw. III.
		Rich. II.	1 Hen. IV.
		9 Hen. V.	Hen. VI.
Great Bedwin . .	Ditto	8 Edw. II.	36 Edw. III.
		37 Edw. III.	7 Rich. II.
		10 Rich. II.	1 Hen. IV.
		2 Hen. IV.	9 Hen. V.
Luggershall . . .	23 Edw. I.	4 Edw. II.	1 Edw. III.
		4 Edw. III.	9 Rich. II.
		10 Rich. II.	9 Hen. V.
Old Sarum . . .	Ditto	24 Edw. I.	34 Edw. III.
Wotton Basset . .	25 Hen. VI.		
Marlborough . . .	23 Edw. I.		

Counties, Cities, and Boroughs.	When first summoned.	When discontinued.	When restored.
WORCESTERSHIRE.			
Bromsgrove	23 Edw. I.	24 Edw. I.	
Dudley	Ditto	Ditto	
Kidderminster	Ditto	Ditto	
Pershore	Ditto	Ditto	
Worcester	Ditto		
Droitwich	Ditto	5 Edw. II.	Ph. & M.
Evesham	Ditto	24 Edw. I.	1 Jac. I.
Bewdley	Jac. I.		
YORKSHIRE.			
Doncaster	23 Edw. I.	24 Edw. I.	
Jervale	Ditto	Ditto	
Pickering	Ditto	Ditto	
Ravenser	33 Edw. I.	12 Edw. III.	
Tykhull	23 Edw. I.	24 Edw. I.	
Halifax	Commonw.		
Whitby	Ditto		
Leeds	Ditto		
York	Ditto		
Hull	33 Edw. I.	34 Edw. I.	12 Edw. II.
Knaresborough	1 Mary		
Scarborough	23 Edw. I.		
Rippon	Ditto	24 Edw. I.	1 Edw. II.
		2 Edw. II.	Edw. VI.
Heydon	Ditto	24 Edw. I.	1 Edw. VI.
Boroughbridge	1 Mary		
Aldborough	5 Ph. & M.		
Malton	23 Edw. I.	27 Edw. I.	Cha. II.
Thirsk	Ditto	24 Edw. I.	1 Edw. VI.
Beverley	Ditto	1 Edw. II.	5 Eliz.
Northallerton	26 Edw. I.	27 Edw. I.	Cha. II.
Pontefract	23 Edw. I.	Ditto	19 Jac. I.
Richmond	27 Eliz.		

Counties, Cities, and Boroughs.	When first summoned.	When discontinued.	When restored.
CINQUE PORTS.			
Hastings	43 Edw. III.		
Dover	Ditto		
Sandwich	Ditto		30 Edw. I.
Hythe	Ditto		16 Edw. II.
New Romney	Ditto		19 Edw. II.
Rye	Ditto		18 Rich. II.
Winchelsea	Ditto		20 Rich. II.
Seaford	26 Edw. I.	27 Edw. I.	1 Hen. IV.
		31 Edw. I.	16 Car. I.
		17 Edw. II.	
		20 Edw. II.	
		19 Rich. II.	
		21 Rich. II.	
		2 Hen. IV.	
Calais, in France	27 H. VIII.	3 P. & M.	
WALES.			
Twelve Counties } Twelve Boroughs }	27 H. VIII.		
SCOTLAND.			
Thirty Counties } Fifteen Boroughs }	6 Anne		

By the above Table it appears, that SEVENTY-ONE Boroughs, exclusive of Calais in France, which formerly sent members to parliament, are now disfranchised; and that boroughs have been created and annihilated, from the reign of Edw. I. to that of Char. II. at the whim of each successive monarch. We may here be allowed to ask the enemies of reform, whether the constitution would receive a greater injury from the disfranchisement of Old Sarum, Gatton, Castle Rising, or Midhurst, than it has at present sustained from the disqualification of Leeds or Manchester? It surely becomes necessary to abolish the existing rotten boroughs; or, according to the argument of our opponents, to make the constitution complete, by restoring the seventy-one which have been discontinued.

CORRECT

CORRECT TABLE

OF

PARLIAMENTARY PATRONAGE.

PATRONAGE OF PEERS.

Names of Patrons.	Nominations.	Influences.	Total
Duke of Norfolk	—	2 Carlisle 1 Arundel 1 Leominster 1 Hereford	5
Duke of Richmond	1 Seaford	1 Sussex 1 Chichester	3
Duke of Grafton	—	1 Thetford 1 Bury	2
Duke of Beaufort	—	1 Monmouthshire 1 Gloucestershire 1 Monmouth	3
Duke of Bolton	—	1 Totness	1
Duke of Leeds	—	2 Helston 1 Penryn	3
Duke of Bedford	2 Tavistock	1 Bedfordshire 2 Bedford 1 Oakhampton	6
Duke of Devonshire	2 Knaresborough	1 Derbyshire 1 Derby	4
Duke of Marlborough	2 Woodstock 1 Heytesbury	1 Oxfordshire 1 Oxford	5
Duke of Rutland	1 Bramber	1 Grantham 1 Scarborough 1 Newark 1 Leicestershire	5
Duke of Ancaster	—	2 Boston	2
Duke of Portland	—	1 Nottinghamsh. 1 Buckinghamsh. 1 Cumberland 1 Wigan	4

Names of Patrons.	Nominations.	Influences.	Total
Duke of Manchester	—	1 Huntingdonsh.	1
Duke of Dorset	2 East Grinstead	—	2
Duke of Bridgewater	2 Brackley	—	2
Duke of Newcastle	2 Aldborough	1 Newark	6
	2 Boroughbridge	1 East Retford	
Duke of Northumberland	2 Launceston	1 Northumberl.	5
	2 Newport, Corn.	—	
Marquis of Buckingham	2 Buckingham	1 Buckinghamsh.	6
	2 St. Mawes	1 Aylesbury	
Marquis of Lansdown	2 Calne	2 Wycomb	4
Marquis of Stafford	—	1 Staffordshire	4
		1 Litchfield	
		2 Newcastle, Staff.	
Marquis Townshend	—	1 Tamworth	1
Marquis of Bath	2 Weobley	1 Bath	3
Marquis Cornwallis	2 Eye	—	2
Marquis of Hertford	2 Orford	—	2
Earl of Derby	—	1 Lancashire	2
		1 Preston	
Earl of Pembroke	2 Wilton	—	2
Earl of Exeter	—	2 Stamford	2
Earl of Northampton	—	1 Northampton	1
Earl of Westmoreland	2 Lyme Regis	—	2
Earl of Thanet	1 Appleby	—	1
Earl of Sandwich	—	1 Huntingdonsh.	3
		2 Huntingdon	
Earl of Carlisle	2 Morpeth	—	2
Earl of Shaftesbury	1 Dorchester	—	1
Earl of Berkeley	—	1 Gloucestershire	1
Earl of Abingdon	2 Westbury	—	2
Earl Poulet	—	2 Bridgewater	2
Earl of Oxford	—	1 Herefordshire	3
		1 Radnorshire	
		1 Radnor	
Earl of Orford	1 Castle Rising	—	1
Earl of Portsmouth	—	1 Andover	1
Earl of Warwick	—	2 Warwick	2
Earl Fitzwilliam	2 Malton	2 Peterborough	5
	1 Higham Ferrers		
Earl of Powis	—	1 Montgomerysh.	2
		1 Montgomery	
Earl of Egremont	2 Midhurst	—	2

(479)

Names of Patrons.	Nominations.	Influences.	Total
Earl of Guildford	1 Banbury	—	1
Earl of Hardwicke	1 Ryegate	1 Cambridgeshire	2
Earl of Darlington	1 Winchelsea	1 Durham County	2
Earl of Radnor	2 Downton	1 Salisbury	3
Earl Spencer	—	1 Oakhampton, 1 St. Alban's	2
Earl Bathurst	—	1 Cirencester	1
Earl of Aylesbury	2 Great Bedwin, 2 Marlborough	—	4
Earl of Clarendon	—	1 Wotton Basset	1
Earl of Uxbridge	1 Milborne Port	1 Anglesea, 1 Carnarvon	3
Earl of Lonsdale	2 Haslemere, 2 Cockermouth, 1 Appleby	1 Cumberland, 2 Westmoreland	8
Earl Grosvenor	—	2 Chester	2
Earl Camden	—	1 Bath	1
Earl of Mount Edgcumbe	2 Plimpton, 2 Leftwithel, 1 Bossiney	1 Fowey	6
Earl of Beverley	2 Berealston	—	2
Earl of Dorchester	—	1 Dorchester	1
Viscount Bolingbroke	—	1 Wotton Basset	1
Viscount Falmouth	1 St. Michael's	2 Truro	3
Viscount Sydney	1 Whitchurch, 1 Luggershall	—	2
Lord Petre	—	1 Thetford	1
Lord Craven	—	1 Berkshire	1
Lord Onslow	—	1 Guildford	1
Lord Walpole	—	1 Lynn	1
Lord Pelham	—	1 Sussex, 1 Lewes	2
Lord Bute	1 Bossiney	1 Cardiff	2
Lord Brownlow	—	1 Grantham	1
Lord Rivers	—	1 Dorsetshire	1
Lord Harrowby	2 Tiverton	—	2
Lord Foley	2 Droitwich	—	2
Lord Dynevor	—	1 Carmarthensh.	1
Lord Grantley	—	1 Guildford	1
Lord Camelford	2 Old Sarum	—	2
Lord Eliot	2 Liskeard, 2 Grampound, 2 St. Germain's	—	6

(480)

Names of Patrons.	Nominations.	Influences.	Total
Lord Bulkeley	1 Beaumaris	1 Carnarvonshire	2
Lord Delaval	—	1 Berwick	1
Lord Malmesbury	1 Christchurch	—	1
Lord Grimstone	—	1 St. Alban's	1
Lord Somers	1 Ryegate	—	1
Viscountess Irvine	2 Horsham	—	2
Total number of Members returned by Peers			195

PATRONAGE OF COMMONERS.

Names of Patrons.	Nominations.	Influences.	Total
W. Drake, Esq.	2 Agmondesham	—	2
P. C. Crespigny, Esq.	2 Aldboro', Suff.	2 Sudbury	4
Joshua Iremonger, Esq.	—	1 Andover	1
Sir Robert Palke	1 Ashburton	—	1
Earl of Lisburne	—	1 Berwick	1
C. A. Pelham, Esq.	2 Grimsby	1 Beverley	3
Lord Westcote	1 Bewdley	—	1
Lord Clive	2 Bishop's Castle	1 Ludlow	3
Sir Robert Clayton	2 Blechingley	—	2
George Hunt, Esq.	—	1 Bodmyn	1
Sir H. G. Calthorpe	1 Bramber	1 Hindon	2
Sir Charles Morgan	—	1 Monmouthshire, 1 Breconshire, 1 Brecon	3
Tho. Whitmore, Esq.	—	1 Bridgenorth	1
Charles Sturt, Esq.	—	1 Bridport	1
—— Trefusis, Esq.	2 Callington, 1 Ashburton	—	3
John Mortlake, Esq.	—	2 Cambridge	2
Sir Jonathan Phillips	2 Camelford	—	2
B. Howard, Esq.	1 Castle Rising	—	1
Sir S. B. Fludyer	—	1 Chippenham	1
James Dawkins, Esq.	—	1 Chippenham	1
George Rose, Esq.	1 Christchurch	—	1

Names of Patrons.	Nominations.	Influences.	Total
Thomas Lifter, Efq.	1 Clitheroe	—	1
P. A. Curzon, Efq.	1 Clitheroe	—	1
John Bond, Efq.	1 Corfe Caftle	—	1
Henry Bankes, Efq.	1 Corfe Caftle	—	1
Edmund Baftard, Efq.	—	2 Dartmouth	2
T. W. Coke, Efq.	—	1 Derby	1
James Sutton, Efq.	—	2 Devizes	2
Sir Jofhua Vanneck	1 Dunwich	—	1
Miles Barne, Efq.	1 Dunwich	—	1
J. Buller, Efq.	2 Eaft Looe 2 Weft Looe 2 Saltafh	—	} 6
Sir Francis Buller	—	1 Totnefs	1
Sir Charles Davers	—	1 Bury	1
Sir John Rufhout	—	1 Evefham	1
Philip Rafhleigh, Efq.	—	1 Fowey	1
Robert Ladbroke, Efq.	1 Gatton	—	1
Wm. Currie, Efq.	1 Gatton	—	1
John Robinfon, Efq.	2 Harwich	—	2
Edw. Milward, Efq.	2 Haftings	—	2
Lord Milford	—	1 Haverford Weft	1
Baron Dimfdale	—	1 Hertford	1
Beilby Thompfon, Efq.	—	1 Heydon	1
P.W. A. A'Court, Efq.	1 Heytefbury	—	1
Wm. Beckford, Efq.	—	1 Hindon	1
Sir Geo. Yonge	1 Honiton	—	1
Sir C. F. Radcliffe	—	1 Hythe	1
Wm. Evelyn, Efq.	—	1 Hythe	1
R. Troward, Efq.	2 Ilchefter	—	2
Wm. Præd, Efq.	2 St. Ives	—	2
Alderman Harley	—	1 Leominfter	1
Tho. Anfon, Efq.	—	1 Litchfield	1
—— Everit, Efq.	1 Luggerfhall	—	1
Sir Harry Burrard	2 Lymington	—	2
I. H. Strutt, Efq.	1 Maldon	—	1
C. C. Weftern, Efq.	1 Malden	—	1
—— Wilkins, Efq.	2 Malmfbury	—	2
Tho. Williams, Efq.	1 Marlow	—	1
W. Lee Antonie, Efq.	1 Marlow	—	1
Sir Francis Baffet	—	1 St. Michael's 1 Penryn	} 2
W. C. Meddlycott, Efq.	1 Milborne Port	—	1
J. F. Luttrell, Efq.	2 Minehead	—	2
Rev. L. T. Holmes	2 Newport, Hants 1 Yarmouth, Hant	—	} 2 1

Names of Patrons.	Nominations.	Influences.	Total
J. C. C. Jervois, Efq.	1 Yarmouth, Hant	—	1
T. P. Leigh, Efq.	2 Newton, Lanca.	—	2
Sir John Barington	1 Newton, Hants.	—	1
Sir R. Worfley	1 Newton, Hants.	—	1
Henry Peirfe, Efq.	1 Northallerton	—	1
Edw. Lafcelles, Efq.	1 Northallerton	—	1
Hugh Barlow, Efq.	—	1 Pembroke	1
Wm. Jolliffe, Efq.	2 Petersfield	—	2
B. Lifter, Efq.	—	1 Poole	1
J. Jeffrey, Efq.	—	1 Poole	1
Sir John Carter	—	2 Portfmouth	2
Sir Tho. Dundas	2 Richmond	—	2
Sir Edw. Deering	2 Romney	—	2
Tho. Lamb, Efq.	2 Rye	—	2
P. Stephens, Efq.	—	2 Sandwich	2
Lord Mulgrave	1 Scarboro'	—	1
Rt. Hon. T. Pelham	1 Seaford	—	1
Paul Benfield, Efq.	—	2 Shaftefbury	2
Sir John Honeywood	2 Steyning	—	2
T. F. Barham, Efq.	2 Stockbridge	—	2
Robert Peele, Efq.	1 Tamworth	—	1
Sir B. Hamet	—	2 Taunton	2
Sir T. Frankland	2 Old Thirfke	—	2
Richard Barwell, Efq.	2 Tregoney 1 Winchelfea	— —	} 3
Sir F. Sykes	2 Wallingford	—	2
John Calcraft, Efq.	2 Wareham	—	2
Clem. Tudway, Efq.	—	1 Wells	1
Wm. Pulteney, Efq.	2 Weymouth 2 Melcombe Reg.	1 Shrewfbury —	} 5
J. B. Church, Efq.	2 Wendover	—	2
Cecil Forefter, Efq.	1 Wenlock	—	1
Sir H. Bridgeman	1 Wenlock 1 Wigan	— —	} 2
Vifcount Middleton	1 Whitchurch	—	1
Richard Gamon, Efq.	—	1 Winchefter	1
Henry Penton, Efq.	—	1 Winchefter	1
Sir W. W. Wynne	—	1 Denbighfhire 1 Flint	} 2
R. Middleton, Efq.	—	1 Denbigh	1
Mrs. Allanfon	2 Ripon	—	2

Total number of Members returned by Commoners . . 155

PATRONAGE OF THE TREASURY.

	Nominations.	Influences.	Total
	2 Queenborough	—	2
		1 Dover	1
		1 Rochester	1
		2 Plymouth	2
		2 Windsor	2
Total number of Members returned by the Treasury			8
Total sent by Peers, Commoners, and the Treasury			358

SCOTLAND.

PATRONAGE OF PEERS.

Names of Patrons.	Nominations.	Influences.	Total
Duke of Hamilton	—	1 Lanerk C. 1 Renfrew C.	2
Duke of Buccleugh	—	1 Berwickshire	1
Duke of Gordon	—	1 Aberdeen 1 Bamff C. 1 Inverness C.	3
Duke of Queensbury	—	1 Dumfries C. 1 Roxburgh C. 1 Dumfries B.	3
Duke of Argyle	—	1 Argyle C.	1
Duke of Athol	—	1 Forfar C. 1 Perth C. 1 Perth B.	3

Names of Patrons.	Nominations.	Influences.	Total
Countess of Sutherland	—	1 Sutherland C.	1
Earl of Eglintoune	—	1 Ayr C.	
		1 Peebles C.	2
Earl of Galloway	—	1 Kirkudbright	
		1 Orkney	
		1 Wigtoun	4
		1 Whitehorn B.	
Earl of Hadington	—	1 Hadington C.	1
Earl of Lauderdale	—	1 Jedburgh B.	1
Earl of Elgin	—	1 Elgin C.	1
Earl of Leven	—	1 Kinrofs C.	1
Earl of Dundonald	—	1 Sterling B.	1
Earl of Bute	—	1 Bute C.	
		1 Irvine B.	2
Earl of Hopeton	—	1 Linlithgow C.	
		1 Kinghorn B.	2
Earl of Fife	—	1 Fife C.	1
Total patronage of Peers			30

PATRONAGE OF COMMONERS.

Names of Patrons.	Nominations.	Influence.	Total
Sir John Sinclair	—	1 Caithnefs C.	1
William Pulteney, Esq.	—	1 Cromarty C.	1
Lord F. Campbell	—	1 Dumbarton C.	1
Rt. Hon. H. Dundas	—	1 Edinburgh C.	
		1 Edinburgh City	2
Sir Thomas Dundas	—	1 Stirling C.	
		1 Dingwall B.	2
Alexander Brodie, Esq.	—	1 Elgin B.	1
Sir John Anftruther	—	1 Craill B.	1
Total patronage of Commoners			9

N. B. All the Members for Scotland are fent to Parliament under the influence of Individuals, though the Author has not been able to procure the names of all the Patrons; which makes the total number, fent under the influence of Proprietors of Boroughs and Patrons, to be 430.

FINIS.

www.ingramcontent.com/pod-product-compliance
Lightning Source LLC
Chambersburg PA
CBHW021424300426
44114CB00010B/627